THE CLAIMS OF LIFE

THE CLAIMS OF LIFE

A MEMOIR

DIANA CHAPMAN WALSH

THE MIT PRESS   CAMBRIDGE, MASSACHUSETTS   LONDON, ENGLAND

The MIT Press would like to thank the anonymous peer reviewers who provided comments on drafts of this book. The generous work of academic experts is essential for establishing the authority and quality of our publications. We acknowledge with gratitude the contributions of these otherwise uncredited readers.

This book was set in ITC Stone Serif and Avenir by New Best-set Typesetters Ltd. Printed and bound in the United States of America.

Library of Congress Cataloging-in-Publication Data

Names: Walsh, Diana Chapman, author.
Title: The claims of life : a memoir / Diana Chapman Walsh.
Description: Cambridge, Massachusetts : The MIT Press, [2023] | Includes index.
Identifiers: LCCN 2022059844 | ISBN 9780262048491 (Hardcover) |
    ISBN 9780262376280 (epub) | ISBN 9780262376273 (pdf)
Subjects: LCSH: Walsh, Diana Chapman. | Women college presidents—
    Massachusetts—Wellesley—Biography. | Wellesley College—Faculty—Biography. |
    Wellesley College—History.
Classification: LCC LD7212.1 .W35 2023 | DDC 378.744/7
[B]—dc23/eng/20230120
LC record available at https://lccn.loc.gov/2022059844

10   9   8   7   6   5   4   3   2   1

This book is dedicated to:
Chris
Allison
Thomas
and
Sean

CONTENTS

A NOTE ON SOURCES AND NAMING

Everything I describe here happened to me to the best of my recollection, augmented by extensive notes I kept for many years in journals, memoranda, speeches.

In some few cases, to preserve individual privacy, I have changed names or descriptive details of people or places.

I learned a tremendous amount in my interactions with Wellesley students while I was president, and I tell some of those stories.

I do not, however, reveal identities of any students. Some may recognize themselves, but none expected that I would be recounting our stories someday far off in the future.

It's my hope that some students, faculty, staff, trustees and alumnae will be reminded by these stories of the ways in which they helped "hold the college in trust" during those 14 years.

I am grateful to you all.

1

WE TWO FORM A MULTITUDE

I am at the hospital, beside my husband's bed. I drove in early this morning from Wellesley, about 12 miles to the west. He was admitted on Friday, under observation. What looked like a straightforward procedure—maybe a stent or two—flipped to a medical emergency in a nanosecond when the angiogram revealed a blockage known as the widowmaker. The cardiologists' consolation, "You're a good candidate for surgery," has carried us to this point.

In a few minutes the medical staff will arrive to transport him to the operating room. I'll be taken to the family waiting room to sweat out the five hours until I can see him again. I brought a briefcase of work to do while I wait. A report to the board, and my speech to Wellesley's graduating seniors. Ha! Fat chance I'll get to them. All I can do is fight back the dread that he won't make it through. We are both terrified. But we're keeping our fear under wraps.

I am seated in a small black armchair, tipped forward on its two front legs so I can lean into his bed and hold his hand. He's not wearing his wedding ring.

"Where's your stuff?" I ask.

"In a bag, I think. Maybe under the bed."

I glance down and see a plastic bag, bulging with his clothes and shoes, labeled with his name. His watch, wallet, and ring must be in there too. I stroke his hand and my eye falls on the plastic ID bracelet on his wrist. I look away. It gives me the creeps. This is how they'll know him when he doesn't know himself. I change the subject to the daughter we both dearly love. Our only child, she is a young physician in training at Massachusetts General Hospital, down the street.

"Allison hasn't been crying," I say. "But I've been a mess all weekend. She's been my rock, and sees this as a disaster averted. I told her I'm crying not because I think we might lose you—I just wish you didn't have to go through this ordeal." My throat constricts.

He nods. I sense I'm pushing too far. Chris needs his control. Ceding that to him is the least I can do. He tells me that when he woke in this hospital bed, he spent about a half hour thinking about us. How like him it was to quantify his rumination, always the scientist, always on task. I ask what he thought about, and he says, all the places we've lived in our 34 years, all the jobs we've had.

"Not about vacations we've taken," he adds.

"There were quite a few," I say. "And I would never have had all those jobs if I hadn't married you. I would have been a secretary somewhere or an administrative assistant."

He replies, "No, you would have been in Philadelphia running something."

"Yeah, the DAR." I grimace.

"No," he insists. "You would have escaped that fate."

I come from a family that traces its roots to the founding of Philadelphia, to Quaker abolitionists who arrived at the time of William Penn. Our family's genealogy was a source of pride to us. As a child I was less conscious of our privilege than of our ancestors who had stood up and sacrificed for what was right. I wanted to be worthy of them.

We lived in Chestnut Hill, an affluent neighborhood of Northwest Philadelphia. My family was comfortable but not wealthy. We were far from the pinnacle of the social hierarchy in our community and my parents were socially insecure. Only gradually did I come to see that I was a product of WASP privilege, and to catch glimpses of what a cocoon that was. The discovery made me wonder why I was born in this time and this place, in this body and this class.

When I was eleven and twelve, I had a friend who lived in a grand house with a swimming pool and a squash court, and the first television set I ever watched. It was fun to visit her there . . . when it wasn't scary. Betsy was bolder than I, a risk taker, transgressive. I looked on helplessly—there was no diverting her—one day as she straddled a Reading Railroad track, taping a quarter on the rail so the next train along would flatten it. Her previous attempt had sent the quarter flying and we had searched for it in vain. Maybe the tape would slow its trajectory so we could retrieve it? But the second quarter went the way of the first. To my relief, we abandoned the experiment.

We walked back to Betsy's house, went into the library, locked the door, and spent the rest of the afternoon buried once again in a coffee table book almost as thrilling as the railroad tracks. *The Family of Man* showed many naked bodies, love making, graphic pictures of babies being born. It depicted birth and death and rage and joy and dancing and grieving and every kind of emotion. I was mesmerized by the people of all ages, all races, all cultures. On two pages toward the end were seven photographs of couples, standing or seated, together. They looked directly into the camera, and each picture had the caption: "We two form a multitude."

I met my husband of fifty-seven years at a Harvard mixer, over a cigarette. I was with my college roommate, Joan. We were both in our sophomore year at Wellesley College. I had recently been named Vil Junior, the counselor to the dorm's incoming students, and we had brought a group of freshmen to the party. Chris walked over and introduced himself. His suitemates were hosting the party as members of the Leverett House social committee—his alibi.

"Can I bum a smoke?"

"Sure," I said, and handed him my pack of Lucky Strikes. We three spent the evening together, standing back in our semi-official roles, affecting the practiced detachment of disinterested observers. When it was time for Joan and me to round up our charges for the bus back to Wellesley, she excused herself. Chris stepped forward.

"Could I ask a question?"

I thought he wanted Joan's number, but he asked for mine.

Early the following week he called to ask me out on Saturday.

"I can't go out on Saturday," I said. "I have to play golf."

"I love golf! What do you mean you have to play? Where are you playing?"

"Wellesley has a nine-hole course," I explained, "and I am on my honor to play once a week all semester because I failed gym this winter."

He chuckled and asked if my honor would be violated if he were to come out and play the round with me.

"Certainly not," I laughed. "I can sign you in as my guest." I told myself I had to play anyway, so why not with this eager person?

On that spring Saturday morning in 1964, Chris hitchhiked from Cambridge to Wellesley with his bag of clubs. I met him on the first hole of the Nehoiden Golf Club, "an unpretentious . . . golf course with a fascinating past," according to a 2005 centennial history published long after our fateful game and dedicated to me as a Wellesley president "familiar with the course." Not familiar enough, apparently, with the first hole, a par five. I disgraced myself with nine strokes. The first went straight into a brook, the second bounced off the trunk of an oak.

This is going to be fun, I could hear Chris think to himself, as he recorded his bogie and my pathetic nine. Then I pulled myself together and shot par on each of the remaining eight holes to his astonishment and delight. He rushed back to announce to his suitemates that he'd met the woman he was going to marry.

"She is such an obviously fantastic athlete. She shot eight pars like a PGA professional golfer. And she is beautiful. Slim with a classic jaw, a ski jump nose and bright blue eyes. And amazing legs."

What I hadn't mentioned was that, at age eleven and twelve, I had been the junior-junior golf champion of Philadelphia. I was the family athlete all my life, and excelled in many sports. At Wellesley I had chosen swimming to complete the physical education requirement my sophomore fall. But after each class I had a twenty-minute walk back to my dorm in the dark and the cold. I always arrived late for dinner with my wet hair literally frozen to my head. So I decided to stop attending the class and engage in a minor rebellion, which was out of character. The instructor said she would fail me if I didn't make up the missed classes. I told her I understood but wouldn't be returning. I received the F on my transcript and was told I could expunge it by spending another semester in any sport. I chose golf.

After our golf adventure Chris continued calling for dates. I began to warm to him, but still had hesitations. One evening he arrived in his father's car, which he'd hitchhiked home to borrow. It had a Saint Christopher's medal on the dashboard. Now it dawned on me that his family was probably Catholic. This would be a problem for my family, I was sure, and thought maybe I should disengage before we became too involved. When I gingerly broached the religion question, he was unequivocal.

"My family is Catholic," he said. "But I am not."

"Why did you rebel?" I asked him years later.

"Because you shouldn't have to have heaven and hell hanging over you to be a good person. That's how they keep you in check. I have issues with authority. I believe in honesty and hard work, integrity, in all of the virtues and qualities I admired in heroes I read about as a kid. It wasn't an external threat that motivated them, it was a set of personal values. It was qualities of character."

Chris Walsh was named for his father, a troubled and difficult man, a pharmacist and regional detail man for Hoffman LaRoche. His mother was a substitute teacher from a family of nine who lived nearby. It was obvious to all that her husband was mercurial and emotionally abusive. She escaped into her extended family—visiting, playing cards—or sometimes solitaire bridge alone at her kitchen table. She was kind and smart and agile with numbers but had neither ambition nor advanced education, nor any way to imagine a way out of a crushing marriage. As a teenager Chris would sit with her and try to convince her that they could leave his father, that they would manage, that he would help. But she knew she was trapped.

Chris found his way out. He became a reader. When he was eleven, he won a full scholarship to a private boys' school, Roxbury Latin. RLS, he often says, changed his view of life, taught him that he could make a living thinking. About what, he didn't know, but mental labor that would distinguish his life from family members who had preceded him.

At Harvard College, Chris worked with an assistant professor, John Law, in a collaboration with the famous biologist, E.O. Wilson. Together with Konrad Bloch, they published a paper in the journal *Nature*, a big deal. That same year, 1963, Bloch received the Nobel prize in physiology or medicine for the biosynthesis of cholesterol. Biomedical research looked enticing, a chance to advance the health of many rather than caring for one person at a time.

Chris abandoned his plan to be a doctor, sure his father would explode when he heard the news. But he was ready to hold his ground against a father's expectations built up over twenty years of piled-up indignities inflicted on a salesman who spent his life in supplication to physicians. To have his son become a doctor would be his ultimate vindication.

We dated regularly through that spring and decided not to date others while we were separated during the summer of 1964. I lived at our family vacation home at Pocono Lake Preserve, where I had spent all of my summers. I ran the dining facility—the Dining Camp, it was called. I handled reservations, recruited kids to wait on tables, trained and supervised them. I greeted and seated guests and kept the books. I celebrated my twentieth birthday there at the end of July. Chris came down from Cambridge.

In the fall, back together with me for my junior year, and his last at Harvard, Chris was considering applications to graduate school in biomedical research. I thought medicine, his plan when we met, was a career that promised security and also the social status that would reassure my mother. My father was a research engineer, with just a bachelor's degree, directing an R&D unit at the Atlantic Richfield Company. I knew that was different from what Chris had in mind. But I didn't know anyone in academic science and had no idea what such a career might entail or demand.

It didn't matter to me whether Chris became a doctor or an academic scientist; I hardly knew the difference. What I knew was that I wanted to marry him. And I wanted us to be engaged before my senior year, when he would be away in graduate school, maybe far away in California. He had plane tickets to fly there for interviews but decided first to look into the Rockefeller Institute (later University) in New York City. With its low profile in the world of graduate education, it appealed to his nonconformist streak.

He spent the morning of his visit in interviews with faculty and, right before lunch, he was scheduled for a perfunctory meet-and-greet with the president, Detlev Bronk. Knowing that Bronk had been president of Swarthmore College, Chris mentioned that his fiancée's great-grandfather —mine—had been chair of the board for many years. About a minute later, Bronk called out to his assistant in the adjacent room.

"Mable, cancel my next appointment. I am taking Mr. Walsh to lunch." Over lunch, the president extolled the virtues of Rockefeller's research faculty in comparison to Chris's top choices, MIT and Berkeley.

Over coffee he sat back and asked, "Are you ready to sign up for Rockefeller?"

"Yes," said Chris. He scrubbed his trip to the West Coast, fully realizing, as he would later say, that it was my genealogy that sealed the deal with Bronk.

Some months later I took Chris to meet my great-grandmother, the widow of Charles Francis Jenkins, the former board chair at Swarthmore. We went to see Granny at Far Country, the Germantown, Pennsylvania, estate where they had raised their children and, over many years, hosted Thanksgivings for the large extended family. I had memories of running down to the pond with my sister in our Mary Janes to feed the ducks, poking under the chickens in the back garden to feel for eggs, playing hide and seek with cousins we hardly knew. My great-grandfather, a publisher and history buff, had spent years collecting stones, one each from the threshold of the birth home of every signer of the Declaration of Independence. The stones were embedded in a grass lawn in an unobtrusive arc off the front entrance to the house. We used to skip along the path—the Signers' Walk—fifty-six stones. Button Gwinnett's was the final stone, the one that completed Grandpa's collection. On the day I brought my fiancé to meet her, Granny was ninety-seven, seated on a lounge bed. We were escorted into her parlor. She rearranged herself.

"One sits up straighter when a Harvard man enters the room," she said.

Back at Wellesley, I was loving my junior year. I saw Chris every weekend, came to know his Harvard friends, discovered pizza and Chinese food. Meat and vegetables and potatoes at home were our regular fare. We almost never went out to eat. My father was too impatient, and my mother considered it a needless extravagance. She was a child of the Depression, as she often said. Mom went to the market every day to be sure the meat was fresh. She'd return with standing rib roast or top of the round steak ground for hamburgers. Or we'd have roast chicken, unadorned, and frozen vegetables, sometimes scorched. When the cocktail hour ran long the smell of burning peas would waft up the stairs. My brother, sisters, and I avoided the living room scene. The sound of my father's ice cracker would signal another round of high-balls and with it the prospect of another family dinner in stony silence, bruised feelings, or bitter rancor. Black spots on the bottom of the pot after dinner told the tale of the forgotten peas.

I loved the peace, the freedom and adventure at Wellesley, feeling like an adult and a leader in my role as the Vil Junior in my dorm. And I loved falling in love. I was taking only electives and enjoying them: English literature, my major, philosophy, political science, all favorite subjects, my distribution requirements safely behind me. I narrowly made it through a chemistry course my first year, not knowing that, on top of my having a father who was a chemical engineer, my sister would become a chemistry professor and I would fall in love with a chemist.

I was working hard, reading every assignment—every word—taking copious notes, pulling all-nighters when papers were due, a suboptimal pattern I established from the beginning of my college career. I was stressed out a lot, always trying to do more than I had time to complete. I arrived at college and graduated with the belief that I wasn't smart enough, that I had to work especially hard to hold my own. I believed I had been admitted, early decision, for mysterious qualities of character that I wasn't sure were real, yet felt obliged to try to discover and develop. That's what the admission director had seen in me, I thought, and so I threw myself into college government.

Wellesley's studious culture stood in stark contrast to the Harvard ethos. Chris and his friends struck me as pseudo-laid-back and covertly cutthroat, with an overlay of arrogance. In the fall of his senior year, Chris was taking all science courses except for an elective on the history of Western thought, taught by a famous professor, Crane Brinton. It met two mornings a week, Tuesday and Thursday.

"I'm not going on Tuesday," he said casually one Sunday afternoon.

"Why not? Where will you be?"

"Nowhere. Not just this Tuesday. I'm not attending the course. Not ever."

"What do you mean you aren't attending it? How will you pass?" A reasonable question from the woman who had failed swimming.

"I want to see if I can ace the course without going to even one lecture."

At the end of the semester he had an A on the final paper, an A on the exam and an A for the course. He'd raced through the reading at semester's end and had proven, once again, how effortlessly he learned, how independently. Later he would look back on the victory as Pyrrhic. He'd wasted a whole course. The professor's perspective would surely have been interesting.

Chris carried a dazzling compendium of facts in his head, on any and all subjects, so it seemed. At first, I would suspect that he was making them up on the spot when a topic came up in conversation. But invariably he'd be proved right. "You can always tell a Harvard man," would run through my head, "but you can't tell him much." Chris had a delicious sense of humor, and I loved laughing with him. My family didn't laugh often when I was growing up. Life seemed precarious then, as though we were on quicksand.

I think it was Chris's sense of humor that won me first. That and his unwavering conviction that we should be together, that we could create a life that would be extraordinary, a life in which both of us would grow, each in our own direction, with respect and support for the other. Jointly we would create possibilities neither alone could even imagine. We would free ourselves of constraints that were holding us back. We would escape, just we two. Together.

We decided we did want to be engaged before Chris moved to New York the next fall. But first, we had some hurdles to clear. I had met Chris's mother, his close ally at home. We sat at her kitchen table with her on several afternoons. She was warm and welcoming. I could see how much she treasured—and trusted—Chris, that she wanted for him whatever he wanted for himself. She could see he wanted a life with me and seemed fine with that.

I heard indirectly that Chris's father objected. He wanted us to be married in the Catholic church, to raise our children in the church. Chris was adamant that this was out of the question, that it wasn't about me, that he had left the church long ago. I wanted a Quaker service. That was no church at all, by his father's lights. Why is she being so stubborn? What's it to her? Chris was convinced we could work something out and rock solid in his certainty that he would not let his father control his life, or ours. In the meantime, I had yet to tell my parents I was going to marry Chris.

I arranged to fly to Philadelphia on a random weekend—a rare event— offering no indication of why I was coming. It was early spring. My parents met me at the airport and drove me home by way of Fairmount Park. The Japanese cherry trees that edged the Schuylkill River were in full bloom and the lawns were emerald green, weeks ahead of Boston. It was gorgeous. But I was preoccupied. I was nervous about telling them, but unsure what it was I feared.

I had a return ticket for late Sunday afternoon. All day Saturday and Sunday, when I wasn't studying, we walked Dad's springer spaniels, cooked meals, read the Sunday *New York Times* Mom had ordered for me. She betrayed no hint of curiosity about what had brought me home. Less than an hour before we had to leave for the airport, I still hadn't found an opening. I was perched on the white metal clothes dryer in the kitchen, my feet dangling over the edge, my suitcase and green canvas bookbag on the linoleum floor below, packed and ready. My heart pounded in my chest. My mouth was dry. What would I tell Chris if I arrived back in Boston having botched the mission?

"Chris and I have decided we want to be married," I mumbled. "I've come home to tell you. That's why I'm here."

The rest was a blur. A few of the obvious questions all came from my mother: Are you sure? We'll need to meet his family. When do you envision the wedding? Not before you graduate?!

I assured her we'd marry after I graduated the following June. My mother had left Swarthmore at the end of her junior year to marry my father who had graduated from Penn a year ahead of her. She had always regretted not finishing her degree but feared she would lose him when he moved to Waynesboro, Virginia, for his first job. She felt he was ready to settle down. That parallel had not occurred to me nor, for a moment, had I thought to forfeit my senior year.

On the ride back to the airport I told them more about Chris, emphasizing that he had long ago broken decisively from the Catholic church, and was inured to his father's pressure on the topic.

"He's a scientist through and through," I said, "and totally independent. Clear about who he is, he knows what he believes, knows what he wants."

They were glad of that. But what they didn't do, what they couldn't do, was speak about their feelings. I couldn't do it either, speak to and from my heart. We didn't have the language. Or the practice. Or we couldn't trust our feelings. Or we didn't have the nerve. Why was it so hard? I didn't know. It was the best our family could do with the skills we had, I consoled myself on the flight back, relieved to be returning to Boston with their support.

When Chris was ten, he started a coin collection. He would go to banks and buy rolls of coins, sort through them for the rare ones, then return the rest for a fresh supply. He organized them in blue Whitman folders and took special pride in his mint-condition buffalo nickels and standing Indian quarters. He sold the coin collection to buy me a diamond engagement ring. We went together to the jeweler who helped us select an affordable diamond set off in a delicate setting. I wore it with pride. He didn't tell me that he sacrificed his coin collection for my ring until years later when I happened upon the mostly empty blue folders.

That summer, 1965, was the first in my life I spent away from Pocono Lake. I was teaching tennis to wealthy New York teenagers at a Quaker boarding school in Bucks County, Pennsylvania and living with them in a dorm. I received a letter from Chris and wrote him back almost daily, which captured the attention of the camp director who would tease me about my obsession with the US Postal Service.

Chris was in New York, living in the lap of luxury. Rockefeller's campus was on the Upper East Side, nestled in a lush oasis where East 66th Street ends at the junction with York Avenue. Lunch was served in a grand dining room overlooking the East River, with Nobel laureates and other scientific luminaries at small tables in intense conversations. Students had all their meals in a formal dining room, served by uniformed wait staff.

We made plans to meet on holiday weekends at Pocono—Memorial Day, Fourth of July, Labor Day, and at the end of July, for my twenty-first birthday. Friends in New York who drove back and forth on weekends were happy to have a passenger. Chris was good company. He enlivened our family gatherings for everyone. My brother, Bill, and sisters, Sally and Muffy, took to him instantly.

Pocono Lake Preserve (PLP), founded by Quakers in 1904, was austere initially but evolved into an exclusive family summer community, somewhat like a multi-generational summer camp. Everyone was assigned a color for life—red or blue—and your loyalty to your color ran deep. Colors alternated through families to heighten competition. I was a blue. Chris, as my guest, was assigned the color red. From that day on neither of us would think of drinking from the wrong color coffee mug. Chris was a sought-after player in the Saturday softball game. He was an asset to the reds, to my counterfeit chagrin. I was proud of him.

He was adjusting gamely to an alien world. We PLP natives had grown up taking overnight hikes, sleeping in the woods, cooking over campfires, making s'mores, telling ghost stories. We mucked around in the streams, sailed and swam and played tennis, and, when we were older, tapped a half keg of beer to drink at Wolf Spring. We would huddle around the fire and sing slightly off-color songs. So much of this took Chris beyond his comfort zones. Nature was not his friend, except through a microscope. He had alabaster skin that burned easily. He wasn't preppy and hated all bugs, spiders most of all: a genuine case of arachnophobia.

On his first visit—or maybe it was his second—I was helping him settle his things in the small guest room when he noticed something on the bed, pulsating or bouncing. He thought it was a toad. Just then the creature unfurled its black wings to fly erratic circles around our heads. It was a bat. Chris tried to contain his panic. I dashed to the next room to grab a tennis racket, propped Chris's screen door open and swung at the bat in flight. Eventually it scooted out the door after several minutes of ducking and dive-bombing. If Chris had left that night, never to return, I wouldn't have blamed him. But he recovered quickly. This was an ability—like his memory—he could depend on in a pinch.

My mother felt an obligation, in her capacity as mother of the bride, to reach out to Chris's parents. The proper gesture, she felt, was to invite them to Pocono for a get-acquainted weekend. The visit was awkward to say the least. Chris's parents had no way to comprehend this strange place where people of obvious means lived as though they were Okies. There were bugs, and garter snakes, slamming screen doors with holes, and strange noises from the dark woods. The beds sagged. The Army blankets scratched. It was cold. To us, it was Pocono. We Chapmans did our best to pretend the Walshes were enjoying their visit, while we counted off the minutes until the ordeal would end.

Back at Wellesley for my senior year, I was on the college government cabinet. I'd been elected the previous spring to chair the house president's council, the student government body for the thirteen residence halls. The cabinet met weekly with Margaret Clapp, in the final of her eighteen years as president. On behalf of the house presidents, I was petitioning to extend the Friday night curfew from 10:30 to 11:00 p.m. I would present proposals to the formidable Miss Clapp who would send me back to gather more information. This went on all year long. She never budged.

I was enjoying my courses. I would visit Chris in New York every couple of months, and he would travel to Wellesley in months between. But the long-distance relationship wasn't working for me, the episodic and frequent visits. The version of Chris in my mind wasn't matching the one who showed up. I was getting cold feet. Or I feared I was. I feared I wasn't able to conjure the feelings I thought I should have for him. I felt alone and confused. I was living in a single room next door to my former roommate, Joan, my closest confidante. She would listen sympathetically as I agonized.

"Why don't you make an appointment with the college shrink," she suggested one day. "Maybe he can help you sort it out."

"I don't want that on my record," I replied. She laughed.

"Wait a minute, Diana. Aren't you the one who is constantly reassuring everyone that visits to the campus infirmary are held in strict confidence? Isn't that your job? As chair of HPC?"

So I made the appointment and told my story to the psychiatrist. His first question was along the lines of, "How is the sex?" I brushed him off with irritation and made a silent note that of course his first question would be about sex, what else would be on a shrink's mind? I beat a hasty retreat and decided I wouldn't go back.

Later I wondered if that shrink hadn't been on to something. What should love *feel* like? A powerful lightning strike? Certain? Unshakable? How deeply did it need to be felt to be reliable? To be real? Chris wasn't the preppy ideal that populated Pocono and Chestnut Hill. And *he* was so very certain of his love for me. What an amazing thing to be so deeply loved. Why would I throw that away? I decided I ought to be honest with Chris, take my doubts to him and trust him to be the one to help me sort this out. The next time he came to Wellesley I gently broached my uncertainty. I did it tentatively, as just a whisper of a worry. I'm not as sure as I was.

He took it well, and responded honestly.

"Fine if you don't want this," he said. "If you're sure you don't, then tell me so. I will just go away and never bother you again."

At first this hit me as an ultimatum. Be careful, don't push this too far or he will bolt. But, as he talked, I could see it was something else, something fundamental to how he saw our future. He wanted to give me room, to let me be who I wanted to be. He wanted true equality, not a relationship driven by his perceptions, his wants and needs.

"Having seen my father behave so badly," he went on, "seeing my mother suffer, and loving her as much as I do, I know I will not be the kind of person who will cause pain—not inflict it at least. I believe that to have this marriage is going to be the central thing in my life. I really want it to be great. I will do whatever I can to make it work. I'll be a good husband; I'm sure of that."

Chris never had a moment's doubt about the possibilities before us. And here I was consumed by doubt. What was the matter with me? I couldn't tell him it was something about the way he looked, about a physical attraction to him I worried I lacked. What could he do about that?

"This is such good fortune," he was saying. "I spent my life in fantasy. All the books I read. Hoping for a life that would be different from my parents. I believe you are it: the central part of it. I want to make a life for us. That's where life has meaning for me. Because I'm a hopeless romantic, I suppose. Maybe it's mystic Catholicism. A little Celtic mysticism. But I see this special relationship as Ecclesiastes' idea of exultation. I see a marriage that will be an exultation for me every day. But it has to be one for you too, or it will not work. That's for you to decide."

I nodded, gathering myself.

"And aside from all of that," he added, as if to seal the deal, "if you marry me, I will take you to Australia." We both laughed. I had no desire to go to Australia. It was the farthest thing from my mind, and he knew it. He had wanderlust. I did not. But his vision of who we could be carried me back all the way to the possibility that two people, together for life, could form a multitude. I remembered how much I loved him, trusted him, needed him. I remembered how it felt to be in love with him. We were back together dreaming a beautiful future.

Then tragedy struck. Chris's mother suffered a massive heart attack. She was in intensive care in critical condition. He flew up from New York, rushed to the hospital and called me from there.

"It's very bad. It's doubtful she will make it. And if she does it's unclear she'll have any kind of life." Her heart had stopped long enough to starve her of oxygen. Surgeons had to amputate one leg at the hip. The next few weeks were awful. Eventually Chris's father arranged to have his mother moved back home to a hospital bed in the living room with twenty-four-hour care. She was never the same.

In his grief and desolation—and his narcissism—Chris's father decided that we had caused the coronary. He told everyone that the prospect of our being married outside the church had broken his wife's heart. Of course, this was pure projection. He was the only one obsessed about the church. We had his mother's blessing. But that no longer mattered. His father insisted that we postpone or cancel the wedding. If we didn't, he would forbid any members of his family to attend. His priest was behind him, he said. But my parents stood by us. So did my brother, Bill. During the worst of it he took it upon himself to invite Chris to Pocono for a family conclave on how to go forward.

My parents were stalwart and generous to a fault, clear that they intended to support me—support us—in any way they could. I was their first-born daughter and the first of their four children to marry. I knew I had their love. They wanted to host a beautiful wedding for me and for my friends, for Chris, and his, and for their own friends too.

We found a Presbyterian chapel in Chestnut Hill not far from our house. One we had attended a few times, years ago, for the Sunday school that was livelier than the tiny one at Friends' meeting where Mom sometimes taught. Chris and I met with the minister who was sympathetic. With his help we designed the lovely wedding my mother had in mind. On June 18, 1966, two weeks after my graduation from Wellesley, we were married. But not a single soul was there to represent the family of the groom. Chris's older brother, John, in a doctoral program in oceanography at the University of Miami, declined to come. I never quite forgave him. Chris's groomsmen, including my brother, deftly avoided the conventions that would have called attention to the imbalance.

My father walked me down the aisle, foggy and unsteady from a drunken episode the night before. My Aunt Phyl had hosted a rehearsal dinner that evening, standing in for the family of the groom. Champagne flowed. After Chris and I went back with Mom for the night at my family's home, Dad took off alone in his car and went missing. We learned the next morning that at 2:00 a.m. the wedding party had gone on a search. The police had come upon Dad, semi-conscious, parked on the side of a road and had taken him to the station. He managed to carry on through the wedding, and so did we. But he had let me down on the day we had all worked for months simply to muddle through. And he knew it. We never spoke a word about what happened that night. We never—ever—mentioned his drinking.

Chris's best man, a friend at graduate school, had organized a collective present, a honeymoon in Puerto Rico. It included a wedding night in New York at the Plaza Hotel, then a helicopter to LaGuardia for the flight to San Juan. We ducked through the flying rice into the airport limousine and didn't look back. We were setting out on our own. Starting over. Escaping.

2

THE NEW YORK YEARS

New York City was hot that summer. Beastly hot. We were newly married and back from our honeymoon. Relief from the heat came in the evening breezes off the East River.

I had a job at Barnard College that would begin in the fall. Until then, I'd been instructed to learn to type. I left the sylvan succor of Rockefeller early every morning, boarded a cross-town bus, and then a grimy subway shuttle to Times Square where I walked the last half block to the dreary storefront that housed the cheapest stenography school in the Yellow Pages. It had no open windows, no air conditioning, just large fans rotating with a constant whir. From nine to five, in a row of metal desks each equipped with a manual typewriter, I and my fellow aspiring typists did our drills. My perspiring fingers slipped off the keys while my classmates tapped faster and faster leaving me in the dust. Was this my new life: hotter than hell with a new college degree, learning to type and failing at it?

I was discouraged but tried to hide it from Chris. One sweltering evening as my bus pulled into the York Avenue stop, I looked out the window and saw him standing there alone, grinning behind a hand-made "Welcome Home!" sign. I took his arm and we walked to our apartment in The Abby, number 401. On the door he had taped a sign, "401 Club," and inside he had set up a small card table, with a menu: club sandwiches, the limit of his culinary capabilities. He had produced a private dinner for two.

In our second year I prevailed on Chris to abandon student housing so that we could move beyond the cosseted comfort of the Rockefeller campus. We packed our few possessions and took up residence in a fourth-floor walkup across York Avenue in a mustard-yellow brick building.

We shared 500 square feet of space with cockroaches who took over the kitchen as soon as the lights went out.

"Their total body mass probably exceeds ours," Chris groaned one day.

I read a lot, tried to make my own sense of all that was stirring and new. The *New York Times* every day. The Sunday *Times* all morning and, through the following week, threads that unwound from it—books, arguments, controversies. I read to fill my gaps, read as a student reads: the latest novels, African American writers, feminist polemics, nonfiction. I would take notes, look up words I wanted to be able to use, write them on half index cards, meanings on the back, alphabetize and memorize them. Words like orthorexia, argute, kakistocracy. I filled journal after journal with ideas I wanted to track, theories to parse. I read as a writer reads, carried along by the music of phrases. I read about writers and writing, the life of it, craft of it, struggle of it. I hung a calligraphy over my desk that said: "Writing is easy. All you have to do is stare at a blank sheet of paper until beads of blood form on your forehead." Where any of this was taking me was my blank page.

Chris on the other hand knew exactly what he was doing. He was on task, moving forward. He chose to do his thesis work in the laboratory of Fritz Lipmann, a Nobel laureate who characterized ATP (adenosine triphosphate) as the energy currency of all cells. Chris worked on enzymes and, with his lab mate, John Hildebrand, started a seminar series. They invited senior scientists who ran the labs they thought they might want to join as postdocs.

My father gave us money to buy a car. Rockefeller gave us free parking. We bought a blue VW bug, the first car for either of us, another ticket to adulthood and freedom. We would drive to Philadelphia or Pocono for all major holidays and some weekends. It never occurred to me that my father's act of generosity was also a talisman of sorts, a way to keep us coming back.

Every winter weekend we left Rockefeller at five on Friday afternoon, drove six hours to Vermont or New Hampshire and stayed in the cheapest guest house we could find. We skied all day Saturday and Sunday and drove back that night, exhausted. My father loved to ski and had taught me when I was little. In my earliest memories, I am bitterly cold, terrified of the blue ice on the scariest pitches of the trails, and not heavy or strong enough to manage the T-bar lifts. Dad was an impatient teacher. Sally and I cried a lot. But I took to the sport and expected to ski all my life.

"Irish don't ski," Chris had announced when first I proposed a ski outing, but he cut me a deal and instituted a five-year plan. He would ski twenty days a year. If at the end of five years he still hated the sport, I'd be on my own.

So we rented decent equipment and enrolled him in ski school. Over the next couple of years, we both skied in classes, at different levels, until the day came when Chris could keep up with me on all terrain. A Swiss guide once instructed us to follow him, one inch behind. From then on one of us would take off and call to the other, "Follow me! One inch!" We would tear down the mountain, breathless together back in the lift line. I loved the way it felt. I loved going fast. I loved Chris for fulfilling his pledge to me, and then some. I always loved skiing with him; it was one of my life's great thrills.

Squash was a different story, although part of my childhood, too. I played while in high school and at college. During a tour of Wellesley in the summer before my junior year my mother inquired if there were any squash courts. I was the junior club champion at the Philadelphia Cricket Club where we were members.

"Are those the small white rooms that look kind of mental?" the guide responded. When I arrived as a Wellesley freshman the squash coach invited me to join the team. So did the coaches of hockey and lacrosse. I declined them all. At Springside, the private girls' school I attended, I played on all the varsity teams and reveled in the camaraderie and the competition. But at college I decided not to be a jock. I was determined to cast off that element of a childhood identity that was more my mother's construction than my own. Sally was the smart one. Bill was the affable one. Muffy, who came along later, was the cute little one we all could love. I was the natural athlete. I did make one exception while I was at Wellesley: at the end of squash season I would sign up for the open squash tournament and surprise myself and everyone else by winning every match and retiring the title, four years in a row.

Chris hadn't ever played squash until he met me. Rockefeller had two courts. He was a quick study in all things. He scrambled for the ball. He never gave up. We played ferocious games. After a few years he started beating me consistently and it stopped being fun for me. I quit. No five-year plan, no honest effort, an F in marital squash. If Chris always recovered, I sometimes withdrew, and wondered about our different relationships to competition. Or to defeat? My sixth-grade English teacher once slipped me a note: "Getting angry is sometimes better than going away."

Chris never got angry; that wasn't in his DNA. He avoided conflict. What he did was believe in me, in all of my abilities, all of my potential. I had grown up convinced that I was athletic but not smart, not like Sally was smart. Numbers never made much sense to me. My first report card, in kindergarten, declared that I was getting along well with the other girls, but was "not well oriented in time and space." Mom would quote this many times. "Where are you, then?" she would ask with a chuckle. When I got my driver's license she asked if she would ever see me again.

I worked hard. Too hard, my parents worried as I grew older. After dinner most nights I did homework in my room with the door closed while the family watched TV: *Perry Mason, Maverick, The Ed Sullivan Show*. But I was happy alone. I would stand in front of the mirror and practice over and over—to tame my stage fright—the poems I had selected to recite in front of our sixth-grade English class. I still know them by heart: "Jabberwocky;" Hamlet's soliloquy, "To Be or Not to Be;" Rudyard Kipling's "If." In upper school I would write and rewrite papers until they were flawless. I was a perfectionist—except in math, where I was mostly mystified.

Toward the end of my sophomore year, Mom scheduled a conference with the head of school. I could drop advanced math, she told us, but the top colleges expected to see it on their applications. This decision would probably put them out of my reach. Mom turned to me.

"Dad and I hate to see you staying up so late every night," she said. "We don't want you to get sick. There are many good colleges." I accepted as inevitable the verdict that I wouldn't get into a Seven Sister college. Turns out it was premature.

Springside School awarded three special deeded honors at graduation in addition to other prizes for the seniors. When I was in ninth grade, Miss Potter, our venerated headmistress, read the citation for the Laurel Wreath Award, recognizing "a student who exemplifies the school motto, *laurus crescit in arduis*, 'honor comes through hard work.'" And then—to my astonishment—she said my name. My heart pounding, I ran down the aisle and up the steps to the stage, shook Miss Potter's hand and curtsied, accepted the prize and dashed back to my seat, my cheeks burning.

In eleventh grade I won the next remaining prize. I was thrilled but told myself I was a teacher's pet, always trying to please, and that's why I was being singled out. Then came my own graduation and the announcement of the third deeded prize: the Caroline Susan Jones Pin, named for a former headmistress. Given "by vote of the three upper classes and the faculty to a senior who is respected by all for courage, cheerfulness, fair-mindedness, good sportsmanship, for influence widely felt and for the courage of her own convictions." And my name again! So much for my teacher's-pet theory. I was honored, grateful, proud. But also challenged. What were my convictions? How and when had I stood up for them? With courage? Whatever all those people saw in me, I didn't see in myself. I was enrolled in a merciless self-improvement campaign. Any stupid misstep sent me into a tailspin and from there to the privacy of my journal where I wrote about the incident, remembered it, tried to transform it into a bracing lesson so that I could hope to avoid it the next time, at least try to. I could try to be a better person.

Labor Day 1966. The first day of school. There were no new pens and notebooks to mark this one. Excited and a little jittery, I boarded my crosstown bus for the West Side subway that took me up Broadway to Barnard College for my first real job, as secretary in the Office of College Activities. The office, just inside the main entrance, sat on a campus that was a scant four acres in contrast to Wellesley's 500. Barnard was one of the exalted Seven Sisters, as was Wellesley, but was in a unique sibling-like partnership with Columbia. Sally, who later spent her career on the Barnard faculty, sometimes referred to it as "the bag lady of the Seven Sisters."

Elizabeth Y. Meyers, known as Wiff, was my first boss. I worked for her for two years and grew to love her. She was friendly, informal, funny and maternal, qualities in other women that invariably drew me to them. She took an interest in Chris and me as a couple, invited us for golf at her Maplewood, New Jersey, country club and to her home for dinner. We could talk to her about anything. One day I mentioned that we might never have children.

"We just feel that we two are enough, all we need to be happy."

"That's great," she replied. "You're happy. Savor it. But wait and see. You may change your minds. Raising a child together is one of the most meaningful things a couple can do. A family doesn't diminish that bond but strengthens it."

"We are a family," I said. "That's my point. But you could be right. We'll see." I filed her comment away as the advice of a woman I admired and trusted, a woman with no stake in the outcome. My parents were biding their time and hadn't uttered a word about grandchildren. But I could already feel their subtle pressure.

After two years working for Wiff, I was invited to move to the public relations office in a larger role, as manager of special events. Barnard had a new president, Martha Peterson, and her inauguration on April 29, 1968, would be the biggest event of that year. Not for a moment did I imagine that I would be inaugurated as president of a sister college, exactly twenty-four years later to the day.

By spring 1968 civil rights and antiwar protests were sprouting everywhere. Columbia was ground zero. Students for a Democratic Society (SDS) had established a foothold in Morningside Heights. Protests were gaining traction on campus. Chris had a five-year draft deferment as a full-time graduate student until 1970. After that, his work as a research scientist would likely earn him another pass and keep him out of uniform. We were lucky that our direct stake in the antiwar movement was more political than personal, but it was still visceral to me, as was my support for the civil rights movement. I was sure that the war was wrong, the worst sort of American imperialism. In my heart I sympathized with the students' agenda, despite reservations about some of their tactics.

On April 23, 1968, SDS took over five Columbia buildings and the office of the president. With megaphones and red armbands they leaned over the window ledges of the massive classic buildings, called out to each other, tossed food back and forth. The scene had a carnival quality, with music blaring, people dancing. Some 200 Barnard students joined the occupation, and I admired their moxie.

But I had other things on my mind. I had to get Grayson Kirk to Martha Peterson's inauguration at Riverside Church. No Barnard president

had been installed without the participation of the President of Columbia University. No such absence was imaginable. I made an appointment
to see Kirk, who was holed up under armed guard in the basement of
Columbia's Low Library. I presented him with my plan: I'd give his two
bodyguards graduation robes to wear so they would blend in as he walked
the academic procession down the aisle of Riverside Church. He agreed. I
ordered the extra robes. Mission accomplished.

I was relieved but a little bit miserable. I had crossed over, hadn't I?
Three years ago I'd been a student leader at Wellesley. Now I was on the
side of the administrators, the oppressors of the student rebels. Kirk never
addressed the students' demands. On the day after the Barnard inauguration, eight days into the occupation, he charged the occupiers with tres-
passing and called in the police to clear the buildings.

That evening, April 30, I watched New York's Tactical Police Force
advance in formation through the Columbia gates. A few were on horseback, most were on foot, all were helmeted and armed with heavy shields.
They slashed their riot clubs through a crowd of protesters, dragged students from buildings and shoved them into police vans. Among those
arrested were over 100 Barnard students.

The portent of what I watched was mostly lost on me. Only later did
I understand that I had witnessed the power of the university presidency
erode before my eyes, a casualty of leaders who, like the proverbial deer
in the headlights, were blinded by the glare of oncoming danger they
could not fathom.

But that wasn't all. That same spring our office was plunged into a
media maelstrom that was ours to manage. My boss, Sarah Johnson, the
director of public relations, was a departure from Wiff Meyers. Sarah lived
media relations. She and her administrative assistant, Karen Kushner,
resonated at frequencies I'd not before seen in a partnership. Karen was
from Sheepshead Bay in Brooklyn, with a strong New York accent and a
vocabulary laced with Yiddish terms, plus a few profanities.

The pace accelerated the day the *New York Times* broke a story on
unmarried students living together. Cohabiting. Illicitly. An unnamed
Barnard sophomore from New Hampshire quoted in the piece was easy
to identify: Linda LeClair. Upon returning from a medical leave she wrote
on her housing form that she would be living off campus for the semester

as a live-in babysitter. But then she moved into an apartment on West 110th Street with her boyfriend, Peter Behr.

Columbia men were free to come and go at will while Barnard women were bound by stringent curfews, as we had been at Wellesley. I watched Linda LeClair draw condemnation from outside the college. The *New York Times* followed the scandal in near-daily articles, several on the front page. We were hearing from trustees and many alumnae who were horrified to perceive Barnard's reputation in tatters. A letter to the editor in *Time* magazine managed to push all our buttons. It appeared in the May 10, 1968 issue whose cover story featured a photo of LeClair.

"I don't know what kind of student Linda LeClair is or what kind of a mistress she makes," wrote Harriet Wagner from Northbrook, Illinois. "But judging from the picture of her apartment, she makes one lousy housekeeper. Doesn't Barnard College have a Home Economics department?"

"No!" I wanted to shout. "That's not what Barnard's about."

Meanwhile, LeClair and Behr rallied their fellow members of SDS to picket outside her Barnard administrative hearing, one of their first "gendered actions," she later bragged. The committee announced the penalty—a temporary suspension. President Peterson invited LeClair to return in the fall if she agreed to abide by college policies.

"I decided not to go back," she said years later in a retrospective of the incident, "because what I had thought Barnard was—namely a place to support feminism, to support the empowerment of women—at that point wasn't so true." She was right, of course, but at the time even I was irritated, as others were, by her *chutzpah*, her smug disdain for the college's reputation. Would it ever recover, I wondered? It did. Another lesson.

In June 1968 Sally graduated from Smith College at the top of her class. She planned to go on to a doctoral program at Yale in physical chemistry but took a gap year in a job at the Metropolitan Life Insurance Company in Manhattan. Mother Met, we called it, I never knew why. The job was mind-numbing; its only virtue was that she had a lot of free time. One of the perks for Rockefeller students was a steady stream of "twofers," half price tickets to theaters for same-day admission. I went with Sally and Chris to many plays, mostly off-Broadway and occasionally on, and out to cheap restaurants all over the city. My two years with my sister in New York provided a chance for us to bond as adults.

As children, Sally and I grew up at an emotional distance caused in part by a competitive dynamic my mother set up between us. It was probably unconscious but, as we looked back, we saw our dance reflected in the mirror of Mom's lifelong rivalry with her own sister, Phyllis, two years younger, a superior athlete and more adept at making friends than Mom was. She was less insecure, more fun.

The taboo of my father's covert alcoholism was surely another factor that kept Sally and me apart. It was a heavy unspoken secret. My mother told stories, some to cover up, others with a moral. One of her favorites was from the time I was nine and Sally was seven. A new baby was on the way, our sister, Muffy. My parents had found the new house they wanted, unoccupied and being sold from the deceased owner's estate. They took us there to show us where our rooms would be. Mine, as the oldest sister, was on the second floor next to the baby's room. Bill and Sally were relegated to the third floor, an injustice Sally always resented. We five were examining the third floor while the realtor waited downstairs. My father wanted to convince Bill and Sally that each would have a sizable separate room, so he kicked down a flimsy partition wall. It looked temporary, but Mom was horrified.

"Don't you dare breathe a word about this to anyone," she said. "We don't own this house." In the early afternoon of the next day, the story goes, Mom received a call from Sally's teacher. She had not uttered a single word all day and refused to open her mouth, even at lunch. Mom rushed to school to pick her up and the minute they were alone in the car turned to Sally.

"What's wrong?"

"I can't open my mouth," Sally said. "The secret might slip out."

Ironically, it was Sally, of the four of us, who did occasionally venture a question or a crack about Dad's drinking, although never within his hearing. My mother would cut her off.

"Lay down your ax, Carrie Nation," she would say, and all of us got the message.

The LeClair Affair presaged the rise of feminism that would follow, second-wave feminism launched by Betty Friedan's explosive 1963 book, *The Feminine Mystique*. A young Barnard faculty member, Kate Millett, was finishing a doctoral dissertation at Columbia that would set off the next explosion and land her on the cover of *Time* magazine in August 1970 when her revised thesis came out as a book. Sexual domination is "the most pervasive ideology of our culture and . . . its most fundamental concept of power," Millett wrote in *Sexual Politics*. Although an axiom now, this declaration was mind-blowing then. One member of her Columbia dissertation committee famously said of her book that reading it "is like sitting with your testicles in a nutcracker." A second Kate—Catherine Stimpson—was also at Columbia, teaching part-time in Barnard's English department. Stimpson had studied at Cambridge University; Millett at Oxford. They occupied adjacent desks in an office in Barnard Hall, four floors above mine.

I would see either or both from time to time, attend seminars they organized, read works they cited. The two Kates and their colleagues were gutsy women who called out the patriarchy, advanced women's studies, made men uncomfortable and made women think twice—and then again—about gender and power. They made me think about things that hadn't crossed my mind, like how power operated in my parents' marriage and in my own so far. And what accommodations and sacrifices true equality of the sexes might require. I wondered how I would begin forming my own opinions on these loaded topics that had been unspeakable.

In a larger sense, the intellectual and political foment in the air around Barnard and Columbia in those years challenged my basic assumptions about who I could and would be, what claims life would make on me. They set me on a course unrecognizable from the one I had automatically expected to follow. Gradually I came to believe in the vision Chris had for us, that I would pursue a career every bit as demanding and prominent—and as central in our marriage—as his would be. Chris had launched himself while I had spent my time in New York mostly putzing around. He had secured a postdoc at Brandeis University in Boston, and I decided it was my turn for graduate school. I looked into two master's programs at Boston University, mostly because they were affordable, one in social work, the other in journalism. I knew I wanted to write, and I thought social work might provide me material to write about. That didn't go over so well in the interview. Anyway, I had in mind that the journalism program was the logical next step. With the job in media relations it would be a pathway into a career as a writer.

In May 1970 Chris defended his dissertation in a formal lecture, open to the public, in Rockefeller's domed auditorium. My parents drove up from Philadelphia and we sat together. My stomach churned as he started. I felt the tension in his voice. Then he loosened up and delivered an impeccable talk, "Purification of the Citrate Cleavage Enzyme." Chris presented a series of slides with many numbers and graphs and chemical structures, and a few schematic diagrams like cartoons that carried the listener through the logic of his experiments. How this molecule over here in green attached itself to that one over there in yellow. He did it so smoothly that I had the illusion I was following along. But even after four years of living with him and his dissertation, the whole thing went over my head.

In those four years I absorbed a lot, though, about the culture of science. Some faculty were gifted collaborators, connectors, generous mentors to all, eager to learn from others, to see their fields advance and their colleagues succeed. Chris was one of those. Others were hoarders. They locked their labs. They swore their coworkers to secrecy lest someone come along and steal their ideas. All of the graduate students worried, necessarily, about being scooped before they could finish their project and publish it in a respected journal. Years of work would be for naught if the findings were not original.

I also began to glimpse firsthand the connected community scientists have, the dedication, passion, and reverence that animates their questions, and the satisfaction of unlocking, piece-by-piece, the mysteries of life and the universe. There are elements in the world of empirical reductionism as transcendent, compelling, and inspiring—and ethically-alert—as there are in any pursuit I know. I wanted to be part of a community with that sense of vocation and promise, but it wouldn't be in science. That was not where my gifts would take me.

Two weeks after Chris's lecture, we dragged our few belongings from the fourth-floor walk-up down to the sidewalk on East 65th Street and into a twenty-foot U-Haul. Chris threaded the van through the chaotic city traffic, and I followed in our VW, toward Interstate 95 North to Boston. I was sorry to see the New York skyline disappear in the rearview mirror but excited at the prospect of claiming my own life.

3

A WRITING STICK

We had very little money in those first years in Boston. Chris won a fellowship from the Helen Hay Whitney Foundation that paid $300 per month, and we lived on that. We found a one-bedroom basement apartment for $100 a month in Jamaica Plain, a neighborhood of Boston. The living room had a couple of windows high up on the wall that were flush with the sidewalk outdoors, a side street where residents parked overnight. On cold mornings they would leave their cars idling to warm their commute. With our coffee, we inhaled their exhaust fumes.

My father loaned me money to cover my BU tuition. I was enrolled in a one-year master's program in journalism at the School of Public Communication. For my commute I bought a new English bike equipped with three gears, a basket and a lock. All for $59.50. My prized possession. Every day I biked through the parks to get to school.

My BU courses were easy. I liked the ones rooted in social theory and social research or in ethics: studies of culture and communication, early Marshall McLuhan, readings on the history of the press and press freedom, responsibilities of the fourth estate in a democracy. The course on general semantics was interesting if its relevance to newspaper work was less than obvious. The instructor wore Birkenstocks and told us one day that he preferred women with unshaven legs, and armpits. Not that we asked. He enthusiastically displayed his countercultural credentials and was enamored of the Polish philosopher Alfred Korzybski, founder of general semantics. "The map is not the territory," was the theory's core axiom. "There are two ways to slide easily through life," Korzybski averred, "to believe everything or to doubt everything; both ways save us from thinking." This was a course on thinking and common logical errors: "uncritical inferences," and "the is of identity." I would build a framework from these early concepts as reminders to question my premises and assumptions, to be conscious of what can't be fully known and what can't be captured in words. This interest in thinking about thinking, an extension of the philosophy I'd studied, stayed with me from then on.

One morning as I biked to school, I ran over a twig on the cement path. I watched it fly up as if in slow motion, lodge between two spokes of my front wheel and, in the same instant, I felt myself catapult over the handlebars onto the ground. I lay on the sidewalk unsure if I could move. A bystander called 911 and a police officer appeared in minutes, drove me to Beth Israel Hospital and called Chris. In short order the ER team had me sutured, casted, cleaned up and wheeled to a recovery room. Chris soon arrived, rushing. My strongest impression was how happy he seemed, ebullient. It took me a minute to register how the call from a police officer must have hit him. He had imagined the worst. Chatting cheerfully, he drove me home and the next day I was back in school, being met with sympathy. Except in general semantics.

"What happened to you?" the instructor asked.

"I had a freak accident," I replied and revved up to tell my twig story. But he cut me short.

"What do you mean by 'freak'? Would you agree that an 'accident,' by definition, is unexpected? Freakish in that sense? A superfluous conditional then." Our colloquy went on from there and my mishap became the day's object lesson in misplaced modifiers and misattributed causality. Territory without a map.

The capstone of the journalism program was a master's thesis on a topic of our choice. Mine followed a controversy over the port authority's proposed expansion of Logan Airport. Residents of East Boston, the working-class neighborhood separated from the city by the Callahan Tunnel, had long endured the noise and pollution of constant air traffic. They organized against the approval of two new runways. East Boston denizens would pay the price; wealthy suburbanites would reap the benefits.

I attended public hearings and neighborhood rallies, interviewed legislators, industry spokesmen, travelers from outlying suburbs, and East Boston residents: leaders of the resistance versus neighbors whose livelihoods bound them to the fortunes of the airport. I wrote about the racket of jumbo jets taking off and landing at all hours of the day and night. I would sit in living rooms and on back porches and not hear a word my host was saying, nor even a thought I was thinking. All I could do was close my eyes, take a breath, and wait for the noise to subside, but only momentarily. The next jet would accelerate loudly and rattle the porch windows. Most houses were inherited, multi-family homes passed down through generations. Long-time residents sold and fled as they were able. Many couldn't afford to move. They felt forgotten and dismissed. They were powerless. There had to be a better solution than doubling down on these people.

My thesis was nearly done when I broke my hand. Chris typed the final draft with two fingers, hunt and peck, ironic in light of my summer learning to touch-type. That failure was redeemed by success in journalism school. I won the award for the best thesis: "Troubled Waters in Boston Harbor: The Expansion of Logan Airport." Chris claimed some bragging rights for typing the finished copy. I graduated at the top of my class.

After my graduation, we found an apartment on the third floor of a three-family house in Waltham, near Brandeis, where Chris would post-doc. It was wood frame, double front entry, ours with stairs and an exit to the second story. Every floor in our unit was painted ebony black. To cheer it up we spent the first weeks with rollers painting every wall in every room a different color, all highly saturated and intense. This was the first of many times I would be the beneficiary of Chris's flair for interior design. Only later did a routine eye exam reveal that he was red-green colorblind, and explain his penchant for vibrant colors. Waltham was the third of thirteen moves we made in fifty-four years, always with Chris more interested than I in interior aesthetics. The views I needed to feed my spirits were in the natural world outside. That was not Waltham's long suit. We didn't see ourselves putting down roots here. Anywhere but greater Boston, we thought. Chris was still so skittish about his father's attempts to control him that we paid to have an unlisted phone number.

My job search lasted longer than anticipated. Six months into it I had sent letters with resumes to every newspaper within roughly an hour's radius. How naive I was to imagine that my stellar BU record would open doors. When I did score an interview, the outcome was always the same.

"For now, we have our woman reporter," the interviewer, invariably male, would say without compunction. Or "the women's page is covered." I decided to go back to the Wellesley placement office to see if they could help again, since they had set me up in the Barnard job.

"Well, there are a couple of administrative jobs here at the college," the career counselor said as she flipped through a large binder. "But I'm guessing you won't be interested. You've been painting on a wider canvas." I didn't expect this, but it struck me as an affirmation of a belief that, until that moment, had been subliminal. I wanted to keep moving forward, testing myself, exploring my limits. And, conversely, the lure of a place of comfort could too easily become a prison.

She turned a few more pages and found a listing from the Planned Parenthood League of Massachusetts (PPLM). They were looking for a new director of information and education. The position required a master's degree. I thought it sounded promising. Okay, so I wouldn't be a journalist, but the degree did give me my entree. I applied and was hired. Back in New York, I'd opened a fortune cookie in a Chinatown restaurant and read the little slip of paper, "He who has a writing stick shall never have to beg." I'd saved it in the coin compartment of my wallet. And now it was officially validated. Not "he," though. Me.

At PPLM, I met two redoubtable women who founded the organization. Lorraine Leeson Campbell and Mary DuPont Faulkner. Both were in their mid-sixties, classic Boston Brahmins. They told me stories about Margaret Sanger and about how hard it was to recruit physicians to support family planning, a third rail in Catholic Massachusetts. They reminded me of my mother, whose outside life revolved around golf and volunteer work in politics and social welfare. One of her many causes was the Philadelphia Home for Incurables. Years later the board renamed it Inglis House. When I was young, she sometimes took me with her. I was dismayed by the misshapen bodies of residents warehoused in that place, especially the kids whose heads were so enlarged by hydrocephalus that they couldn't hold them up. It amazed me to watch my mother greet them as her friends. They lit up when they heard her voice, excited to see her return with new books to read to them. I doubted I could ever be as kind and caring a person as she was on those visits. We didn't speak— then or ever—about my doubts, nor about her affinity for that place. As with so much else between us, those unspoken feelings were stranded on ice thinner than we dared venture out on.

In Massachusetts, birth control came under federal and state Comstock Laws passed in 1873 to punish "lewd, lascivious, immoral, and indecent" behavior. They forbade the Commonwealth's medical professionals from recommending or providing contraceptives of any kind. Private gynecologists, it was well known, discreetly made them available to their married patients, but poor and single women were on their own. Margaret Sanger wrote about a physician who counseled an indigent woman to "tell Jake to sleep on the roof."

Our office, in contrast, buzzed with trained volunteer counselors who took shifts on the telephones. They answered questions—without judgment—from all comers, provided referrals and gave encouragement. "Children by choice, not chance" was the goal. My job was to spread the word and to patrol the policy horizon for signs of possible new points of leverage.

My Barnard public relations experience came in handy when the US Supreme Court ruled on two crucial reproductive rights cases. In 1972, *Eisenstadt v. Baird* extended to unmarried women the right of privacy that ensured their access to medical contraceptive services. In 1973, *Roe v. Wade* extended the *Eisenstadt* logic in a landmark decision that legalized abortion for all women. We were ecstatic. Champagne flowed. I issued press releases, held press conferences and thanked our many supporters for staying the course toward these hard-won freedoms that culminated a three-decade struggle. We believed that we had opened the door for good, had won the battle, once and for all.

What we failed to foresee was the backlash the decision would ignite, and the soul searching that would ensue among legal experts, including Ruth Bader Ginsberg. Was the Roe case decided on sturdy enough logic? The earlier *Eisenstadt* case set the precedent as a right to privacy. But in retrospect, gender equality might have laid a firmer foundation. In 1998, I had the opportunity to discuss this road not taken with Justice Ginsberg. We spent a November afternoon alone together in the living room of the Wellesley President's House. I asked about the *Roe* decision, and she hoped it would endure over time. We spoke of her life's work advancing women's rights and equal justice under the law and I had a chance to express my indebtedness to her.

I told her that when we were celebrating *Roe v. Wade* at PPLM it never occurred to me that, in the years ahead, my friends and I would take our teenage daughters to Washington, repeatedly, to march in massive rallies in support of *Roe*. We sensed the need to imprint on them that they would have to fight for *their* reproductive rights. My favorite poster at one of those rallies read: "post-menopausal women nostalgic for choice." There we were, a full generation later, fearful that the clock could turn back, although never really believing that it would, unable then to foresee the shocking *Dobbs* decision, announced on June 24, 2022. On that day, for the first time in US history, the Supreme Court overturned any ruling that for almost five decades had guaranteed a constitutional right—in this case, to abortion.

In the moment of victory, though, with our champagne toasts, we were swept up in the excitement of the historic ruling. We felt validated, liberated, respected as autonomous adults capable of making our own decisions. Now we were free to control our own bodies, our reproductive lives, our destinies. It was a heady time for a nascent women's health movement.

A local leader in Zero Population Growth became a friend. He was in his twenties and had had a vasectomy. He urged other young men to follow his example. We read *The Population Bomb* and *The Limits to Growth*, with growing concern that we humans were expanding beyond the carrying capacity of the Earth. I continued to study the population problem. On behalf of PPLM, I reached out to a state legislator, Robert Wetmore, who chaired a commission on population growth. I attended the hearings and ghostwrote the final report in 1971. It left little room for doubt that our species was headed for trouble and largely blind to the danger ahead.

National Planned Parenthood, to its credit, began to emphasize population control in combination with its core vision that every child could be wanted. This new focus was launched on a sly bumper sticker, "Trouble parking? Support Planned Parenthood." But soon the sticker became a liability as community activists and leftist scholars brought to public attention a documented history of racism, colonialism, eugenics, even genocidal intent, in white-sponsored programs to limit minority populations. My counter-culture semantics teacher would have known better than to accept population control as an unalloyed good. I took a razor blade and scraped the parking sticker off the bumper of my VW.

Around this same time, I became acquainted with members of the Boston Women's Health Book Collective, initially a small group of college-educated women in their late twenties and early thirties who were a lot like me. They were writing a book called *Our Bodies Ourselves*. Over the next thirty years, they would sell millions of copies in multiple editions and languages around the world. The 1973 edition began with a chapter, "Our Changing Sense of Self," which pushed me beyond my comfort zone. It raised questions that led me to second-guess choices I was making. The authors discussed ways in which their lives were less than satisfying—as privileged as they knew themselves to be. I saw them going out on a limb with no way of anticipating where the conversation would take them. This seemed brave to me, risky. What demands would their inquiry make of them—to change their lives, maybe radically? They hoped to become "fuller, more integrated women," they wrote, whatever that meant. I wished I knew. Their words were tapping into an unspoken dissatisfaction I had kept at bay, not ready—not yet—to consider the leaps they were taking. My hope was to grow in directions they seemed to be describing, but that voice inside me was still a private murmur, a tendril of the self-improvement campaign I had been conducting since I was a child, privately, by and for myself. It occurred to me that I was missing the essential element that spurred them on, a community, a sisterhood. But I had neither the insight nor the nerve to know how or where to seek that out.

I did learn at PPLM all I needed to know about sex. The women in the office tossed diaphragms around like they were frisbees. I went off the pill and, in early March 1973, learned I was pregnant. Chris announced that he'd carry me around on a blue silk pillow, but didn't try, fortunately. I discovered that Planned Parenthood was the ideal work environment into which to bring a baby. Everyone there loved babies. At a statewide conference in early September I stood up to make a point. I was eight months pregnant at the time.

"I'm from Planned Parenthood," I started out. The moderator interrupted.

"Well, yes you are. We can see that!"

Gone were the early reservations I had expressed to Wiff Meyers. Gone were the more recent concerns provoked by *The Limits to Growth* and ZPG. To have one child was responsible. Chris had long felt unsure he could be a good father, the kind he had sorely lacked. But his doubts faded as we watched good friends take the plunge. They were muddling along, making it work and, we could see, having fun.

We lived in Cambridge, nearer MIT now, in a one-bedroom apartment off the Common, a location that reminded us of our New York City days. We liked it there, but had to move again to make space for three of us. We found a small house in suburban Waban, a village of Newton, west of Boston. My father loaned us the money for a down payment, and I braced for another DIY move with another round of painting every wall. This time the task fell mostly on Chris. But we shared all the rest. Childbirth classes together. Naming the baby—Allison. Labor and delivery, an all-day ordeal. Mercifully, I blocked that out of my mind by the time I healed. Was this nature's way of preserving the species—the forgetting and, even more so, the tug of love that caught me completely off guard? That first night, in my hospital room, I cried as I watched Chris in the chair by my bed, our new baby in his two cupped hands. He looked deep into her eyes and told her tales of enzymes.

My mother was thrilled that we had finally started a family after dithering for eight years. She came up from Philadelphia to stay with us and help, a relief to me and Chris. We'd read all the books but were still clueless. I nursed the baby for the first couple of weeks and intended to continue. I loved the intimacy—and the peace—of cradling her in my arm, breathing in the sweet scent of her soft head, overtaken by a love with a force I'd never felt before, never imagined. I was stunned by it.

But Mom was convinced the baby wasn't getting enough nourishment. I didn't have the energy to resist. Whatever her reasons and without much discussion she set us up with bottles and formula. Now she and Chris could take turns feeding the baby so I could sleep. She insisted I needed more sleep. Ever the peacemaker, and not wanting to deny Chris his fair share of time with our new daughter, I capitulated. But I chastised myself for caving in. I'd failed the first test of motherhood, if not the last.

As my five weeks of maternity leave came to an end, Chris and I began to look for a babysitter. I planned to return for three days a week during the first three months, then to resume full time. I wasn't going to risk stepping off the treadmill and losing the momentum I'd worked so hard to stoke. I was sure I'd be ready to return to work by the end of my maternity leave.

A PPLM volunteer told us about Mary McCarthy, who came to the house to meet us. Chris and I sat on the sofa, and offered her the arm-chair. Between us sat Allison in her little blue scoop-seat balanced on the coffee table. Mrs. McCarthy exuded both confidence and competence. She had experience, rules, and boundaries. She had raised four children who now had their own families. After her husband died, she cared for infants in their homes, infants only. She had no interest in chasing after toddlers at her age, or wrangling with terrible twos. We had to under-stand that this arrangement would be for one year only. We agreed, and sensed she would be taking charge. This was a bargain I struck, a year of accommodation to her superior knowledge—her stronger will—in return for assurance that our baby would be nurtured and safe.

She instructed us to call her May and we agreed on a salary, a rough schedule for the year, and a starting date. With mounting dread, I watched it approach. The days at home with my baby were sublime. I couldn't imagine giving them up. Sitting on the front lawn one sunny afternoon in early October, Allison lying face up on a blanket, I stared into her eyes and promised I'd be there for her. I would love her, protect her, celebrate her—all the days of my life. It felt like a solemn vow. I would not forget that moment.

But then came the day of betrayal. It was time to return to work. What could be more fulfilling than the days with my child? How could I walk out the door and leave her behind with May? I cried all the way to the office. I returned home for lunch that day and May put up with me then, but soon made it clear that Allison would be on a schedule and her days would go far more smoothly without my dropping in. I conceded that ground, glad to have the two days a week, still, that were all mine with my daughter. Departing in the morning continued to be agony, the ordeal of watching Allison's face watch me go.

On my off days, I frequently took the baby to the office. When we needed a photo for a new brochure, she was our poster child for a wanted child, which she surely was. I returned to full-time work, on schedule, after three months, but never found it easy to walk out the door.

Sometimes Chris took the baby to his office. He was at MIT, a beginning assistant professor in chemistry and biology. Negotiating the joint appointment almost cost him the MIT offer. But he needed to attract graduate students from both departments to pursue the scientific questions he wanted to tackle. Now he served two masters. He had nightmares that he wouldn't have enough creative ideas to fuel his lab. Against the advice of the chemistry head, he designed and taught a graduate course on enzymes that bridged biology and chemistry. He believed in his own strategic instinct and proved himself right, as he had before and would do again in a lifelong string of many such proofs. The course was a big draw, attracting brilliant students to the Walsh lab, and quite a few faculty auditors to the course. And—a bonus—he converted it into the textbook that underwrote Allison's education. All of it, through medical school.

The year after Allison's birth, I secured a federal grant to host a PPLM conference on new directions in contraceptive technology. I reserved space at the Worcester Foundation for Experimental Biology, birthplace of the birth control pill, and lined up a roster of speakers—scientists and physicians—on the frontiers of contraception research. For the luncheon speaker I invited the Massachusetts Commissioner of Public Health, William J. Bicknell, MD, recently recruited from Berkeley.

On the day of the conference, there was no sign of our featured speaker. I stood outside, shifting from foot to foot. Who would I dragoon as a fallback if he didn't show? Then, a nondescript black limo with state plates pulled up, braked abruptly, and disgorged Bill Bicknell from the back seat. His blonde hair was mussed. He had one shirt tail hanging out on the side, and a daub of what looked like ketchup on his tie. Maybe he stopped for a hamburger rather than wait for our lunch after his talk? A clutch of journalists was waiting to pounce. I hoped they weren't trolling for a negative story about our conference, but they had larger quarry.

"Mr. Commissioner," one shouted, "beekeepers across the state are protesting your aerial spraying of the insecticide malathion. They're calling it reckless endangerment of bee colonies. What's your answer?"

"We're trying to contain a deadly outbreak of Eastern equine encephalitis," Bicknell responded curtly, "I am sworn to protect the public. The humans. Not the bees."

"How do you justify the sweetheart deal you negotiated to come here from California?" another yelled.

"Easy. It's legal. It's proper and was thoroughly vetted. A contribution from the private sector. I took a large pay cut. Now if you will excuse me, I have a speech to give." I escorted Bicknell into the conference hall, introduced him to the waiting crowd, and turned over the podium.

He spoke informally without notes, but I noticed him glancing occasionally at his left hand. It was covered with what looked like scribbled word fragments in blue ink. Was this disheveled guy reading his talk off his palm? Really? The deliverable for my grant was a published conference proceeding. It would be incomplete without his talk. To be safe, I took some notes in case the recording failed and wrote them up that night at home.

The next week I contacted the speakers for copies of their papers. All complied except the commissioner. No surprise. I went to the library with my notes and the transcript to fabricate my best approximation of his luncheon talk. I spruced it up. When I had a draft, I sent it to him and asked if he would approve it for publication. He called me right away and said yes. Then he offered me a job. Big surprise! He needed someone who could write with him. I told him I had a new baby and put him off until February.

Right on schedule Bicknell called me back. The job was still mine if I wanted it. Leaving the warm embrace of PPLM was painful. I'd made good friends there and several board leaders asked me to consider becoming the next executive director. I was flattered but knew I had more to learn before I'd be ready to assume a role that might freeze me in place. This was just an instinct, but a strong one. I sensed that I was not yet where I wanted my career to take me, even though I was still unclear where that might be. When PPLM's board chair asked if I wanted to become a director, I jumped at the chance to learn what it was like to be on a governing board. I served for seven years. My first board experience, the first of many to come.

My remit with Bill Bicknell was to work with him on a column in the *New England Journal of Medicine,* one of the world's premier medical publications. At that time, the NEJM reserved a monthly space for the Massachusetts Department of Public Health, under the auspices of the commissioner. He supplied the topics, I researched and drafted the columns. We shared authorship. Only later did I come to appreciate how progressive these terms were. In future years I met gifted women who wrote for and with men—sometimes their husbands—and garnered at best a prominent acknowledgement, often no mention at all. A well-known case in point—one of countless examples—was Anne Ehrlich, who co-authored with her husband, Paul, the book we'd all been reading, *The Population Bomb*. Bill Bicknell was an early feminist, and it was a stroke of dumb luck that he was my first writing partner. After I worked with Bill I never accepted anything less than full billing.

Bill was fine with my working from home two days a week. On Allison's first birthday Chris and I sat down with May and asked if she might consider staying on for another year. To our surprise and great relief, she said yes. On that birthday, and each one to follow, we performed the ritual. The answer was always yes. May became like a member of our family. Quintessentially Boston Irish, she was rooted in the values of the Catholic Church. In a way, she was a surrogate for Chris's mother. We all loved her, Allison especially. She continued with us until Allison was 10. Some years later I set up an annuity for her through Wellesley's planned giving program. She sent us a thank you note every month without fail on the day the check arrived.

I learned a lot about public health from Bill Bicknell and, by observation, about leadership on a larger scale. We read together, wrote together, argued out our differences, and taught together. Long after I worked for him, I continued to draw on material I first developed with Bill. For all his brilliance and generosity, though, he was a handful as a boss. He was undisciplined and often oblivious of competing demands on my time and attention. He kept me on the phone, sometimes for an hour or more, while he unfurled some half-formed idea he thought we should write about. I think he enjoyed the sound of his rummaging mind. It occurred to me that my note taking—even on the phone—was feeding his ego. When I was home with the baby, there would come a point when I had no choice but to cut him off. This man who had no boundaries taught me essential lessons about how to assert my own.

Bill wanted us to write a "Special Article"—a study—evaluating the impact of a controversial program called Certificate of Need. He sent me to meet its director, Elaine Ullian. Just twenty-six years old, with a master's degree in public health, she wielded new and previously unthinkable financial power over the Commonwealth's hospital presidents. The legislature had passed the Certificate of Need law to require every hospital in the state to petition the health department for advanced approval before adding beds or services. Costs were rising in health care, insurance was footing the bills, and the theory was that hospitals prospered by growing until someone stopped them. That someone was Elaine Ullian. CEOs of even the mighty Harvard teaching hospitals were being stymied by this upstart young bombshell in three-inch heels who knew her stuff and stood her ground. I thought she was fabulous. She wore her power gladly without conflict. I could learn from her. Over the years, our friendship deepened until, like a Calder mobile, it became a centerpiece around which our two lives rotated.

Bill and I published our evaluation of Elaine's program, and ten briefer papers over the next eighteen months. Short articles on arcane topics—the control of Eastern equine encephalitis; the slow diffusion of a proven dental health measure: fluoridation of water supplies; the department's response to the first red tide outbreak in Massachusetts history; a new approach to nursing home regulation; expanded roles for physicians' assistants and nurse practitioners in primary care. It became an advanced course for me in public health, minus the tuition, classes, and exams.

As commissioner, Bicknell was a political appointee. So he was a goner with the election of Michael Dukakis in 1975. But he landed on his feet at the Harvard School of Public Health with a grant to cover his salary and a half-time colleague. From his large DPH team I was the one he chose to work with him there half time. I stayed on at the DPH, also half time, to write with the new commissioner, Jonathan Fielding. At HSPH, a faculty member, Marc Roberts, invited me to lunch. He'd seen a grant proposal I'd written and was curious about my plans.

"It's a fine piece of work," he said, and then asked if I minded some unsolicited advice. Of course not. I welcomed it.

"You have a decision to make. You can go on as you've been doing, supporting others' success. Or you can have your own career, go as far as you want. But if you want an independent role in the academy, you need a doctorate. The *sine qua non*. And the sooner the better."

Marc was right. Sure. But I had an infant at home, two part-time jobs vying with each other for a piece of me, plus a husband in a new job. There was the suburban house, secured with a loan from my father—I wasn't about to go to him for more tuition. And then there was the voice in my head, chiding me: this is a lot to manage already. Do you really want to take more on? And, by the way, who says you're smart enough to succeed in academia?

So I decided to review my current options and make a few inquiries. I instantly received offers from four leading Boston physicians, each prepared to hire me as a full-time writer. All attractive possibilities, worth weighing against each other. The writing stick still had its charm.

And then, unexpectedly, another variable came across my radar screen. It was over breakfast one morning as I idly scanned the *Boston Globe* want ads. I never read the want ads, but now I was feeling restless. What caught my eye was a display ad for a "HEALTH WRITER." I had not thought to define myself with those two words. But they fit. It was an identity I would later see as still too limiting, but, for now, intriguing. I cut out the ad and stepped into a wide new world on the other side.

4

I GET ON WITH MY LIFE

If I stepped off the carousel, I would lose my seat. I was sure of that. I had the health writer ad and was debating whether to apply. Elaine Ullian, my new friend, was in conversation with the brass at Boston University Hospital. I called her for a take on the doctor who sponsored the ad, this man everyone seemed to refer to by his last name, pronounced egg-doll.

"He casts a big shadow at BU, atop the whole show in medicine and health," she said. "Smart, restless, ambitious. But not young. I think of him as the past, not the future. Maybe fifty. Part of the University Hospital crowd. Where would the job be?"

"At the Health Policy Institute," I replied.

"He founded it and spends a lot of time there," Elaine confirmed. "Word is he persuaded President Silber to set him up with it as part of his package coming in. The HPI is his baby, a think tank that plays to national leaders in medicine, health, government, and especially business. He's to the right of Bicknell for sure. To the right of those Harvard health reformers you've been consorting with. He sees private industry as a force to slow inflation in health care costs. That's not who you've been. Is it who you want to be?"

Elaine had bored into the heart of my hesitancy. It was *not* who I wanted to be. Large corporations didn't need my help. I wanted to serve the underserved, women and children in the inner cities. People of color, blue- and pink-collar workers, laborers on minimum wage. The ones barely getting by in a rigged system. The ones being deafened by the planes in and out of Logan Airport. At least that was what I told myself. But did I have a clue how to be that person? Or was it a story I told myself so I could believe I was a caring person, intent on making up for this life of unearned privilege into which I'd landed. And then from a newer voice in my head—one growing weary of self-sabotage—came a pertinent impertinent question: Just a minute here, Diana, how many ways can you torment yourself? This is getting tedious! Get on with your life.

I applied for the job and was invited for an interview. There I found a world apart from the dingy government offices Elaine and I had occupied at the DPH downtown. The HPI filled a historic revival townhouse two blocks from Kenmore Square, with unimpeded views of the Charles River on its way to Boston Harbor. On the far shore were Cambridge and MIT. I was greeted by Dr. Egdahl, who moved like an athlete, trim, immaculately dressed in a suit and tie with short gray hair, a broad smile, and an outstretched hand. He directed me to a chair in front of a commanding desk. A single folder sat at its center.

"You've been busy," he said. "A solid publication record in a short time. I liked your certificate-of-need paper. You're enjoying working with Bicknell, it appears?" He had a sparkle that invited a response in kind. I described my situation. He described his position. He was the general editor of a flagship surgical series into which the publisher, Springer-Verlag, was plowing money. They had agreed to underwrite a more modest series on industry and health care, under his control.

"We've been experimenting with prototypes," he told me. "You'll take a look at them. I want these books to be accessible, inviting, and provocative. Not the usual academic tomes gathering dust. I want them to enter and advance the health policy discourse with new points of view."

We talked for most of an hour, a surprising one. He seemed as interested in what he could do for my career as in what I could bring to his project. He hinted at a future for me beyond the health writing, perhaps. He saw potential in me that felt attainable and real. I could work with this guy.

From his tone and demeanor I sensed that the job was mine if I wanted it. But the premise behind the project weighed on my mind. Would I be selling out, abandoning the moral purity of the public health mission? How pure, in the end, was it? How should I weigh a vague unease about the more conservative politics of this policy institute against my clear sense that of the five job options in front of me, Egdahl's offered the

greatest room for growth? The four Harvard docs had progressive credentials, well burnished, highly regarded. I would learn from them, but as a
hired hand. In contrast, this striving surgeon had power and resources
that he seemed inclined to invest in my development. Would I be striking
a Faustian bargain? I wasn't sure. But I decided to trust my gut and take
the plunge.

In February 1976, I started at the Health Policy Institute. Dick stopped
by my office the first day to show me his prototypes for the Springer
books. I hated them. They were not serious or substantial. They had hardly
any text, mostly illustrations, cartoons in garish colors. I held my tongue
and bought time to figure out how to tell him so. Someone in authority
at Springer must have shared my view because the publisher soon sent
a new set of prototypes that were recognizable as books: a reprieve. The
series would extract much of its material from interdisciplinary working
conferences. Springer had agreed to bring the books out no more than six
months after each meeting to ensure that they were timely. I would have
to write them quickly and to run hard to keep up. I liked that.

On the home front, Chris and I were considering one more move—our
fifth in six years. Our realtor showed us a few houses, all in the city of
Newton where we already had good friends. I especially liked the one she
showed us in a quiet Waban neighborhood, set back on a lot behind a
stand of mature maples and oaks. I imagined it would be almost like living in the woods. Chris didn't say much.

Next, she ushered us into a more formal house on Commonwealth
Avenue in West Newton. This one was brick Tudor with a slate roof and
a spacious step-down living room opening to a brick and lead-glass-lined
sunroom beyond. Chris took one look from the front foyer and whispered to me, "This is more beautiful than any house I ever imagined for
myself." With a silent pang of regret, I abandoned my forest fantasy and
we put down our roots on the busiest thoroughfare in greater Boston.

On Patriot's Day in April, a hidden virtue of Chris's dream house
revealed itself: a ringside seat for the Boston Marathon, a family festival
for the whole 26.2 miles. Lawn chairs, picnics everywhere, people sport-
ing costumes and hand-made signs. Neighbors flowed in and out from
all directions to cheer the runners. We were situated in the heart of it, at

mile 17.5. It became part of our lives, reinforced the sense of community I always craved, and turned me into a runner. The other days of the year, I ran up and down the grass median on Comm Ave early every morning before others were up, even in rain or snow. In three miles on weekdays, five or more on weekends, I earned my endorphin high and managed the stress of my frequent race back and forth on the Mass Pike to be present in my daughter's life.

I was engaged in my work at BU, daily more confident that I'd made the right professional choice. Dick Egdahl was the mentor I sensed he would be. I was learning fast and building confidence in my ability to create. But I feared I was missing the pleasure of watching Allison grow. I was discovering with my generation of feminist trailblazers that our newly claimed freedoms came at a price.

In May, I traveled to a Cornell University conference on health care costs and secured permission to draw on it for the first book in our series. June brought our first Springer conference. Dick was in his element moderating. At the end, he called on a distinguished professor of medical sociology, Sol Levine, for a ten-minute summary of the two days. Those two conferences, both recorded, and with background papers, would form the backbone of the inaugural series volume I would write.

Dick told me the book "would write itself." I disagreed. Whether I'd be able to put my stamp on it remained to be seen. We would address industry, broadly defined. I titled it *Payer, Provider, Consumer: Industry Confronts Health Care Costs*, and spent two weeks in Harvard's medical library with materials from the two conferences in front of me. Using pretty much everything I learned in my years with Bill Bicknell and before that at Planned Parenthood, I wove a narrative that answered my own question: Why care?

"Through industry's window onto the health care system," I wrote as my opening, "it is possible to see most of the urgent policy choices confronting us, along with many of the built-in conflicts that confound those choices." I laid out five that matter for everyone's health, for the national economy, for access to quality care, affordability, and equitable distribution of needed medical services. By the time I completed the draft I'd made my peace with the bargain I'd struck. I could work at the intersection of private industry and health care, make a worthy contribution, and feel whole.

I delivered the manuscript draft to Dick's inbox on a Friday with a note inviting his input. And I looked forward to a free weekend at home with Allison and Chris now that I'd moved the all-consuming project off my desk. Before I left the office, I checked in briefly with Elaine. She and I had begun settling into what would become a deeply nourishing friendship. One that became intimate in ways I never knew existed, or believed could exist for me: an unconditional bond that was naturally reciprocal. It eliminated the usual worries about giving and getting, deserving or owing. We and our other friends knew this as a core friendship for us both. We two, too, formed a multitude. Chris honored it. And it laid the foundation for a whole array of new and astounding friendships that would enrich—and define—the remainder of my life.

Back at work on Monday morning, Dick asked to see me. I saw my manuscript on his desk, the only item there. He was a neatnik.

"I had a feeling the first time we met that you wouldn't have a ceiling," he began. "That you could do whatever you set your mind to. Now I'm sure. The only thing you lack is a PhD. We need to get you one. Then the sky's the limit."

I guessed he liked the draft.

He told me he had a plan. He was a professor of medicine and also a University Professor. As was Sol Levine, the sociologist who had summarized the first conference. President Silber created the University Professors Program on his arrival in Boston as one of his early gambits to up BU's academic game. Elie Wiesel was a University Professor, as was Alasdair MacIntyre, and other world-class scholars including Silber himself. All had joint appointments in one or more BU schools or colleges in addition to UNI as it was known. A small college housed within a vast university, UNI concentrated excellence and valorized interdisciplinary work.

To qualify for the doctoral program, applicants had to propose a project that crossed disciplinary boundaries and enlist a committee from the program's faculty. Dick sent me to see if Sol Levine would agree to cosponsor me. Then on to the Dean of Management, Jules Schwartz, another UNI member. With the guidance of these three I would be free to fashion and pursue my own curriculum for a PhD in health policy.

I could tell Sol wasn't sure what to make of me. Was this young woman with a journalism degree UNI material? We spent an hour together in his book-lined UNI office. He had two others. One was across town on the medical campus where he was active in the School of Public Health as a professor of social and behavioral sciences. The other was a few blocks down Commonwealth Avenue in the sociology department, which he had chaired off and on as its most prominent member. There he was close to the Marxist scholar, Mike Miller, and his wife, Jean Baker Miller, who, at Wellesley College, was unseating Freud's alienating views of women's psychological growth. Sol walked a middle path, a wide, many-laned highway he traversed with gusto and grace. He, too, would become a major influence on my life for the rest of his, as I wended my own way along his middle path.

At this first private meeting—we had met at the Springer conference—Professor Levine was cordial but formal, with a deep voice and the air of someone accustomed to receiving supplicants for an academic laying on of hands. I was prepared and ready to present myself.

"I've learned a lot about public health and medical care systems," I said and referenced some of his writings. "I've worked with physicians who have a natural claim to dominance in health policy. They have legitimacy and specialized knowledge, not to mention professional prestige. If I am going to make a distinctive contribution, I will need my own academic roots." In anticipation of our meeting, I'd read the textbook Levine coedited with two colleagues, the *Handbook of Medical Sociology*, recently released in a second edition. Not long later, in 1989, I would contribute a chapter for the third edition.

"I want to understand the debates and cross-currents in this growing sub-discipline of sociology," I said. "To master those and hold them up against work in other disciplines that are remaking American medicine in what I see as a pivotal period." I did not delude myself that I had won Sol over in our hour together. More likely he agreed to take me on as a courtesy to the colleague who held the BU purse strings for all things medical. But he said yes, and gave me a list of additional faculty to consult. His name opened doors, as did Egdahl's.

A few days later, Jules Schwartz readily agreed to join Sol and Dick on the committee. What remained for me was to design a program of coursework, choose a topic for a dissertation, research and write it. Then defend it. And to shoehorn what would likely be a five-year grind into a full-time job, a young daughter at home, and a busy husband whose career was taking off.

I did pause briefly to ask myself whether this was the path I truly wanted. Surely, it was one of those openings in life that seemed providential and irresistible. After all, I had cast my lot with Chris Walsh, a true academic, now a tenured associate professor at MIT. That he was far smarter than I was self-evident—to me anyway. Yet he believed in me, believed in this path for me. And I was almost ready to believe in it for myself. I relished the research and writing of the NEJM articles and the Springer books, the satisfaction of making new discoveries, constructing new arguments, accumulating a store of specialized knowledge. With Chris's support at home, I felt sure I could complete this PhD.

Already so much more than the nurturing father neither of us had known, Chris delighted in our fascinating daughter as she did in him. He could bring her to gales of laughter. Maybe it was their Irish blood. I would have to count on him to play an even more active role with Allison which, I was sure, would deepen his special bond with her. And weaken mine? A price I might have to pay.

I had been following Alice Rossi, the feminist scholar, who observed that men have as much to gain as do women in the struggle to dismantle rigid gender roles that define parenthood. Rossi, in the 1970s, was early to argue that children could thrive, even from infancy, without "continuous mothering." She resurrected for modern feminism powerful tracts from the 1870s that John Stuart Mill and Harriet Taylor Mill wrote collaboratively and with equal billing. They made the case for, and lived, a marriage that was egalitarian and intellectually productive for both partners. That's what Chris and I would have the chance to improvise together, I told myself, if I were to throw myself now into becoming a true academic.

On a crisp September morning in 1978 I took Allison by the hand and walked her to the local public school for her first day of kindergarten.

From that day onward the shoosh of dried leaves underfoot would fold her five-year-old hand back into mine. Jitters and excitement radiated from her as I fended off the melancholy of the one-wayness of time. Allison did well at the Peirce School in West Newton. She made friends and thrived.

I worked hard to be in evidence when other mothers were, chaperoning trips, attending class presentations, shows, and demonstrations of student work. I tried not to be late or, worse, absent. After one such occasion to which I had sped west on the Mass Pike to arrive just under the wire, I was driving Allison home and blurted out to her: "Maybe I should quit my job and just be your mom." She looked at me and burst into tears. I did not pause to explore—then or later—what stood behind those tears, any more than my mother would have done with me. I retreated behind the old familiar wall of silence. I wanted desperately to take her reaction as an affirmation that she liked things as they were, liked having a mom who worked. But that was far too facile. At some level, I must have recognized my overture as a lame attempt at an apology. Her tears reflected her stress, provoked by my own. I harbored serious doubts about whether I was being a "good mother." And I knew I was being less than honest with her. I had no intention of quitting my job. A "better" mother—one less stressed and distracted—would have stopped the action right there and met the message behind my daughter's tears. Instead, the incident stayed with me, laden with unasked questions and corrosive self-doubts.

But I did carve out time to be with Allison and to admire the person she was becoming. She loved books and stories. I read to her frequently and was saddened when she told me she preferred to read to herself. We went through a period of making hand-made cloth dolls together and sewing elaborate costumes for them. The world's worst seamstress, I managed to muddle through.

The five years I worked toward my PhD while holding a demanding job were the travail I anticipated. Being a full-time employee qualified me for the tuition remission that made the doctorate affordable. Chris had entered an intense phase of his advancing career and was bringing in extra income as a sought-after consultant. He was also assuming more than his share at home without complaint. It felt incumbent on me to complete my degree with all deliberate speed. I took courses many evenings while Chris cooked for Allison or took her out for dinner. They ate at a family-style Italian restaurant called The Chateau. The Shadow, they called it. They played the jukebox and something like table-top shuffleboard with packets of sugar. Chris invented a game of elimination in which he offered pairs of preposterous names from which Allison would choose one, then matched it in another pair. Esmeralda and Cruella often won the sweepstakes. They would arrive home laughing, and I would be grateful as well as happy for them both, but also secretly sorry to be missing the fun.

In the summer of 1981, we toured Australia for a month with Jeremy Knowles, Chris's close colleague and scientific collaborator who would later become dean of Harvard's Faculty of Arts and Sciences. Jeremy, with his wife, Janie, designed the trip that crossed the continent by train and ended in Perth for a scientific meeting. I was along for the ride on this excursion that delivered on that half-joking promise Chris had made to me when we were engaged.

All across Australia I hauled the draft of my thesis, thinking I'd work on it. With no input from me, it weighed more every day. At the Australian National University, Chris bought me a T-shirt that read "Don't ask me about my thesis." The entire month he tried to persuade me that this thesis was not my life's work but a hurdle to clear on the way. He was always focused and disciplined. The T-shirt is now long gone. And the thesis? An ambitious undertaking I later distilled into a book, *Corporate Physicians: Between Medicine and Management*, published by Yale University Press in 1987.

Back in 1982, the year before I defended my dissertation and received my PhD, I became an adjunct assistant professor in BU's School of Public Health. I continued at the HPI and split my time about evenly between the two campuses, teaching two evenings a week at SPH on the medical campus. Dick continued to cover my full salary, another expression of his generous support. The academic appointment opened new doors. I traveled a couple of days a month, mostly in the United States. I gave talks and presented papers at conferences, consulted with corporate executives on their health and medical programs, and, whenever possible, squeezed in interviews of corporate medical directors and other executives for my dissertation.

In addition, I had recently received a grant from New York's Commonwealth Fund, $1 million in start-up funding to design a study to evaluate treatment options for problem-drinking workers identified on the job. I would run that study with collaborators at the SPH, even though the Commonwealth Fund knew me for work I'd done at the HPI on the topic of corporate-sponsored employee assistance programs. I was back to serving multiple masters, still finishing my doctorate with appointments and commitments in two units, quite separate both physically and philosophically.

But the interdependencies held the arrangement together. The design for my dissertation was my entry into qualitative social sciences research, an approach that required collecting and interpreting data, inventing concepts, and producing narratives to capture the layered meanings of social reality. The randomized controlled trial, in contrast, was a quantitative design using standardized measures, the epitome of experimentally tight research in medicine and the social sciences. The two approaches were complementary, as we taught our students in methods courses, and I was deeply immersed in them both.

Allison did well at Peirce, but we began to feel she might have outgrown the school. Equipped with Chris's curiosity, and his capacious mind, she was filing away reams of data from her own voracious reading. All the kings and queens of England and much of European history. Back to the Greeks, too. Every classical myth. What seemed like the greater part of English literature, all the Russian novels of the nineteenth century, and P. G. Wodehouse's total opus, which she read multiple times. From no age at all it was clear that this small person was an intellectual.

We asked her if she would like to change schools. Respect for her autonomy to make her own decisions was axiomatic for us. After visiting several schools, she selected the Winsor School. That spring Mary McCarthy let us know she planned to retire at the end of the school year. The one year had extended to a decade; Allison had won her heart.

For her first two years at Winsor, Allison rode a bus to and from school, while Chris and I coordinated to be certain one of us was home by at least

5:30. She insisted that she had outgrown babysitters and could manage on her own after school. To my mind that made her a latchkey child, the worst sort of child neglect in my mother's lexicon. But Allison was confident and we deferred to her judgment, even though it intensified the pressure to be home on time. Then, it led to a rash purchase.

One gloomy day we three were in the car doing errands and I muttered, out of nowhere, that there was no chaos in our lives. Chris, a master decoder, translated my word chaos to spontaneity and fun. He didn't need to hear more. A quick U-turn to the local pet shop, and we emerged with a tiny fur ball, a headstrong cocker spaniel we named Magellan—an explorer who became a devoted companion, welcoming my latchkey daughter home, and wandering on with us through many future lives.

I received my PhD in health policy at BU's graduation in May 1984 and was promoted from assistant to associate director of the Health Policy Institute. We'd grown the staff and published seven volumes in the Springer series and two more with a new publisher, Ballinger. I distilled my doctoral dissertation into journal articles and the Yale University Press book. I delivered a keynote address on my findings for a national conference of occupational physicians, the group I had studied, doctors who served two masters—their patients and the firms that paid their salaries. I drew on a sizable literature on organizations, professions, and ethics, and made a case that doctors, to be effective in these roles, would have to be especially conscious of moral dilemmas, be politically skilled and astute, and be sensitive to conflicting demands on their loyalty.

Unlike the Springer series, these publications were mine alone.

We had held two conferences each year following the formula that suited Dick's quick and restless mind. He moderated them. I participated actively in planning and leading them, and now I delivered the closing summary that Sol Levine had delivered for the first conference. I braided multiple threads into a tapestry in which everyone recognized pieces of their own contributions and marveled at the richness of the larger meaning we, collectively, had made in our two days together. In the early years I stayed up much of the night straining to pull out the threads and connections. In time I discovered I had a flair for it, this weaving of disparate

ideas. I came to delight in doing it, in creating an integrated shared expe-
rience that would elevate the whole proceeding. It came more easily once
I learned to trust my process, and to relax into this particular intelligence
I was able now to acknowledge.

The house on Commonwealth Avenue in which we lived longer than
anywhere else was ideal for entertaining and we did our share of it, hosting birthday parties for each of us and parties to welcome new colleagues
or say farewell as others moved on. All three of us had good friends there
and the Newton years were happy ones. But by 1987, the year I was promoted to full professor, Chris was becoming restless professionally even
though his career at MIT was everything he had ever wanted and more.
Beyond academia, he had made a mark in big pharma as a consultant and
had brought his strategic intuition to several promising biotech startups.
The dean of the Harvard Medical School, Dan Tosteson, persuaded him to
leave MIT to refound the HMS pharmacology department by merging it
with a separate department of biochemistry. Chris was hired to bring the
combined entity into the twenty-first century. Members of the targeted
departments were sure to respond much as hornets do when their nests
are poked.

Uncharacteristically, Chris was beset by second thoughts for the three
months between his decision to go and the actual move. It was he who
would usually set a new course and never look back. On moving day,
his research group vacated a whole floor at MIT amid "Better Dead than
Med" signs posted by students from other groups. Nevertheless, he rapidly established himself as an HMS player. As chair of the new department
of biological chemistry and molecular pharmacology, he turned it into a
powerhouse among the five preclinical divisions of what he had always
considered "the one true medical school." He was back at Harvard, where
I had met him as a junior aspiring to become a physician. That was before
he was transfixed by the siren song of basic science. He may have taken a
detour but had found his way home.

From the Winsor graduating class of 1991, Allison and two others went
on to the one true medical school and successful careers as physicians,
after attending separate colleges (Stanford for Allison). The night before
Chris was scheduled to lecture for the first time to her Harvard class, he

tossed and turned in anxious anticipation, and was buoyed after the talk by Allison's review.

"They loved your lecture, Dad," she told him. "They say you have my sense of humor."

Back at the BU School of Public Health, the alcoholism study was weighing me down. From the outset I was sure I'd been tapped to lead it because I was a woman. The Commonwealth Fund was looking for promising women to sponsor. The vice president, Tom Moloney, had seen me in action at our HPI conferences and had approached me to consider the project. The study would answer an important policy question, and also set a new quality standard for research on alcoholism treatment, a field long tangled in ideology. That is, if I could pull it off.

Tom suggested that I, as the principal investigator, enlist an SPH colleague, Ralph Hingson, as my coinvestigator. Ralph led a research group that specialized in alcoholism research. He knew more about prevention and treatment than I did and more, too, about the research methodology. This was good advice, and I did recruit Ralph. But the thought that he deserved to be the PI colonized my mind. My insecurity threatened to turn our collaboration into a one-woman power struggle.

It got the better of me one critical day during a high-stakes site visit by an external committee reviewing our proposal for a large federal grant essential to completing the project. The chair asked me a question which I was preparing to answer when Ralph interrupted and took over. Or so it felt to me. The instant the committee left, I lashed out at him, releasing pent-up frustration I'd harbored for a couple of years. His reaction stunned me. He told me how much he respected me, insisting that my understanding of the larger context was vital to our project. Near tears, he said he deeply valued our partnership. More than that, he said, he valued our friendship. The incident cleared the air between us, and we got our grant. But it left me ashamed of how completely I had misjudged Ralph. It was a bitter lesson to me of the poison of insecurity. I was going to have to find better ways to keep it in check.

We drove to the GE plant in Lynn, Massachusetts every couple of weeks. Ralph was driving one day, and I was fulminating about our recruitment and funding challenges. A truck pulled in front of us with a tiger head filling the back panel. An angry one. "Ah, there you are," said Ralph. "You are looking in the mirror." We chuckled, but I took note of Ralph's invitation to lighten up.

And then, unbidden from an unexpected source, came my opportunity to lighten up in the company of new companions. With them, I would wade into and through what I came to see as a mild midlife crisis that I'd been holding at bay.

"This looks like you," Dick said, and dropped a packet on my desk. "Save the whales." I looked up from my computer, but he was gone, back down the flight of stairs between my office and his. It was 1986 and I was in a spacious office atop his where, a decade earlier, I first met him and was dazzled by his view of the Charles River. Now I enjoyed it too.

What had he left for me? A flashy brochure requesting him to nominate candidates for an initiative of the W. K. Kellogg Foundation, a fellowship program for outstanding midcareer leaders on a trajectory to catalyze positive social change.

I was cautiously intrigued. Was this the direction I wanted to go? Away from pure academia? How far away would it take me? What about Chris and Allison? It would take me away from home a good bit, the overview made clear.

I decided to apply. After all, the odds of getting an interview were roughly one in ten, and then only a 50/50 chance of being selected. Dick believed I was a shoo-in and nominated me. I was invited to Chicago for an interview, which, to my surprise, I found relaxing and fun. I felt sure then that I'd be selected.

I was, but I had no inkling that the program would be the transformation it became for me. The first required seminar in June 1987 was an ordeal. Called "Perspectives on Leadership," it oriented Group VIII of the Kellogg National Fellowship in a busy orientation week in Wayzata, Minnesota. I was met by a van at the Minneapolis airport with five other fellows, all strangers making small talk. I hate small talk. By the time we arrived at the conference center and I was directed to my room—which looked like a monastic cell—I was glad for a place to retreat to, alone. Already we were sizing each other up and would continue all week to measure ourselves against the forty-four other lottery winners who nailed the selection process. A frequent topic during breaks was what we took from the interview about who they wanted. Many of us hinted at feeling like imposters. Maybe that was our common denominator.

We were hard drivers working in health, education, food systems, the environment, inequalities—all priorities of the Kellogg Foundation. We were organizers, writers, activists, scholars, leaders, founders of small nonprofits. About a third were academics venturing beyond the ivory tower. We were in our thirties and forties, most married with kids. We were a diverse group: five women and six men of color, and various ethnicities and sexual orientations. Six physicians, half women, and our token private-sector guys, two white male executives.

Each of us was given a primitive laptop computer—our first ever in most cases—and taught to use a primordial version of the internet run out of Michigan State University. "Confer," it was called, and our first experience with email. Remember: this was 1987. None of us suspected, as Confer sucked us in, that the internet would devour our later lives. We were told we'd be in constant connection; the community we would create was an intentional feature of the program. Kellogg saw to that.

This first meeting was designed to plant our community's seeds. We met individually and in groups, spread out among five faculty mentors. On the second day a flamboyant woman broke into her mentoring group, breathless and loud, to announce that her boyfriend tried to kill her the night before and burned her house down. The story spread rapidly and some of us were wide eyed. Others were thrilled to welcome the arrival of a "real person" to shake up the foundation's social engineering. The program director, a former mother superior, took a dim view of the late arrival but remained a model of hospitality and equanimity.

We were marched through small group exercises on styles of leadership. I liked the material and especially the experiential pedagogy. We were encouraged to self-organize into interest clusters on themes of our choosing. Many seemed to be in their element—to have died and gone to heaven—but I felt as though I'd been dropped into a mixer from hell. Everyone seemed to be an extravert. Later I would discover what an oversimplification that was. But all I saw were confident people strutting their stuff, in sales mode, jockeying for attention, grabbing available airtime. And it was only the first day!

Meals were their own dilemma, with tables of eight and no assigned seating. Fellows vied for the seats nearest the people who glittered. At the first meal one table was by far the loudest, erupting in raucous laughter. The second and subsequent meals revealed that Dr. Nancy Snyderman was the magnet, invariably, at the unruly table. Later she became a good friend and, later still, a lifelong soul mate. But that orientation week inscribed me with a permanent memory of the stinging dynamic of in- and out-groups. On the third day, a limo appeared early to take Nancy to the airport for a flight to New York and an appearance on Good Morning America. We watched her on TV the next morning, and she was back with us for dinner. That night her table levitated; like a UFO it hovered above the rest of us.

As the week progressed, I heard reports from optional sessions I'd avoided. People were gushing about them as profoundly meaningful. "Spiritual" was the word I was hearing, softly spoken. Some who spoke it struck me as thoughtful, approachable. Is this what the introverts did? But spiritual was not a word that worked for me. It smacked of New Ageism, anti-science, anti-intellectual. I opted for other sessions. My field was health policy, so I sought out the physicians. I liked them but I lacked the central element of their identity, this guild of card-carrying docs who were policy wonks on the side.

After lunch one afternoon I took a run on a golf course with five fellows and one of our advisors. I'd been thinking some of us might undertake a group project together during our fellowship, shape a contribution by pooling our knowledge and skills with some of the foundation's funds. When I mentioned it, the advisor said no and slowed us to a walk.

"That is not why you are here. The purpose of this program is to invest in you. That's why we selected you. Later you will pay the investment forward many times over in your work through the rest of your lives." W.K. Kellogg's credo was "I'll invest my money in people."

Soon the week was over. Bags were packed, piled by the door, tagged with flight information. Larraine Matusak, the director, mentioned the form we were to sign and return within ten days to confirm our membership in Group VIII. I asked around as we awaited the airport vans. Everyone planned to continue. I hid my doubts. When I landed at Logan

Airport, it was harder to hide them at the sight of Chris and Allison waiting at the gate to meet me.

Over the next few days, I wrestled with the urge to flee. I had done
fine at the meeting, made connections, some potential friends. What was
holding me back? A mild bout of social anxiety I had known off and on
since I was a kid. It was time to leave it behind, I decided, and I signed
Larraine's form. There had always been a force within that propelled me
toward the next hard thing.

When the three years were over, we would say there were no bad partners,
no bad seats on the bus. And we piled into a *lot* of buses for some long
and bumpy rides. At first, I angled for a seat mate I could count on as easy
company. One who would carry a conversation. But with time I came
to relish the Kellogg silences. Preserving those was a surprising aspect of
the fellowship's ethos, amid all the chatter. An aspect that would affirm a
natural preference I found in myself, this comfort in quiet. In time I came
to believe in its strength.

An African American fellow commented that, in retrospect, there were
no "effing racists" in the group. He said this on a COVID-forced Zoom
call that stood in for our thirty-first annual reunion, three decades after
our final seminar in 1990. The racial reckoning following George Floyd's
murder was much on our minds that weekend as we gathered personal
perspectives and swapped readings we'd found of value. Group VIII was
unique within the larger fellowship in our practice of coming together for
a weekend reunion every year, generally with fewer than a dozen members missing. This was testament to the tight bonds we'd forged and our
determination to hold onto this group that had helped many of us find
our north star. We didn't want to lose it.

The bonds took time to form. I went alone to my first outing after the
opening seminar, a weekend conference called "The Power of Laughter
and Play." I doubted anyone else would want to come with me and didn't
inquire. It would be good for me to strike out on my own, I rationalized. I
would anchor this fellowship in an explicit act of personal agency. A week
later I was in a packed hotel ballroom with a bunch of strangers taking

instruction from Steve Allen Jr., son of the entertainer, teaching us how to juggle with colorful scarves. I did not learn how to juggle, but I did learn the *stages* of learning to juggle. Most vivid were stage five, "the guilt-free drop," and stage ten, the "Ta-Da!" Drop the judgments and remember to celebrate. Above all, lighten up. These were goals I carried forward through the fellowship and beyond. I would take myself and my life less seriously. And, in the future, round up at least one partner; guilt-free juggling would have been much more fun with a Kellogg playmate.

Our second all-fellows seminar was strictly business: a week at the Center for Creative Leadership in Greensboro, known, to this day, for its personalized and experiential leadership programs that emphasize assessment and feedback, goal setting, and peer learning. Psychologists with clipboards followed us around. They set up and observed "leaderless group" exercises and documented our behavior through one-way mirrors. They administered batteries of personality tests and leadership profiles. In advance, they asked us to enlist coworkers back home to fill out long questionnaires on what we did well and badly, a "360" which was new to me then, and gave me pause.

My Myers-Briggs Type Indicator test pegged me as INTP, not the most common combination, I was told, especially among women. It described an "absent-minded professor," driven by curiosity and a desire to learn everything possible. Some of that rang true. But I had my doubts about the scientific validity of the whole endeavor. Surely this attempt to quantify human predilections and interactions as they manifest in complex and shifting circumstances could not help but oversimplify. I did, however, listen carefully for habits I should try to break.

One of the fellows described me as intimidating and intense. "She hauls out an intellectual elephant gun in a tough argument." I was amazed. I'd always thought of myself as a peacemaker, never a big game hunter. I resolved to tune into feelings of aggression.

On a test of decision-making styles, I came across as highly inclusive, consultative, almost to a fault. That did ring true. These contradictions could coexist, I realized, as tensions and antinomies to be noted and held with curiosity, humor, and humility. We were identifying traps that can trigger any of us, and did at times trap me, to be less than the admirable leader—the caring human—I aspired to be. I thought of the insecurities that had fed my tensions with Ralph.

Ralph and I were coteaching a methods course together at night. On many days we felt like road warriors pitching the study at GE facilities all over the country. The enrollment was slow at our initial site, GE's aircraft engine plant in Lynn, Massachusetts, and we needed more research subjects. We hoped to line up additional GE plants to hasten the study along. I made several solo trips to GE headquarters in Fairfield, Connecticut and one to a plant in Waukesha, Wisconsin. Together, Ralph and I made repeated trips to Schenectady, New York, where GE started out, and to Appliance Park, in Louisville, Kentucky. There we met at the union hall in a culture of heavy drinking and smoking. We must have come across as aliens, a couple of callow public health purists from Boston. On our first visit my presentation was interrupted before I completed my third sentence. The union president held up his hand to me and turned his head toward a union brother standing by the entrance. "Go get Fred," he said with a drawl. "Tell him to get in here quick with his thee-saurus." Evidently my attempt at clear communication had misfired.

Five months after the leadership bootcamp in Greensboro, another of our weeklong Kellogg seminars involved a two-hour train ride to Battle Creek. I sat next to a psychiatric nurse and nurse educator who recounted her family history. She grew up in Florida, in a family that passed memories of living in slavery down through generations of women. They picked cotton in the fields, lived in constant terror for themselves and those they loved, found strength in faith, in community and creativity. They prevailed in the end with preternatural strength. I said something self-deprecating about my being a privileged WASP. We take much for granted, lack much in the way of culture, and sorely lack survival skills anything like those you've just described to me.

She reacted strongly. If I took inspiration from her stories, she said, fine. But it was equally the case that I came from a world no one in her family could have known anything about. The hand we were now in a position to extend to one another was across the common ground we had found from our vastly different starting points. If I denigrated my own story in comparison to hers then I would vitiate our connection, depriving us both of an authentic encounter with the other.

"Never apologize for who you are," she said with urgency.

From Battle Creek, I split off with a newly formed small group of six fellows for a weekend retreat on "spirituality," the whispered word at Spring Hill that nearly drove me away. We met on five weekends over the three years in rugged or remote settings known for their sacred aura and proximity to nature. We spent time in silent meditation with a facilitator who specialized in what she called "releasing techniques that free the heart, open it to a life of joy, fulfillment and limitless possibilities." We'll see, I told myself.

She did have a calming presence as she guided visualizations in a melodic, almost hypnotic voice. In a circle, she encouraged us, if we chose, to give voice to some of what was coming up out of the stillness. I was moved by stories others told of growing up, one in a large family on a subsistence farm that administered harsh discipline and left him to fend for himself, another in a small immigrant family, abandoned by her father, raised by a loving mother who barely made ends meet. Their stories tapped into a personal sadness that I had always tried to keep under wraps.

At first, I was confused and embarrassed by my unexpected emotions. But in this accepting group, they became a release, a watering of arid ground, a clearing of space. We went more fully inward each time we met. I felt myself becoming a different person, more at peace with myself, more trusting of my emotions, my intuition, and imagination, newly aware of the possibility—and the relief—of unconditional acceptance. I began a meditation practice.

Back home, Chris and I often folded our small family into the larger families of good friends—dinners on the Cape with the Silbeys and their two daughters, summer travel with the Furies and their two boys, Sunday dinners and Jewish holidays at the Ullians. Elaine commented to me one day that she could see me changing, and so could Chris.

"I think he may be worrying that you will grow away from him," she said. "Not that he's said so in so many words, but . . ."

Many of the Kellogg fellows were feeling badly for the spouses we left behind to cover for us during our frequent excursions. Reentry would be an issue, we had been warned, and it was. Chris never begrudged me the time away, but there was no avoiding the impact of my life-altering experiences and deepening friendships with men and women he did not know. Neither of us could be certain where I would come out. When a fellow whose expertise was family systems offered a weekend for anyone who would like to bring a spouse or partner, I invited Chris and he agreed to come.

The couples retreat was in New Orleans. The facilitator spoke of stressors in committed partnerships and then sent us blindfolded into the city to explore how it felt to be a leader or a follower. Chris led me around town and then we swapped positions. It was no surprise that each of us was more comfortable in our conventional role: Chris leading, me following. He was the inveterate map reader with an unfailing sense of direction and I could be counted on reliably to take the wrong turn. He was the focused one, always on task, watching the clock, while I was all over the place, lost in time and space. I kind of enjoyed being the leader, though. It felt like giving Chris the gift of my attention. A gift of love he had been giving me all these years, when I at times wished I could shake loose of his control. I decided to take a firmer hand—greater agency—in my marriage and in my life.

The other moment that stuck with us both was a four-corner exercise back in the hotel meeting room. Each corner was labeled with a sign: Leader, Follower, Obstructor, Observer. Which are each of you most often in your marriages? When the chime rings, head to your corner. Chris and I found ourselves—together and all alone—under the Observer sign, laughing. Everyone in the room, spread out in the other three corners, laughed with us too. Who is *in* that marriage? Actually *doing* it?

In October 1988, Kellogg took us to Brazil for two weeks. We flew to Manaus way upriver where the Rio Negro meets the Rio Solimoes flowing down from the upper Amazon. For more than four miles the two rivers run together without mixing. Two starkly different colors, side-by-side, like oil and water. A metaphor for the time it takes for differences to blend.

I would remember, in the years after the Kellogg fellowship, the flight a few of us took the next morning on a small plane over the Amazon basin. The president of the University of Amazonas narrated the gut-wrenching images below. Smoke and flames billowed into the air for mile after mile as he told us of economic incentives that drove slash-and-burn agricultural practices no one seemed able to halt. This tragedy would accelerate in years to follow. The rainforest was vanishing, the lungs of the planet. This was a wake-up call—a relatively early one for me—to a concern that in later years would absorb much of my attention.

Back in the states, some of us began to discuss whether we had enough mutual trust to expose our vulnerabilities around another theme that would long follow me—race and racism. It was 1989 and much remained unspoken. The fellows the Foundation had carefully selected—expecting us to be real with each other—were the most diverse group of which most of us had ever been part. With that in mind, we planned a weekend retreat with an outside facilitator. Some twenty of us attended, African American, Hispanic, Jewish, whites from a range of backgrounds including a couple of WASPs, men and women in roughly equal proportions. The first thing I discovered on Friday night was that there were as many fracture planes within these identity groups as there were across them. We stayed up late, drinking wine, waxing philosophical, and, toward the end, picking at buried resentments.

First thing the next morning our facilitator poured gasoline on the hot embers from the evening before. His unresolved issues inflamed ours. The group was badly splintered into resentful subgroups. A few members were ready to bolt. Two fellows—both men, one white, one Black—took the situation in hand. They fired the incendiary facilitator and telephoned a potential replacement one of them knew. He arrived within an hour, sized up the situation and promptly had us rearranging furniture. An inward facing circle of about 10 seats was set up in the center of the living room with space around it. People of color were to sit in the circle facing each other, whites to stand in silence on the outside.

He asked those in the center to talk to each other as though no one was watching. To speak as they did in private about what it is like to be a minority in America. What were the everyday incidents that grind them down?

Not that I hadn't thought about race and racism. I had. A lot. For years I'd read and absorbed many of the leading Black writers. I'd taken in the sting of injustice from friends of color and felt the justification for rage. But never had I felt it so viscerally. To see it through the eyes of this diverse group, to hear it in their stories, was to lift the veil on a private conversation that had been closed to me. It cut to the quick to hear these accomplished and sensitive people express their pain.

They nodded in recognition, in sympathy and shared frustration, in controlled rage, about the "talk" they give their sons, the warnings to their daughters, discussed much in later years but new to many of us whites then. A father in our group described the memory of watching his son, now a teenager, take his first step. He felt his boy's joy—his pride and exultation—for only the fleeting moment before the next thought overtook the father: my son doesn't yet know he is Black. As they went around the circle one last time, I registered this as an afternoon I would not forget.

And I didn't. It was with me at Wellesley four years later in my final interview for the presidency. The search committee asked if I had the experience and skills to "build and bind a respectful multicultural community?" The college had been having problems. I found the temerity to say yes and to believe it, because of the debt I owed Kellogg, owed my fellow fellows and what they taught me: how to hear their lived realities with my heart broken open.

The fellowship was nearing its close and everyone was raving about a trip I had skipped, a week in Taos, New Mexico, arranged by Rick Jackson, a good friend who had long followed the writings of an educator named Parker J. Palmer and decided to use the foundation as his calling card to meet him. Parker agreed to facilitate a week-long retreat for up to twenty fellows, the one I missed. It was such a hit that Rick was organizing a reprise. We would study community by living together intentionally for four days, fourteen of us including three married couples. Parker had written ahead to say our themes would be work, love, and death. We'd read poems together.

I loved poetry. I'd long collected verses that spoke to me, wrote them in journals, on sheets of paper, tacked them on bulletin boards, or slipped them into books, where I would discover them years later if they floated to the floor when I opened an old volume that had called me back. In school and in college I filled my mind with fragments of poetry and prose that represented the part of me that was curious about an opaque inner world that I lacked the vocabulary or a sure enough footing to feel safe exploring beyond the secure confines of the literary canon I studied as an English major.

"I am sure of nothing but the holiness of the heart's affection and the truth of the imagination," John Keats wrote to a friend in 1817. Those words remain stored in my memory with scores of similar fragments. Is there a search for one holy truth of which I can be sure? From my time with the spirituality small group, the gossamer language of pop psychology felt less distasteful to me, less menacing. But I still didn't trust it. And here I was in Taos with this man, Parker Palmer—this man with two last names and a profusion of poems.

Nancy Snyderman and I roomed together. We were pals now. Our bedroom had a light aroma of cedar logs coming from a small fireplace molded into a corner of the white walls. At dinner we met Parker, tall with a resonant voice that vibrated with a bemused Midwestern irony. He chuckled at his own jokes, laughed at himself. I liked that. Years later he told me that he had thought I might be an uptight Boston academic, and was pleased to be proven wrong.

The next morning we started with poems Parker had brought, not to analyze them or "beat them with a hose," as Billy Collins wrote of poetry classes. Parker used poems as a "third thing," to stimulate reflection in conversation with what he called "an inner teacher." We sat in a circle, and spoke into it. We welcomed insights that emerged spontaneously out of the silences. I had been slow to speak out in my classes at college, afraid I had nothing original to add. I wanted to speak, knew I should, and yet couldn't summon the nerve. This was different. Parker evoked insights from experience. Freed of the pressure to formulate a clever comment, I listened more intently to what others said and saw new connections. There was no judgment here, no right or wrong, no rush either. The pace was slow. The silences were a refuge as they had been in Quaker meetings when I was a child. They invited us to see through others' eyes what we could not have seen through our own. I found the process magical, light, and playful. Parker loved word play, idea play. We had incorporated the guilt free drop and the Ta Da! into one morning's conversation.

One of the poems that first morning was by a Guatemalan revolutionary, Julia Esquivel. An unlikely selection to open our first day, our day to talk about love. It was a dark poem full of murder and mayhem during a bloody time. "Threatened with Resurrection," it was called, a lamentation over the genocide of indigenous people. Gradually, in the alchemy of our circle, the poem became a living object, a paean to a pure form of love. We were playing with shadow and light, the tensions of opposites. Through years to come as I stayed close to Parker, I would look back and know this as a central theme of his that became one of mine. For now, I heard our small circle find all sorts of unlikely connections to our cushy lives, so reliably safe and secure. Our own moments when unlikely reconciliation moved us toward love.

But lest we take ourselves too seriously, Parker popped in an egregious poem by a Scotsman, William McGonagall—widely hailed, Parker assured us, years after his death in 1902, as the *worst* poet in the English language. He set a bar so low that even we amateurs could clear it. We had fun. I could see why I had to be here.

That night Nancy and I fell asleep right away, but I turned over and checked my watch just after 3:00 a.m. A poem was forming in my mind. I lay in bed half awake and poked at this protean poem. I was used to waking in a liminal space of half-arousal, phrases and sentences forming in my mind as I toiled subconsciously on a writing project. It always seemed brilliant and essential until I awoke to the reality that it was a garbled mess. Was this one of those?

I rose, found paper and pen, pulled on a sweatshirt, tiptoed to the kitchen table, and began writing. Words flowed and took form in interesting ways. I wrote, scratched out phrases, scribbled marginal notes. The words had a form and a drive. I wrote for several hours and then slipped back into bed.

Early the next morning I heard someone in the kitchen, dressed, and went out to find Parker making coffee. He gave me a cup and I told him about the poem that invaded my sleep. We laughed about marauding poems. I offered to show it to him and sensed myself feeling protective of it. I didn't want to insinuate myself into his program, or call attention to myself. But I found I also did not want him to dismiss it.

He suggested I read it to the group after breakfast to start the morning session. I was not sure I wanted to advance myself as a poet. Plus this did not feel like *my* poem. It came from somewhere else, from the circle, or the night. I didn't say this to Parker, and my thoughts sounded rather woo-woo to me. Okay, Walsh, came a Snyderman-like taunt from the recesses of my mind (she called me Walsh), you are really overthinking this. Let it go. La-de-da.

So I did read the poem. I heard myself reading and noticed cadences that pleased me, ones that had required refashioning through the night. I sensed the group listening quietly, taking it in with the open minds and hearts we accorded yesterday's poems. The real ones. Parker gave the poem a few moments of silence. He didn't invite responses or make more of it, just passed out copies of the next poem and we moved on. I would look back and recognize the beauty of this simple decision. How perfectly Parker had read my situation, gently and yet cordially inviting the poems to continue invading my sleep. As they did, night after night.

Taos became a place for me of profound—dare I say?—mystical awakening. A place where a steady outpouring of poems came to me, and—so it felt—through me, day and night. All of us were amused as I emerged in the mornings with one, two, three new poems. Where were these coming from? Each morning Parker encouraged me to read one or more of the new crop aloud to the group. And the noninvasive appreciation that came back to me called forth more the next night. "Volunteers," Parker called them. I left Taos short on sleep but with a sheaf of original poems.

Among them I had poems that went in asking why I worked so hard and came out with my father's drinking as an answer, an unexpected ending that clicked in with the authority of the last twist of a wall safe's combination. There were poems about a midlife crisis, poems that railed at misogyny and the commodification of sex, and a couple that were bits of doggerel of a sort I wrote for fun, as tributes to people on special occasions, or as thanks. With McGonagall as cover, these efforts had a new freedom to hold up their heads with a knowing smile.

I continued writing poetry after that, but never again with the abandon that possessed me in Taos. The poetry became an extension of journals I kept for many years, a doorway to an inner voice I was learning to trust. Parker became a touchstone in my life from then on, and a beloved friend. He showed up for me periodically, and I for him. The poems would show up from time to time too.

Meanwhile, back home, I had the alcoholism study still plugging along. We had secured the additional funding we needed from the National Institute on Alcohol Abuse and Alcoholism, the federal agency where Ralph was respected for his track record in alcohol studies. Our federal grant was approved in 1987 and we gradually recruited the 227 subjects we needed, then followed them for two years after intake. By 1989 we had completed the ground-breaking study and begun preparing papers for publication.

At about this time, I received a call one day from Leon Eisenberg, a Harvard professor of psychiatry. "How's the study coming?" he asked, as if it were only yesterday that we sat with him in the midtown Manhattan offices of the Commonwealth Fund. Tom Moloney had enlisted him to give us advice, back when it wasn't clear that we could pull off the study. I was happy to report now that we had completed it, against all odds.

Months later I learned that Leon was one of three Harvard luminaries conducting a search for a professor and department chair at HSPH, and this was the reason for his call. In 1990, I was selected for that position and had no doubt that the alcohol study was a prerequisite to my Harvard chair. I had moved to Harvard by the time our principal paper appeared in the *New England Journal of Medicine*, accompanied by an article on the front business page of the *New York Times*. Additional publications followed.

All that publicity credited Harvard. But I would always remember the debt I owed BU in my fifteen years there, when a life that once felt fragmented came together into an integrated whole. It took some hard work, some good luck, massive support from a patient husband, a life-altering Kellogg fellowship, and a whole lot of generous help from friends and colleagues and mentors, including, at BU, Dick Egdahl, Sol Levine, and the indefatigable Ralph Hingson who, in 2004, became a NIAAA division head. Later still, I would remember the BU years again when the Harvard professorship, in turn, made me an attractive candidate for the Wellesley presidency.

5

HOW I BECAME A COLLEGE PRESIDENT

"I don't think this is me."

I knew Wellesley was searching for a new president but hadn't paid much attention. Now I was on the phone with someone from the search committee, the vice chairman of the board of trustees, David Stone. I didn't tell him that I'd deflected comments over the past few months from friends and acquaintances who said I'd be perfect for the job, or who went so far as to nominate me. I didn't admit to him that Wellesley seemed long ago and far away to me now, a mere ten miles to the west, but lifetimes apart.

"We can agree that this may be a reach—for you and for us," he continued, "but your predecessor was a reach too." Then the hook: "Anyway, don't you feel you owe your *alma mater* the courtesy of a chat? The benefit of your advice?"

I recognized the advice ploy. I watched it push Chris into progressively larger jobs, stimulating latent ambitions that made him restless, uprooted him. As I listened to the persuasive David Stone's smooth pitch, I thought, be careful, Diana, this is a slippery slope.

"Why don't you sleep on it?" he suggested. He added that the search committee was headed by Mrs. Gail Klapper, the incoming chair of the board, and gave me the phone number of his assistant, who could always find him. I wrote down the number and his name, then rushed off to a meeting and banished Wellesley from my mind until I could take time to reflect.

Later I returned to my office in the Department of Health and Social Behavior at the Harvard School of Public Health. My eye fell on the note I'd left myself. I stood beside my desk and looked out the window at the plaza four floors below. It opened to a white marble quadrangle: the heart of Harvard Medical School, a constant reminder of medicine's hegemony over public health, an imbalance I and my colleagues were working to correct. That wasn't going to happen in my lifetime, but it was core to my belief in a scrappy profession intent on righting wrongs, dedicated to social justice and the prevention of suffering.

The Wellesley presidency? As a scholar and a teacher chairing a small department, I lacked the administrative experience I expected the college would want and need. Plus, the timing was all wrong for me. This was only my third year leading the department I was recruited to revive. We were just building a head of steam. I'd made a long-term commitment to Harvard, as Harvard had to me. This *was* who I was. It was who I wanted to be, a delayed answer to Elaine's question a decade ago when I was considering the Health Writer job.

I told Chris about the call when he walked in the kitchen door that evening. His eyebrows shot up. *Now this is interesting.* Chris invariably found it easier than I did to consider pulling up stakes to move on.

"But I'm so lucky to be where I am," I said as much for my benefit as his. "This search committee isn't going to pick me. I know that. If I start down this path . . . I know myself. We do! My competitive juices will start flowing. And I *really* don't want to be questioning whether I'm happy where I am. What's the point of that, especially now?" The hesitation I did not voice was the deeper worry that I might let my ego get hooked—and then bruised when the committee chose someone else. Why risk *that*?

"Why wouldn't you *talk* to them? You might learn something, and it doesn't mean you have to take the job, even if they do make the offer." He gave me a hug and assured me that I had his support whatever I decided.

Then before he headed upstairs, he turned back one last time and grinned.

"They might pick you, in fact."

After supper I called Sol Levine. I loved this man. Everyone who knew Sol sought his counsel on important life choices. He studied quality of life and had long fantasized that he would write the definitive book on happiness in due course. In the meantime, we all wished we could simply emulate his *joie de vivre*. As I advanced in my career, Sol often said to me, you ought to be running something. Something big. He *kvelled* as I told him about the Wellesley call.

"Knowing the kind of person you are," he said in his deep voice, "you'll have to step up to the plate. All the momentum in your personality will propel you forward. The biggest question I encourage you to consider is the impact on your family, on Chris and Allison." Then he predicted that if I went to the interview, I would become the Wellesley president. "And you won't want to be successful at it, you'll want to be great. So you should consider carefully whether to start down this path."

Next, of course, I called Elaine, who declared this new twist "delicious." She and I were still essentially who we were when we met: she, the no-nonsense realist, I, the scholarly idealist. Our relationship had matured into the embodiment for me of all the security and stability a truly foundational friendship can supply. I told her I was hesitant to venture out onto this steeper slope.

"Don't be silly, Diana," she said, "of course you'll go to the interview. A man would never decline an invitation like this, a chance to see and be seen in a larger role." She was right. I was just looking for the easy way out rather than put myself under a microscope. She tapped into the striving impulse we both knew would spur me on.

Then I called Dick Egdahl, a chief architect of my career. Three years earlier, I had finally left BU, with a nudge from him. Harvey Fineberg, Dean of the Harvard School of Public Health, had made me an offer to chair the school's behavioral sciences department, and reposition it. I would have "a Harvard hunting license," the chair of another department said to me, as a tenured full professor—a position for life—with the added prestige of a named professorial chair. But before I left BU I perseverated for over a month about whether to leave the place that had shaped me, given me to myself. I was well situated there with two professorships, at SPH and UNI, plus the HPI associate directorship. BU was finalizing a counteroffer to up the ante and perhaps entice me to stay. But Dick pushed me out of the nest.

"We can't possibly match this offer you have from Harvard," he said in summary. "It is incomparable. Why would you turn it down?"

When I reached Dick now with the news from Wellesley, he was excited. "What a great bully pulpit for you," he proclaimed. He was sure I would be selected. It was good to hear his voice and I was conscious of how seldom I'd been in touch with him in the short period since I'd left BU. With a twinge of both guilt and regret, I was reminded of the reality that moving on means rupturing relationships. There is always pain in losses, the cost of reaching out for something new and shiny.

David Stone requested five references. Sol, Elaine, and Dick agreed to vouch for me. I added Margaret Mahoney, an early booster of mine and president of New York's Commonwealth Fund, and Joseph Newhouse, a distinguished professor of economics and public policy at Harvard, a renowned health policy scholar I knew less well, but admired. I emailed their contact information with my *vita* and a four-sentence cover note, and tossed my hat into the ring.

A few weeks later I was sifting through a box of material sent to me by Doris Cook, the search committee administrator. I was to meet with the committee at an inconspicuous conference center a few miles from the college, a bit of cloak and dagger. At the top of the pile was a list of committee members: twelve trustees, four faculty, two administrators, and two students—a lot of people for a chat.

Just below the roster was the formal statement of desired qualities for the new president; it was as daunting as it was predictable. I did find a few items I could check off with reasonable confidence: a collegial decision-making style, a respectable academic portfolio, some success as a public speaker, and experience leading teams. But other important qualifications—like financial stewardship, energetic fundraising for a large institution, leading a large faculty—with courage no less—and guiding a board of trustees, these would be *terra incognita*. Oh, and she would be expected to build and bind an increasingly diverse community, a goal my Kellogg experience told me would be as challenging as it would be crucial. Finally, this closing comment: "The president of Wellesley College will need reserves of stamina, energy, optimism, and emotional resilience in order to enjoy success in this role."

I would need those reserves just to survive the first interview.

I focused on learning the names of the committee members and only thumbed through the rest—reports, data, brochures. Otherwise, I went on about my work at Harvard. I would take David Stone at his word that there was really not much at stake. Other than a piece of my pride.

When I arrived for the meeting, Doris escorted me to the dining room, where the committee waited, and introduced me to the chair, Gail Klapper. She was no more "Mrs. Klapper" than I was "Mrs. Walsh." I'd read up on Gail. She founded an all-women law firm in Denver with a public policy portfolio and came close to being elected attorney general of Colorado. She'd graduated in the class of 1965. I didn't remember her, and should have because she was president of college government in my junior year.

After some initial pleasantries, Gail posed the first question. What intrigued me about the job? I paused and admitted that I wasn't intrigued, that I was content at Harvard and not at all sure this would be a good fit for me, or for them. I saw a few raised eyebrows and a couple of suppressed smirks.

"That's funny," said Gail without smiling. "Everyone else we speak to seems to view this as *the* plum job in higher education."

For over an hour they asked me questions: What was important to me about my Wellesley education? That was easy. I believed that Wellesley changed the trajectory of my life, convinced me I could be an intellectual. What had I learned at Harvard about multiculturalism and diversity that might be of value at Wellesley? Not much, so I improvised an answer that harked back to Kellogg. How would I see myself relating to the board? I fell back on my own board service, at Planned Parenthood and Faulkner Hospital, where Elaine had become president. This wasn't highly relevant, but it was something.

Was I good at financial management? Not really. I'd need a good team there. I didn't say what I was thinking: this was my Achilles heel. How would I relate to the students? With pleasure, attention and warmth. I felt sure-footed with students. How would the graduate students I currently taught differ from female undergraduates? I'd taught plenty of women but few undergraduates. I cited my experience with the younger cohort, Allison and her Winsor friends, now spread out at colleges across the country. I didn't say that after attending an all-girls' school, none of them applied to a women's college. They were hungry for a larger world and a co-ed experience. This was a nagging doubt I kept to myself. I would have liked to ask them a question: How relevant is Wellesley today to college-bound women? But I held back.

What difficult decisions had I made professionally and how did I make them? I could have anticipated this question, but rambled a bit, then described the alcohol study as a multiple-year gamble. Pulling it off was a coup. What mistakes had I made? Plenty, but I knew the trick was to cite useful lessons, which I tried to do, rambling again. How did I process mistakes? Owned up to them, made amends if I could, searched for lessons learned, and resolved to do better next time, and wrote all of that down if the mistake were a serious one. What did I do for fun? Family, friends, running, biking, reading, skiing. I mentioned the Kellogg adventures.

What did I imagine I would like most and least about the job? Most, working with the faculty, I started to reply; that's who I was, who my friends were, my husband . . . But I was cut off by a loud "Ha!" from a far corner of the room. "Enough," Gail shot back. Uncomfortable laughter rippled from table to table. The interruption, I learned later, came from a senior professor of classics, a shot across my bow in case I thought the Wellesley faculty would give the new president an easy time of it.

As if to sharpen her point, the same professor asked me a convoluted question later in the evening. I didn't get the reference so I dodged it. She persisted by invoking my daughter, a Stanford sophomore. What did she think of the Western civilization requirement there? I responded with a banal assurance that Allison was enjoying her Stanford courses.

Ah, the next question I did get. What was so great about the graduation talk? They'd heard about a popular commencement address I gave in 1990 at BU's School of Public Health. Obviously they wanted to know I could stand in a graduation tent and command a large audience. It was my first commencement talk and I labored over it. I raised real and layered questions I knew the graduates would live, through their careers and their lives. I laid out specific moral dilemmas in the frame of a larger tension between the public and the private, the reality that much disease is socially produced—by education, income, race and ethnicity, gender, occupation, residence. I didn't tell the committee that part of the talk's appeal was that I closed it with one of the poems I had written in Taos—a risk I took for the graduates but was not ready to take here.

All the way home my mind served up nimbler responses to their questions. I was sure I had missed enough cues, superficially answered enough
loaded questions, and delivered more than enough rambling replies to
obliterate this fork in the road. Under a mudslide?

"How'd it go?" Chris asked as I walked through our back door.

"Not so well," I replied, "I should have taken it more seriously, I suppose, if I'd really wanted the job. But I'm just glad it's over so I don't have
to think about it anymore."

I tried to put Wellesley out of my mind, and mostly did, except when
embarrassing moments from the interview woke me at night. They would
be undercurrents I sensed and missed at the time but now saw, such as
my nonanswer to the Stanford Western civilization question. I consoled
myself with the thought that it might have come across as a skillful *jujitsu*
move, rather than the ignorance of someone worlds removed from the
battlefields of undergraduate education.

Several weeks went by. I did not expect to hear from Wellesley again.
Then, a bolt from the blue: Doris Cook called toward the end of May. The
committee wanted me back and asked that I provide a list of a dozen or so
references they could consult, in confidence, in advance of the meeting.

This still felt improbable, and not worth giving my new Harvard colleagues the impression that I was already poised to jump ship. But something was stirring in my feelings about Wellesley. Was I already caught up
in the chase, my competitive juices unleashed? Or was I interested in the
job? Even intrigued? Maybe.

As a precaution, I wrote a short note to Harvard's president, Neil
Rudenstine, making light of the whole thing, but saying I would not want
him to hear rumors without having heard from me. I spoke to Harvey
Fineberg, my dean. His response was so masterful that I typed it up and
saved it on my hard drive as a model of how to meet a faculty member
who was weighing an outside offer.

"Well," he said. "They're smarter than I thought. This needs a lot of
thought, though. You have to really believe in the mission, in single-sex
education." I launched into the spiel I'd been refining.

"Sure," he broke in. "You must have convinced them that you believe
in it. But you need to be sure you really do. It may make sense now, but

will it be out of sync with reality five years from now?" I admitted that my daughter had her doubts, as did her Winsor friends.

"And you won't be able to make any more scholarly contributions to the field. Don't kid yourself about that." Now he was reading my mind, and stroking my ego. "The alcohol study has already had a big impact and you're poised to make an even greater mark if you stay here." He knew that Chris had recently become president of Dana-Farber and wanted me to consider how different this role would be from his situation.

"They want Chris for his science. He'll still have his lab. But the role of a college president is pure administration. Believe me, that transition is a shock." He was on a roll, triggering all my anxieties. "And it's going to be difficult to raise money after the successful capital campaign Wellesley just completed. You'll spend the first two years trying to convince people that you need more money. And it will be hard to follow such a popular president." Nan Keohane was well known and widely respected, as I well knew. Then Harvey moved in for the kill.

"You need to separate the honor of being chosen from the doing of the job. It is a great honor, but this may not be the right job for you. Tell me if there is anything I can do to make it harder to say yes. Do you want to be dean?" I took this as a joke. And noted to myself that I had absolutely no desire to be dean.

Allison, home from Stanford, was surprised to hear me considering this radical departure. All her life she had known me as a scholar and a researcher. So many dinners out with her dad while I plugged away at my PhD. Why would I give that up for a job that would divert me from my own work? A job that would drag me down with problems and complaints. An administrator. Yuck.

"Anyway," she went on, affectionately, "we know how clueless you are about popular culture. How will you connect with the students? You're like an exchange student from a distant planet." She was not wrong. But when I heard myself marshal a defense, I couldn't help but wonder whether I'd already made up my mind to see this through to the end.

I said to her that if I were in this job, I was sure I would bond with the students in my own way. I would listen to them, care about them. To her first point, I would make the work of leading Wellesley my scholarship, applied and lived in real time, direct and immediate. I would live the questions Kellogg kindled in me. What kind of leader could I make of myself? What kind of contribution could I make in this fractured world? I would approach these questions with the intensity that fueled my scholarly work, gathering the skills and resources I would need to cultivate and deploy.

What I didn't acknowledge to Allison, or to anyone else, was what it might mean to me to meet this test. To win this job and succeed at it over a course of years. Perhaps this might lay to rest the self-doubts that infected my mind, close the gap between how I was so often seen by others—always to my amazement—and how I saw myself. There was the string of awards I had won in secondary school, Chris's unshakable belief in me, and the support I had found in generous mentors over the years. What are others seeing? How real is it really? Can I find it in myself, and trust it?

I drafted a short memo to the dozen people whose names I'd given Doris. I told them they might receive a call from Wellesley, explained why, and asked them to hold it in confidence. It's a long shot, I wrote. I did not anticipate the effect my note would have on them: that many would call me after speaking to a member of the committee to describe the conversation. These reports were far more detailed than the casual update colleagues might normally send each other. My friend Byllye Avery joked that the committee was "as serious as a heart attack."

And not all the news was good.

"They said you didn't make eye contact." My loyal friend and college roommate, Joan Brophy, called me to deliver this reconnaissance. "I said that's because you're an introvert and you wear glasses. But you'd better look at them next time you meet."

"I'm worried for you," said Rima Rudd, another friend and departmental colleague at Harvard. "They want all of you, every bit of you. They will consume you." I asked her what gave her that impression. She ticked off the wide-ranging questions she was asked. I told her about Sol's advice to think about the impact on my family.

"Yes," she said quietly, "but more than that, I'm worried you'll disappear into a black hole never again to be seen by your friends." This touched a nerve. I surely would miss my Harvard friends if I left, not to mention the Harvard professorship that had meant so much to me.

Dan Merrigan reached me one day. He was a Jesuit priest and research collaborator on the BU public health faculty. It was he, in 1990, with whom I tested the idea of reading my poem at the SPH commencement address. I trusted his instincts. Well, *why* would you read it, he had asked back then, and I instantly knew the answer. It would be an offering—from my heart—to students I wished to send off with my admiration and love. That's why the talk was a hit. Dan called to tell me about his conversation with a trustee on the committee.

"I was impressed. She was really digging." Dan let out a slow breath as if he'd just run a long race. He added that they wanted to know about my commitment to diversity.

"And I said you would bring a social science perspective, an empirical and conceptual critique of the conventional wisdom. What I didn't say to them, but will say to you, is that if you take this job, you're going to have to give Wellesley a kick in the shins on some of these issues they're tiptoeing around. That, in itself, is reason enough for you to take this job." I had always admired Dan's lived commitment to social justice. This conversation with him was a turning point for me. While I doubted I'd be kicking the college in the shins, I noticed that I was starting to identify with it and to feel a sense of responsibility for its future.

Gail asked my permission to expand the committee's inquiry to anyone whose name came up and I agreed. But wow, she cast a wide net. All of this input was revving me up. Elaine sat me down one evening after dinner and extracted a blow-by-blow description of all the feedback. After she digested my core dump of data she asked if I remembered Arnold Zenker. He specialized in preparing professionals for the public spotlight, and had spoken at a gathering she had hosted for women in health care management. She suggested I hire him to prepare me for the second interview.

"You have nothing to lose, and no one has to know you did it." I'd endured a weekend of media training during the Kellogg fellowship. I knew how bruising this kind of scrutiny could be to the ego, and, yet, how beneficial. I decided to call him. Another indicator that I was all in.

On June 16, I spent several hours with Zenker. He assumed the role of search committee member and made me feel even more self-conscious in the privacy of his downtown Boston office than I did at my interview with the committee. His whole exercise felt fake. I stumbled through lame answers to his tough questions, and then watched myself squirm as he played back the video.

"You'll never get the job if you perform like this," he said as the tape ended. "It's a wonder they called you back." Apparently building the client's confidence was not part of his package. He told me I had to get my hair off my face and improve my makeup, and to stop looking down. Then he hauled out a list called "Ten Sure Ways to Score with an Audience" and drilled me on more effective responses. The strategy he recommended was to memorize a dozen paragraphs—blocks he called them—key points I wanted to convey. Then I could turn almost any question around and tailor it to one of the blocks I had in the can.

"And, for God's sake, make it interesting or you'll lose them right away." Why was I subjecting myself to this bully?

Zenker dismissed me with instructions to go home and return in a week for a second grilling. In the interim, I heard from a classmate on the search committee who called to offer support and told me to be myself. Zenker had dismissed that kind of advice as "shop-worn. Only the neophyte falls for that." Was I a neophyte? I didn't think so. I had to find ground on which I could stand—well prepared, yes, but authentically myself. And it was crucial to me to find that set point for myself.

I sent Arnold Zenker a thank you note and a personal check for $1,575, his fee. I never told another soul, beyond Elaine and Chris, that I allowed myself to be Zenkerized. The truth was that the session was helpful, but it didn't come close to the impact of the mirroring conversations with people from every phase of my professional life. They freed me to believe that I might be right for Gail's plum job after all.

"I shouldn't be telling you this," Doris Cook whispered, "but I'm pulling for you." Doris had been the personal secretary to four successive Wellesley presidents who spanned more than a quarter century. Here was a woman with a unique perspective on the demands of the office and the culture of the college, as well as a deep reservoir of institutional memory. We were alone in the Council Library awaiting word that the search committee, meeting in the room next door, was ready to meet with me for my second interview.

Gail appeared and ushered me into the room. Committee members were seated around a single table in an open square. I was thankful to see everyone wearing a name tag this time. The faculty member I had taken to be the dean of the college was actually the classics professor, I noted now. Oops. David Stone joked that he wasn't going to say a word this time and engaged in banter with the second male trustee, Walter Cabot, of the storied Boston family who spoke only to God. Another man, seated back from the table, looked dour and spoke not at all. He was never introduced. A spy?

"Do you think you can manage a job as complex as leading Welles-ley?" Gail went right to the point. I turned her question around and delivered my opening from memory. A Zenker move, I had to admit to myself. I invoked Ralph Waldo Emerson who used to greet people with the question, "What's become clearer to you since we last met?" This brought a laugh. "You've been busy," I said, alluding to their calls. "I suspect some things are clearer to you." I sensed supportive attention encouraging me on.

I told them a few things were clearer to me. Like how I would advo-cate for Wellesley. I had ducked that question last time and owed them a better answer. I mentioned a cover story in the *Boston Globe* magazine the previous Sunday about the high costs of college. I saw nods and laid out three aspects of the contemporary Wellesley with which I'd become reacquainted. Strengths well known to those of us close to the college. The challenge ahead would be to demonstrate how we deliver value for money.

I turned to Gail, grinned and said, "Now I've evaded *your* question." This brought a hearty laugh. I pointed out that it was as important to me as it surely was to them that this be a good fit. And I had thought quite a bit about what I might bring to this. I described my managerial experi-ences, distinguished between managing and leading, cited scholarship from the leadership field, and quoted the poet Wallace Stevens, who said, "It is necessary to any originality to have the courage to be an amateur." I might not put that in the search report, though, I added.

Summing up, I said that I learn fast when I focus. I illustrated with a quick review of my rapid ascent up the academic ladder after a late start. I had access to many resources—personal, family, friends. Wellesley does too. I'm not afraid to ask for help. If we were to do this, I concluded, I think we would muddle through the first year or so and then begin to soar. I was channeling feedback from the interviews and feeling more at ease. It was as though we were shifting from an interview to a session of improvisational jazz, one and then another of us picking up the melody.

Mr. Cabot asked whether I was any good at picking people. Yes, I replied. That's important and will be, to fill in my gaps. I discussed hiring I'd been doing at Harvard. Another committee member asked what resources I would need to succeed in the job. Zenker had anticipated this one and I was prepared. The most critical resource would be trust and support from the constituencies the committee represented—the faculty, alumnae, students, staff. Most especially the trustees. Without their support I, personally, wouldn't want the job, and without it I didn't believe anyone could succeed at it.

"What if you don't have all the support you need?" The logical next question. I said I'd always been tenacious, and glanced at Pam Lewis, one of my two classmates on the committee. She was smiling.

"I've already told them," she said. Oh dear. This was a reference to a story from our freshman year. Pam was our class president and asked me to help her race the sophomore class president to our class tree on Tree Day, an ancient ritual familiar to all in the room. Pam and I were running in a small pack and saw the sophomore class president suddenly take off. She had spotted our tree. We'd failed to discuss the details of exactly how I was going to help. So, I tackled her. Brought her down hard. I skulked off in a hurry, embarrassed and a little ashamed. I turned to Gail and said I hoped she wasn't the sophomore class president.

"Nope." said Pam. "Couldn't have been. She was eight feet tall." Laughter. The dean of the college stepped in.

"This is an unfair question," she began, and I was braced to hear what was unfair in it. "The faculty are going on a retreat to talk about the curriculum. What do you think belongs in the core?"

If I weren't here, I said, I would be at a similar retreat at Harvard right now. And I believe in periodic review of the curriculum, even if it doesn't lead to major reform. I wanted to signal to the dean that as president I would support her in this project I could tell mattered to her.

I expected questions about race and multiculturalism, given the controversy I'd heard about. To prepare I'd sought ideas from Byllye Avery as well as friends at Swarthmore and Earlham, and, in several extended conversations, from my friend Susan Silbey, now a professor in Wellesley's sociology department. When the questions did come—from a trustee and then a student—I told them I appreciated the work the college was doing, understood how difficult it could be, and was tuned into issues of diversity in higher education. I spoke about strategies to support students who wanted to connect with others from their own backgrounds, without encouraging too much self-segregation. I invoked Kellogg experiences and work at Harvard in regard to how to handle conflict when it arises. I did not kick anyone in the shins, but Dan was right that this issue would not be going away.

"I may not be allowed to ask this," Luella Goldberg, the outgoing board chair said tentatively. "So don't answer if you don't want to. But where does your husband stand on this?"

"I might have listed him as a reference," I joked, "if I thought you'd have considered him objective. He's my strongest ally and greatest asset. And a Wellesley fan whose picture made it into our class yearbook." I told them how we met, the story that ended with my whupping him in a round of golf. He would be nothing but proud were I the Wellesley president.

To a variant of "tell us about your weaknesses," I offered my mother's story about my first report card and my disorientation in time and space. I'd learned to compensate, I said, but did get lost. You'll have a driver, a trustee interjected. Another fault was my intellectual elephant gun, I added, and referenced the Kellogg fellowship. I'd learned to recognize and modulate it, I said, but did not let on that I knew the committee had questions about an intensity they saw in me. I wanted to signal that I was aware of it.

One of the two junior professors, Andy Shennan, raised the question of what my poetry meant to me. Ah, I replied, as an English major I had no illusions my poems would pass muster with the literature faculty. I mentioned the Taos retreat and said the poems tapped insights and especially emotions that eluded linear prose. I was cautious, I added, about when and how I exposed them. One of the Kellogg fellows brought back from Africa a proverb that seemed right to me: We share our gifts with those who pass by; our pain we save for our friends.

By now, I had shaken off the confining structure of a formal interview and had coalesced the group into a conversation I could tell was engaging us all. Well maybe not *all*. A trustee in an Hermès scarf and a proper demeanor stepped in. A PhD economist, I later learned, proud of an affiliation with the Harvard School of Public Health. And exacting. That I saw already.

"I haven't read *all* your work. Can you summarize what it's all about and how it might be relevant to Wellesley?" I felt myself tense at the tone behind the question. Not so very relevant, truth be told. I spoke of my own studies of alcohol abuse and smoking. And the new direction I'd charted for my department, examining the social determinants of health and illness. Our society and health program had taken off, I said, and began to describe its key elements.

"It sounds exciting," Gail interjected. "How would you feel about giving it up?"

And there it was. The turning point in the interview, the moment, looking back, when my world rotated a fraction of a degree on its axis, and nothing was ever the same. I didn't have a quick answer to Gail's question. Pausing to think about it clarified for me where I was. "I've never been the mad genius type bent on solving a particular problem," I spoke into the silence. "I've always been interested in a broader set of questions and in the policy implications, the so what? To lead Wellesley would be to stand on a higher platform and take up that more expansive applied thinking. And it would be an incomparable chance for me to learn and grow."

The interview continued, with a number of additional questions. What would I change at Wellesley? Who were my heroes or mentors? What would the college have to do to maintain its excellent liberal education? I recognized in them all the questions I would be asking myself if I were in the job. I'd prepared a closing statement, as Zenker had urged. But I decided to ditch it. We'd moved so seamlessly into a spontaneous interchange that it would have struck a false note now. As if reading my mind, Gail slid a piece of paper toward me.

"Here, read this," she said, "in case you are wavering about whether you want to do this." I struggled at first to make out the small and blurred words on the fax machine paper. Then I recognized my poem "Potbound" from the Taos retreat and recited it from memory down to the last line: "When is it that I know I have to go someplace else? When I have to grow—Or die."

We sat in silence. The meeting felt like it was over. I looked around the room. "However this comes out," I said, "this has been a tremendous honor. I'll remember it all my life. And I want to thank you for your dedication to Wellesley."

That afternoon, Gail, on her way to the airport, left messages on my answering machines at home and at work. She wanted to let me know what happened after the meeting. That's all, no clues. All day Friday, I was on tenterhooks waiting for her to call back. I left my office around 5:30. Still no call. When I arrived home, she had called there twice. I sat around for two hours with Chris and Allison and three of her friends. Everyone received a phone call except me. I made them return their calls on the fax machine to keep the other line open. My brother Bill and his son arrived for a visit. When it was time to go to dinner, Allison's friend, who had the only cell phone among us, suggested we take it. As we pulled into the restaurant parking lot, I finally reached Gail on it.

"They fell in love with you. You were fabulous. Our difficulty is that the board instructed us to bring them three names. We're unanimous that we want to recommend only you. But we have to sell the board. A dinner has been scheduled on July 14 for the Boston trustees who can be there." I would meet the others later. If I could give her an answer soon, she could "wrap this up." I was excited and relieved that I hadn't misread the signals.

"We are totally sure about you. You just can't say no to us."

Couldn't I? Had I crossed the Rubicon? My family had gone ahead of me into the restaurant. I took a deep breath and thought about what to say to them. A truck passed by with the name Walsh painted over and over in rows along its side. An exclamation point?

I hung up and knew that I would not say no. And I noticed, to my surprise, that I, too, was "totally sure." I who tormented myself for weeks before I could leave BU for Harvard. Who struggled for far too long with second thoughts about my marriage. I had had only two encounters with the Wellesley search committee, and I was totally sure.

Over dinner, I tried to keep my excitement under wraps.

When, finally, Chris and I were alone together he said to me, affection in his voice:

"Lives have defining moments. This is one for you."

The rest of the summer had the erratic tempo of a waking dream. Gail hastily arranged two days of meetings, July 20 and 21, for all the major campus constituencies to vet "a leading candidate" for the presidency, language she artfully crafted to downplay the reality that I was the only one.

At Harvard, I wrote a hasty memo to Dean Fineberg who phoned me immediately. This is wonderful news for Wellesley, he said. They're going to find out very soon how lucky they are. Minutes later he was at my door with a warm and elegant note written by hand in fountain pen. He advised me to take some time off before the announcement. Things will move very fast as soon as word is out.

The campus meetings would begin and end with trustees. The summer was absolutely the worst time to ask the board to accommodate this schedule on short notice, Gail's memo to them ended. "But given the search committee's enthusiasm and the outstanding nature of this candidate, we know that you will understand why we wish to move so quickly." The trustees elect the president, and she wanted them all to meet me before they voted.

I arrived at the Wellesley Inn, down the street from the college. I was to have dinner there with a small group of local trustees. I was early, waiting outside the dining room, wondering why there were so few signs of life. A stylishly dressed woman about my age arrived and sat down across from me. After a few minutes, I broke the silence and asked if she was a member of the Wellesley College board of trustees.

"No," she replied guardedly. "Are you?"

"No." Then, after a few more minutes sitting in silence, "Are you here to meet with the trustees?"

"Yes. Are you?" Her tone and affect were just short of hostile.

"Well, yes," I said, "I'm discussing the presidency with them."

"So am I," she said flatly.

"As a candidate?"

"Yes."

"Are you far along in the process?" My heart was pounding.

"Yes, very."

"Well I am too." I figured we might as well be honest with each other. "Though I thought I was alone in that."

"Well, you're not," she said. My mind was on fire. Should I walk out right now? Drive home? Call my dean and tell him I wouldn't be leaving Harvard? How could I have so completely misread Gail? I was about to bolt when a woman hobbled in on a walking cast. I recognized her as the alumnae association president from the search committee. She looked at the two of us in horror, sized up the situation, and shifted into take-charge mode.

"You," pointing to me. "Come with me."

"You," turning to the mystery woman. "Stay here, I'll be right back." She and I rushed out to her beat-up Volvo.

"The trustees are waiting to have dinner with you at the College Club, not the Inn. I'm having dinner alone with that woman. She's a last-minute candidate the committee is seeing as a courtesy to someone important who's been promoting her." She sped around the circular driveway at the Club and hit the brakes. I jumped out and watched her pull away, working to tame my toxic doubts. I told the trustees what had happened. Gail apologized profusely. Still, the entire evening felt surreal. I needed to put the incident behind me but it left me with a residue of caution I hadn't felt until now.

It didn't help that I was shuffled around the table roughly every ten minutes to sit next to another trustee. I would be partway into a conversation when Gail would tap me on the shoulder, take my napkin and water glass, and move me down the table to a new seat. A silent parody of musical chairs. The only conversation that stayed with me was when an older alumna on the board whispered as soon as I sat next to her.

"You're not going to let those lesbians use our chapel for their weddings, are you?"

"Gee, I don't know," I mumbled, relieved no others were listening. "We haven't talked about that. I'll have to find out what the issues are." I wanted to push back without creating an incident. "I do know," I added, "that my daughter's generation is much more relaxed about these things than yours or mine ever were. It is their liberation movement." We moved on easily to my daughter and her doings, but I would long recall this cursory interchange as the first of many alerts that sexual orientation was going to be a delicate subject with older alumnae, including some trustees. And, more generally, that I would inherit issues which had buried histories and aroused strong passions beneath the surface of friendly decorum.

Dinner with a larger group of trustees was scheduled to close this two-day visit. I was waiting again in the Council Library, with Gail and the search committee next door in the President's Dining Room, presenting their case for me. When Gail emerged and escorted me in, the trustees applauded loudly for a very long time. I could feel the twelve trustees from the search committee pulling for me with a kind of parental pride, and the momentum of all the earlier probes with them carried me through this vital test: the scrutiny of the board. The search committee had so thoroughly done its homework that I was sure they knew me—warts and all—as well as I knew myself. In some ways maybe better. The committee's decision to do their own interviewing, rather than entrusting any of it to the silent headhunter—as it turned out, the spy in the back of the room—helped lure me into the job. It gave me unfiltered access to the thinking of committee members, and they to mine. By now I was convinced that we had seen each other whole—clearly, candidly, and with nothing to hide. A great way to begin an enduring relationship.

I opened by saying I wanted to paint for the trustees who hadn't met me the most honest picture I could of who I really was. What I was just beginning to recognize, but didn't mention, was that I was already a different person—not the one who dialed the phone on the last day of March to return David Stone's call. I described how I was pulled deeper and deeper into the process through a subtle lamination of insights that had revealed to me what I could bring to the job that might be distinctive, and why I might not be such an illogical choice after all—for the college or for me. I had been inventing and reinventing, or discovering and rediscovering, myself ever since my graduation, as I suspected we all had been doing in this unprecedented period of ascension of women in American society.

I closed with four issues I believed Wellesley would have to attend to closely in the coming years. When I looked back fourteen years later, these were issues that had in fact been central to my presidency. First, I said, we would have to invest wisely to ensure that we continued to compete successfully for the best and brightest students. To do so we would need to address the issue of "college life, the downside of remaining single sex." We could do that, in part, I argued, by ensuring that our educational programs were "anchored in the real world," in "pragmatic attention to the major issues of the day."

Second, we would have to bring ingenuity to the next phase of "multiculturalism," create real incentives for diverse cultures to come together and learn from each other. We would also need to accelerate the pace at which we diversified the faculty, staff, and student body. These efforts would "cut to the very heart of the intellectual qualities a liberal education seeks to produce," I added, "flexibility, open-mindedness, cosmopolitanism, a tolerance for ambiguity and the endless pursuit of a truth that is rich, textured and always provisional and conditional."

Third, I noted that Dean Kolodny was leading a review of the curriculum to make sure it remains vital and at the cutting edge. She would need the support of the president and the board in this work.

Fourth, and finally, I hinted at financial pressures on the horizon. We would need "accountability and sound management through a time of shrinking resources." Our commitment to need-blind admission was going to become increasingly expensive, I predicted, and added that we would also need to create financial incentives to help us counter "the erosion of middle-class students in highly-selective institutions like Wellesley."

I ended with a story to telegraph that I was now committed to this new future with them. After the call from David Stone, I said, Doris sent me not one, but two FedEx packages. I admitted at the first interview that I hadn't made my way through them. By the second interview I'd read everything—except the bylaws. "Tonight, I can report to you that yesterday afternoon I left my office, walked over to Harvard's Countway Medical Library, and read every word of the bylaws. And the faculty's articles of government too."

The full Wellesley board would elect its next president on August 5. In the meantime, I met one-on-one with three trustees who had missed the earlier opportunities, and by telephone with the fourth: the presidents of MIT and Spelman College, the head of Harvard's Memorial Church, and a Wellesley alumna and executive en route to China, who had introduced GM cars there. By now, Gail was sure that the board would affirm her search committee's decision. So sure that she scheduled a celebratory dinner immediately after the board vote, an opportunity for me to introduce Chris and Allison. Press releases had gone out, embargoed until 6:00 that night, and Wellesley's public affairs director, Laurel Stavis, was trying to keep a lid on the news.

Two days earlier, an enterprising education reporter at the *Boston Globe* picked up the scoop and Laurel managed to persuade her to write her story as speculative, pending the board's vote. It ran under the headline "Harvard Professor May Lead Wellesley." One of my friends, an ardent feminist, called me to divulge that her immediate thought on seeing the headline was that Wellesley had elected a male president. We laughed over a mistake that any of us might have made. Harvard professors were still mostly male. She and I took this as an affirmation of the work Wellesley still had to do, countering unconscious limitations on women's appropriate roles.

On the night of the official vote, Chris, Allison, and I were in Chris's car on the way to the dinner. NPR interrupted its programming with a bulletin that I had been elected president of Wellesley College. It was not yet 6:00 p.m. and I winced briefly for Laurel who had worked valiantly to hold the embargo. But then a spark of excitement shot through me, along with a mix of recognition and disbelief.

The dinner was in the main dining room of the College Club. I was greeted with a standing ovation. A sustained one. I was learning to stand less awkwardly as the center of attention. In truth, I was starting to enjoy it.

Taking Dean Fineberg's advice, I spent August 1993 with Chris on Cape Cod. I read everything I could find that might help orient me and I wrote speeches for welcoming ceremonies to mark the opening of the coming

Diana's mother, Gwen Jenkins Chapman, her brother Bill, and Diana, 1946.

Chris walking Diana's mother down the aisle at Diana's brother Bill's wedding, with Diana's father, Robert F. Chapman, following behind, March 1969.

Chris, Diana, and Allison in Chris's new office at the Dana-Farber Cancer Institute shortly after he became president, Fall 1991.

With Dick Egdahl (left), Academic Vice President for Health Affairs, Boston University, and unidentified participant (center), at a Springer-Verlag conference at Boston University, 1986. Photographer unknown.

With Oprah Winfrey (left), and Gail H. Klapper (right), board chair, at Commencement, June 1997. Courtesy Wellesley College. Photographed by John Mottern.

With the Honorable Ruth Bader Ginsburg, at Wellesley to give the Wilson Lecture, November 1998. Courtesy Wellesley College. Photographed by Rebecca Sher.

With Victoria K. Herget '72 (center), incoming board chair, and Gail Klapper (right), out-going board chair, June 1999. Courtesy Wellesley College. Photographed by Nancy Carbonaro.

academic year. When I was not doing that, I rollerbladed. I bought my first inline skates that summer and resolved to master this new skill while I still had time for it.

Almost every day I skated the thirteen-mile round trip along the path beside the Cape Cod Canal, watching the cormorants on the lampposts unfurl their crooked wings to dry in the breeze. An inelegant solution, it seemed to me, to the obvious burden an aquatic bird would carry with waterlogged wings. How had natural selection led to this? Then, again, who was I to judge? Here I was in the August heat, a forty-nine-year-old woman wearing pads on my knees and wrists and elbows, a bicycle helmet with a visor, large sunglasses, blue jeans and a long-sleeved T-shirt. I was not crashing as often anymore, but I had not figured out how to stop in a hurry. I cruised along the path, on alert for convoys of kids on teetering bikes while I evolved a kind of mantra for my new job. It went through many iterations. Each reflected anxieties I had about deficits in my leadership. By the end, it coalesced around six self-commands.

Be tough. Be clear. Be honest. Be fair. Be true to yourself. And keep your own counsel. I knew that under pressure I would take setbacks too personally. I knew that in my eagerness to take in diverse perspectives, I could be too slow to articulate a clear position. I knew I would want to be honest and fair but that I would hesitate to hurt anyone's feelings and might send mixed signals, especially when I had to referee a dispute. I knew that being true to myself was the most important commitment I could make, but sensed that conflicting demands on me might cloud the picture of how best to be faithful to my own ideals. And I was sure I would have to keep secrets, which would run against the grain of the openness that was one of my strengths.

6

THROUGH THE LOOKING GLASS

I had a housekeeper and a cook and two drivers, not to mention this mansion on a lake, with a pair of swans and who knew what other exotica. Chris and I would live here as a condition of my employment.

"We'll help you sell your house if you want," Gail added. "Do you have a financial advisor?"

I did. Chris had lined up what he liked to call his personal banker when he became president of Dana-Farber and needed to create a blind trust for stock holdings from his biotech start-ups that might otherwise have created conflicts of interest for a hospital CEO. The advisor was George Kidder at Hemenway and Barnes, I said. David knew him, I could tell, but he didn't comment. Only later did I notice David's middle name: Barnes. There were insiders here to be ferreted out, in intricate webs of connection. Gail suggested I pay George a visit. All of this spoken casually, as though it happened every day.

We were sitting on three straight-backed chairs in the vacated living room of the President's House. I was being inducted into an alternate universe, ushered through a looking glass. And it was all I could do to take it in, to silence the "Wait? . . . what?!" my mind served up with each new item on the list.

The cook and house manager would take care of all our family's needs, Gail said, and coordinate with the staff in the President's Office to plan many events at the house. Every comment amplified how all-encompassing this job would be, how all consuming—not that I didn't expect that— but also that many strange new responsibilities would cross boundaries between my private and public life. Like overseeing the staff in the house, approving menus, guest lists, seating plans, and who knew what else?

The college would own my car and it would come with two drivers. A couple of days later, one of them, Jim Ralli, met me early in the morning in my West Newton driveway. It was the first time he'd picked me up there. He and his colleague, John Mulhall, chauffeured the trustees and VIP visitors back and forth to the airport and enjoyed their insider status. There was much juicy gossip in rides to and fro, especially during a high-level search, when they weighed in on how candidates treated them. I had spoiled their fun on this search by driving myself—a local candidate they never met until the deal was sealed. But all was forgiven now. Jimmy had bought us both a latte.

"For you, Boss," he said with a grin. He didn't reveal until months later that he had left home at the crack of dawn on this, the morning after his wedding. The fact that he abandoned his marital bed to pick up the new president, with a latte, did become part of his karma.

Chris drove us to Boston in his car for our appointment with George Kidder at H&B. We sat down in George's office and I told him why we'd come. He stood up, walked across the office, closed the door, and turned to me.

"Be careful." George had been a Wellesley trustee for eighteen years, we found out now, another unexpected connection. He spoke obliquely of Ruth Adams, who became president in 1966, the fall after I graduated, and served for a scant six years during a tumultuous period in higher education. In the turmoil of the late 60's that I had witnessed at Barnard and Columbia, Ruth was treated badly, George hinted, and counseled me to negotiate a strong contract. On my next phone call with Gail, I broached the contract.

"Wellesley does not do contracts," Gail declared with finality. "It's a year-to-year appointment." I was too far down this road to turn around now, obviously, so I would hope not to meet whatever fate befell President Adams. She did come to mind from time to time when the going got rough.

Back at the college, I had a meeting scheduled with the associate director of resources. Roger walked in carrying a jumbo loose-leaf notebook as though it were a precious gift.

"These are your new best friends," he declared. He placed the black notebook on the table in front of us and opened it.

"Who are they?"

"The 100 people we predict will be the largest donors to the college during your presidency." He flipped the pages and stopped at the profile of an alumna who graduated in the 1950s. It listed her giving history, and every contact of hers with the college since she graduated. Her professional and personal activities and priorities through her life, her husband's professional vita and income history, her family and their whereabouts. The profile ended with best estimates of her giving potential in the years ahead.

"Where do you get all this?" He pointed to excerpts from "call reports" written by staff of the leadership gifts program he directed. As scouts, these LG officers went out in advance of the president to find prospects ripe for a visit from her. Presidents, too, wrote call reports, detailed ones I gathered from excerpts in the profile. I asked Roger to send me samples so I could get the hang of this peculiar literary form.

"You'll meet the top twenty or so prospects in their homes this year," he said as I stood up to escort him out. "Next year we'll send you out on a tour across the country. The Welcome Diana Tour."

Officially I was the "president elect" until October first. This had been my choice. Through September I spent half of my time at Harvard to ease the transition, the other half at Wellesley where I spoke at one opening event after another, introduced by Luella Goldberg. As outgoing board chair, she stood by all summer to step in as acting president if needed. Ending an eighteen-year term on the board, and with two Wellesley daughters, Luella had made the college a focal point of her life. I could see that she relished the chance to live in the President's House and lead the college, so I told Gail I would need September to wrap up things at Harvard while we sold our house and prepared to move. I hadn't anticipated what fun it would be to spend my frenetic first month at Wellesley in the company of a wise and warm companion who quickly became a friend.

Chris was plenty busy himself in year two as president of the Dana-Farber Cancer Institute (DFCI), a position he had added in 1992 to his job as professor and chair of one of the five preclinical departments at Harvard Medical School. He was always supportive, and sharply focused. A friend observed that when Chris took on a project, it was as though the Army Corps of Engineers had arrived to set up an instant town. I sat at my desk writing speeches while Chris did the lion's share of packing up our house in West Newton. I would see him haul bags of trash out to the sidewalk and occasionally would run after him to rescue a book of family photographs or some other memento I couldn't bear to toss.

I borrowed from Chris's assistant an abbreviation she used in his calendar: YSAFW, for 'you say a few words.' My next official act as president elect was to welcome the incoming first-year students and their families at their orientation assembly in the Chapel. When I wrote that talk the previous week I thought about the dramas playing out in the homes of these families as their daughters prepared to break away and strike out on their own. I remembered seeing Allison off to Stanford two years earlier. In the folder with my talk—offering predictable college advice and reassurances all around—I tucked a copy of a poem that came to me after Allison left. I didn't know whether I would conclude with it, but wanted to have it, just in case.

Allison flew alone to San Francisco for college, after insisting that it would be easier for her to say goodbye to us in Boston, at the airport, with no audience. We resisted as long as we could, but she convinced us that this was how she needed to manage the separation. At that point, there was nothing for us to do but respect her decision, as we had honored her judgment from the time she was very young. She had never failed us, never failed herself.

From the Chapel pulpit I looked out at the rows of attentive faces, felt their rising wave of sorrow, slid the poem out and described its provenance. It began with a question from Chris. "Shall we watch the plane take off? / You ask as I try not to cry. I shake my head, No / And we walk to the car. Unburdened except for the pain. / It's not as though there wasn't time to see this coming, / You say. Cautiously, half question, half joke, as if to help. / But I am blinded by a loss beyond envisioning. / We approach the car. Just two of us now. / No child to sit in the back. / Empty electric chair at the end of death row. / Let's go back, I blurt. Gently, you say, / No. It's time to go on."

I would haul out that short poem thirteen of the fourteen years I spoke at the close of that emotional day. Seniors would hark back to it, with a theatrical groan about the electric chair, in a reminiscence each graduating class wrote and performed at the baccalaureate service before their commencement. One year, a dean of students suggested I forgo it. She was uncomfortable seeing me "make parents and students cry." Her comment set me worrying that my instinct to read it might have reflected a need of mine, not of the audience, and so I took her advice, reluctantly. Afterwards I knew she was wrong. My poem had eased, not heightened, the unavoidable pain of parting, eased it by giving it a name, coaxing it out into the open, shining a light on it to reduce the shadow it cast.

That first year, after we exited the chapel an intense and chic woman, flanked by two mortified-looking teenagers, elbowed her way to the front of the disorderly receiving line that had just formed behind me while I wasn't paying attention.

"These are my daughters," she announced for all within earshot. "They are twins. They are my pride and joy. My life's work. And I am counting on you to take good care of them."

"I'll do my best," I replied and cast the wincing twins a glance of solidarity. "I'm new, too, as you know," to the twins. "I'll bet you're as eager as I am to get settled and get started. It's going to be great; that's my prediction." At least we can hope so, I added only to myself.

I'd learn later to anticipate the crush of parents who craved a moment with the president, ached for confirmation that their daughters would be seen here, appreciated, even, dared they hope, loved. Many told me pointedly, as the twins' mother had, that they were commending their daughters to my care, a reminder of the mantle of responsibility I had assumed, *in loco parentis*, whether I liked it or not.

Around us were clusters of strangers all feeling their way. We'd snaked in a caravan of sorts, an impromptu parade, along the path by the lake from the chapel to the sloping lawn down from the President's House. How was it possible that only two years earlier I had sat with my Wellesley classmates on this lawn that edged the lake, a random member of the class of 1966 back for my twenty-fifth reunion? In the photo from that occasion framed on my dresser I was leaning into my former roommate, Joan, delighting in her company and blithely indifferent to the large white house above us, off in the distance. Had someone suggested on that sunny June afternoon that I'd be its next occupant, I'd have laughed.

For me those early weeks were a total immersion in a whole new world, a formative time. I signed scores of letters every day, sometimes hundreds, and occasionally an enormous check. I received big checks in the mail, and called donors to thank them personally, often from my car phone as I was being driven. I learned a new email system, a new telephone system, new names, new acronyms, a Byzantine array of committees, rules, and procedures.

Each day brought more advice. What I should read, who I should hire, what I should fix first and place at the top of my worry list. Gratuitous offers of help came rolling in. But I didn't have any idea yet what help I needed, as sure as I was that I would need plenty. My situation reminded me of another of my mother's stories, the one about the first time my sister went to the dentist all by herself. He took one look at her and said, Sally, you don't have your moral support. She dissolved in tears. "I don't know what that is," she sobbed.

I was learning to pay attention to what I said to whom. All through orientation week I'd been claiming an honorary membership in the first-year class. They liked that. But at Opening Convocation everyone was back on campus. And I was unaware of a new tradition since my day. Because the senior class was wearing their academic robes for the first time, they expected special recognition. When I called myself an honorary first year, they fussed, hissed, and booed in mock horror. I quickly aligned myself with the seniors and the faculty. Those of us in our academic robes.

At the end of one especially long day—all the days were long—I was instructed in how to shoot the pistol to start the Wellesley invitational cross-country meet. I returned to the track an hour later, after a few more calls in my office, to hand out the prizes. I realized that I didn't know whether it was appropriate for me to show special partisanship toward the Wellesley winners. I tried to give them extra warm handshakes on the sly.

As I walked back to my office, I was reminded of how completely defined I was by my new, visible role. Three students walked toward me on the path, smiled and said a polite hello. But as soon as they passed, I heard one of them shriek.

"My god, that was the president, I've just spoken to the PRESIDENT." Her tone reminded me of Lucy in the Peanuts cartoon howling, I've been kissed by a dog!

Chris and I were told to make an appearance at the show the junior class put on every fall. My assistant had alerted me to wear yellow, the color of the junior class, so I was in a bright yellow blazer. We walked into the auditorium through a side door. Everyone leapt to their feet and let out a great shout followed by a round of loud applause. Chris looked puzzled for a moment, wondered what the fuss was about, and then suddenly registered that the cheering was for me.

Home later that night, getting ready for bed, he commented, "I guess a person who's been the object of five standing ovations isn't ever quite the same person again." It was quintessential Chris to quantify such a statement and pose it so gently and yet analytically. It was not entirely clear to either of us what exactly he meant. Except that we were both adjusting to a dramatically new role for me, and a changed dynamic for our marriage.

My role at Wellesley felt starkly different from his at Dana-Farber. DFCI's annual budget at the time was $160-million compared to Wellesley's $100-million. DFCI was known for its grateful patients, and a Grand Prix resource development machine, the Jimmy Fund. Even so, we were realizing that the Farber lacked the emotional claim on its large and loyal constituencies that Wellesley enjoyed—the durable ties that bound graduates to one another and to the college. The college presidency had a different resonance and symbolism; it felt both more personal and more eternal.

Both of us were aware of the aura around a college president. How much people read into the role. I found it disconcerting at first. Sometimes elderly alumnae literally stroked me, so excited to be meeting this new president, the embodiment of their beloved college, so eager to wish her well. Others, pulling back to reserve judgment, would say so bluntly, standing in the back of the auditorium, waiting to see whether I could possibly measure up to the standard set by Nan, whom they revered. A former president of the alumnae association said it all with a call to me shortly after hearing the news that a fellow Philadelphian would lead her alma mater.

"From now on, you ARE Wellesley College," she signed off. I wondered for a moment about a merging of identities that called to mind the moment in *Wuthering Heights* when Catherine cried, "I am Heathcliff," betrayed her own nature and unleashed forces of chaos. I was sure I did not want to BE Wellesley College, and I was getting the message that the role could become cloying. The academic dean had already hinted as much.

"You may not like this," Nancy said, "but the President is a princess at Wellesley. Everyone looks up to her. She's on a pedestal." I knew I would never see myself as a princess, and the pedestal conjured up a Shelley poem on the transitory nature of human power I had read in my senior year. "Ozymandias."

Shortly before October 1, I was surprised to learn that Gail was flying in from Denver for my official first day in office. Together we walked over to Severance Green at the center of the campus. Rounding the corner with her I was shocked to see a huge festival underway, a party the trustees and staff had planned without letting on to me. How did they pull this off? I was learning that if I thought I ran the place, I might be kidding myself.

Two members of the faculty sang folk songs they'd written for the occasion and the three student *a cappella* groups performed. Every kind of food was everywhere in profusion, including a truck with fried dough the students especially loved. A DJ played loud music and students danced on the green. Everyone wore white painters' caps with the words Welcome Diana in blue script across the front. The hats kept showing up for years, as did the fried dough truck. Gail made a speech and invited me to make one too. The YSAFW that had become second nature to me here already.

The day before the surprise festival was my final day at Harvard, a day of farewells. I packed up my rolodex, my telephone directory, my laptop, and the few remaining items I'd left unpacked in case I might need them right up to the end. I signed the final letters to funding agencies transferring my grants to other faculty, dismantling a twenty-year research career with a few strokes of the pen. A reminder of how expendable any one of us is; how suddenly we can shift what felt like stable priorities.

I had lunch at the Museum of Fine Arts with the faculty in my department, reminiscing, laughing, and eating too much. We marveled together at all we'd accomplished in just the three years since I'd arrived; a total makeover of the department. I was going to miss it. All afternoon, I said goodbye to a steady procession of students, colleagues, and friends who'd stopped by my office. We exchanged contact information and promised to stay in touch. But we knew how unlikely that was, given the pressures I'd be facing. I walked out of the building right at five o'clock, waved a last goodbye to the guard who had been whistling Hail to the Chief to me all month, and looked up at the clock to realize that as of that very moment I was no longer a tenured Harvard professor. Right on time, I walked away from the "appointment without limit of time" that I had thought would be the apogee of my career. Remarkably, I was walking toward an appointment that seemed to have few formal limits of any kind.

Six months later, in early April, I was out for an early run with Magellan off leash, the morning chilly, dawn just beginning to backlight the horizon behind us. Our feet were splattered with mud from puddles along the path. We were nearing the end of our daily three-mile circuit around the lake, feeling alive and alert. We emerged from a wooded glen onto a grassy incline, Green Beach. Straight ahead was a sight that stopped us both in our tracks: the Big White Tent, or BWT. That's what the students in their online commentary had named this apparition.

"What's up on Severance Green?" "Looks like a tent going up." "How much did it cost?" "We should camp out in it."

And now here it was, fully assembled for my inauguration. It was shiny and white, almost phosphorescent in the pink light of dawn. Yards of walls with plastic windows were topped by a rolling roof that peaked in pointed turrets. I coaxed Magellan to follow me into the gaping interior and we stood there on the dewy grass in the morning silence.

I tried to envision the huge space filled with chairs, people, music, warmth—and words: my words. I'd been working on my inaugural address, off and on, for several months. I felt my stomach twist, stood for a long moment, caught my breath, then pivoted and ran back to the house. Although no longer the anxious girl who practiced poems in front of the mirror to manage her stage fright, this was by far the largest venue—and the highest profile—I had taken on. What I didn't know was that I would learn not just how to manage, but how to *relish* presiding over crowds in the BWT. By the end of my presidency, the thought of never doing it again would rank high among the losses I would find most bitter to swallow.

New presidents sometimes confided in each other that we would as soon "elope" as spend the institution's money on an extravaganza designed to place us in the spotlight and on a pedestal. Many had been scholars at heart, introverts recasting themselves for an extravert's role. What we all came to recognize was that the official object of an inauguration was not the person of the president. It was to create a memorable moment for the community to reconnect to its past and recommit to its future. It also served a latent function as another step in the socialization of a new leader into a new role.

The committee had been meeting all year to plan a day and a half of events: discussion panels, musical and theatrical performances, an early-morning fun run sponsored by the athletic department, a zany parade with banners designed by students in their residence halls. The zenith of the ceremony would be the moment when Gail, on behalf of the board, would confer the title of president upon me. She would present me with three emblems of the office: the original charter of the college, the bylaws, and three antique keys to the college, one each for the library, the residence halls, and the chapel. There had been a minor panic when the committee couldn't find these keys. After some speculation that Nan had taken them with her to Duke, and a suggestion that we could just borrow some replacements from Harvard, they had eventually been located safely in the hands of the college archivist, framed in a shadow box.

Victor Kazanjian, the dean of religious and spiritual life, had arrived in my office some months earlier to advocate a multi-faith baccalaureate service for the eve of my inauguration. This was his second year on the job and he spotted an opportunity to showcase his new program. I wanted to be supportive and encouraged him to go ahead. As his plan took shape, he returned to ask if I had friends outside Wellesley I'd like to invite to speak. It would be meaningful for everyone, he suggested, to hear voices from beyond the community, people who could trace the thread from my previous life to my new beginning here. I suggested two friends from my Kellogg fellowship, Sandra Daley and Parker Palmer.

And so it was that on the night before my induction into the presidency, Parker Palmer stood towering over the large congregation assembled in Houghton Chapel. He read a Mary Oliver poem, "The Summer Day," and touched on our experiences together. Then closed with a public charge to me:

"The world needs presidents who are also poets," he said. "Keep your poetry alive." Later that evening at the President's House, my sister Sally, the Barnard chemistry professor, found a private moment to ask me a question that was on her mind.

"When did you become so spiritual?" She stretched out the last word as if holding a smelly object at arm's length. She, like many of my friends in the academy, especially scientists, was suspicious of that elusive word, as I, too, had been before I spent time with Parker. I'd watched how carefully he used it, used all words. As poets do. I, too, was careful with the word, but not afraid of it. And I was determined to keep my poetry alive.

It rained all that night and straight through my inauguration, a dark cloud cover emitting a chilling drizzle. The procession was led by the delegates, in academic regalia, in the reverse order of their institution's founding date, starting with Oxford. Our faculty followed, then the platform party that included outside speakers to bring greetings from the Commonwealth of Massachusetts, the Town of Wellesley, and the academy at large, and also speakers from the college's major constituencies, faculty, staff, alumnae, and students. Gail and I brought up the rear, preceded by the thirty-four trustees.

Gail opened the proceedings. Victor delivered the invocation. Neil Rudenstine presented an erudite and witty salutation on behalf of the academic community. Nancy Kolodny, speaking for her faculty colleagues, enjoined me to take good care of *their* college. Two staff members presented a cutting from the century-old camellia that belonged to the founder's wife and was still being kept alive in the college greenhouse. Last up was the student speaker, the president of college government, a tall, striking woman with poise beyond her years.

She stepped up to the podium carrying a wooden hoop wrapped in a blue ribbon. Wellesley was known for the seniors' annual hoop rolling race in the spring, a tradition that dated back to the late 1800s and had become a parody of itself. I had won the race in my senior year. The student speaker said a few words and then referred to problems we'd been having on campus. I felt the members of the platform party stiffen and inhale. Where is she going? With easy finesse, she said a few more words to convey that students were counting on this new president to make things right. She walked over to me and presented the hoop. As a collective exhale moved across the dais, I felt anything but release. With that gift in that moment, I knew I was accepting responsibility for the residual racism of an elite white institution moving glacially through a historic transition in its demographics and self-conception. I propped the hoop against a leg of my chair and rose for the installation ritual.

Gail's role was to present me, one-by-one, with the three symbols of my office, which we had agreed I would pass to Nancy to hold during my speech. As we proceeded, a faint ripple of laughter in the faculty section alerted me to the irony. The board was giving me my implements of authority and I was turning them over to the head of the faculty, who had just referred to the college as *theirs*. So when Gail handed me the keys to the college and Nancy reached for the box, I grinned and, with a flourish, tucked it under the sleeve of my academic robe and moved to the podium.

I took a deep breath and scanned the rows and rows of guests in the tent, easily 2,000 or more. I employed one of the techniques to carry me past my initial stage fright: over-learn the ice breaker. If I could think through carefully how I would begin each talk, who would be in the audience, and how to connect right away, then I would avoid the sense of isolation, judgment, and self-consciousness. Once I learned to feel an intimacy with the audience, whatever its size, I could speak from my heart and not just from my text. When I could bring everyone assembled into a circle of common care, then we could come together as fallible human beings doing our best to find the deeper meaning and truth in the topic at hand.

My address drew on all I'd learned in my first eight months on the job. First, I took a tentative step out onto a limb that would become a theme of my presidency, the possibility that education is a spiritual journey, not merely an intellectual one. Then, for protective cover, I reverted to Wellesley stories, followed by my thoughts about work we would have to do. It was already obvious to me that making choices was difficult for an institution with a large endowment and an ambitious culture that prized individual autonomy and resisted authority. Fine leadership, no less than fine scholarship, glancing at the faculty, required the exercise of critical discernment. Discrimination in the intellectual sense. Women, in particular, must be honest and clear about authority, must have the courage to acknowledge and use power with integrity, must make hard choices, openly and fairly, standing behind them and confronting and managing the unavoidable challenges and conflicts.

Wellesley ended official gatherings by singing "America the Beautiful," written by Katherine Lee Bates, an alumna and lifelong English professor at the college. Some time after I graduated, the students had established a tradition of shouting out sisterhood where the word brotherhood appears. Years later, the president of Amherst, a coed college, a veteran of inaugurations, told me he envied the spirit and solidarity he witnessed at mine, with the exuberance from Wellesley's students.

"I've never seen anything like it anywhere, before or since," Tom said to me. "I don't know whether it's because your students are all women and have a stronger sense of community, or whether they feel differently about their president. But it sure made for a special day."

Later, back at the house, my father declared my speech too long. As much as his comment burned, I had to admit he was right. Learning to say more with less was going to be a challenge.

Another review of my inaugural address came from a beloved senior professor of economics.

"That was a great speech, boss," Chip said. "You did yourself proud."

"Thanks," I said, touched.

"We'd already figured out that you are nice enough to succeed at this job," he continued as though speaking for the whole faculty—as he kind of did. "But you showed us today that you are smart enough." I tried not to look as crestfallen as I felt. Chip had touched an old wound I tried to hide, one that went back at least to my days as a Wellesley student. Was I smart enough?

But his comment clarified an ambition I had for the college to which I had just been given the keys. I did not want us to go around classifying people according to how "smart" they "are." I saw that as a snare and a delusion, with an edge of both arrogance and cruelty. It implied a static condition, a narrow definition, a marker of status in a rigid hierarchy. Surely this must not be the test of whether you belonged at Wellesley. As a student. As a faculty or staff member. As a president. I wanted our emphasis to be on learning and character. On intellectual, and emotional—and, yes, spiritual—attainment and development. From the inside out and back from the outside in. The question I wanted us to ask ourselves—often—was, are we *learning* enough? All of us.

7

FROM THE INSIDE OUT

I had flown in the previous night to Durham, North Carolina. I was there to show the flag for Wellesley at Nan Keohane's inauguration as Duke's president. At lunch, I was seated with the outgoing president. Nan's predecessor with her successor. I asked about his plans.

"I used to think I would write when I had time," he replied. "My reflections on higher education, a memoir, something in that vein." He paused and I waited. "But the words have gone away." I froze. Oh, no. This cannot be the price a college president pays. I wished I hadn't heard it. I was only half listening as he moved on to presidential advice.

I'd already had enough gratuitous advice. In the previous week a stranger, a campus neighbor, accosted me with an urgent problem. The sixth hole of our golf course, the blind shot to the green just short of Route 16, was dangerous. This was news to me. Days later, I received a letter from a daily commuter upset about the forsythia at the entrances to the circular drive up to the President's House. They looked like pom poms, he complained. Free the forsythia! I checked with the groundskeeper who was happy to stop trimming them. Everything should be so easy. I mentioned the golfing hazard and forgot about it until much later when I passed a crew planting a cypress hedge to screen the road. Years later—my final week in office. Wasn't so urgent after all, I concluded.

I tuned back into my lunch partner in time for the end of his tip. I should solidify my support systems in concentric circles, from the inside out. First make sure the staffing of the president's office and house are working well. Then move on to the senior staff, the faculty, the students, the trustees, alumnae, donors, and outward from there.

I found the perfect person for my administrative assistant, the role closest to me, in Jane Bachman. She'd worked in other parts of the college for a decade or so. I'd taken an instant liking to her; she was even-keeled, always cheerful, and wore well on everyone. I felt sure she'd have my back no matter what, and that we would have fun together. She would keep track of my calendar and my life and represent me to all who sought me out. With her help, I could begin to learn who was who and what was what.

The search committee had told me I was inheriting a strong senior team and would want to keep them in place. The Senior Staff, as the team was called, comprised seven members. I already knew Nancy Kolodny from the search. Gail, David, and Luella had stressed that I could lean on her and Will Reed as I scaled the learning curve—Will for finance and administration, Nancy for all things academic. Will made it clear from day one that he wanted me to succeed. Nancy did too. She was extremely helpful to me, sharp, clear, organized, on top of details. Her associate dean, Jens Kruse, an amiable professor of German, also had a seat on Senior Staff, giving the faculty two voices.

Peter Ramsey, the vice president for resources and public affairs, ran Nan's record-breaking fundraising campaign. It was intimidating that everyone referred to it in exactly those terms. Peter showed up on my first day in office and handed me a sealed envelope.

"It's my resignation letter." I held my breath. "I want you to have it in your top drawer so you can call it in any time you lose confidence in me. Or just want a different person. Fundraising," he continued, "depends on relationships, beginning with ours."

"Gallant gesture," I said. "But no dice." I had a lot to learn from Peter and he was close to the trustees. He was close to Will Reed too, especially when tensions arose. They were cut from different cloth, those two, but respected each other and cleaved together when outflanked as minority males in a matriarchy. Both became coaches and mentors to me: the money guys.

Molly Campbell had been dean of students for nine years. Another alum who didn't stray far after she graduated in 1960, she had been a math instructor, and a class dean, too. She was close to Peggy Plympton, the IT vice president. Both of these women were close to Nan, and I could tell that they had their doubts about me.

Janet Lavin, director of admission, was the final member of the Senior Staff. In her third year at Wellesley, she was popular with everyone, including the trustees. They were proud to see our applications booming, as was I. Janet was the youngest member of Senior Staff. She graduated from Williams College in 1981 when wider choices opened to women as the top men's colleges went co-ed. I was glad to have her perspective as an antidote to my team's Wellesley parochialism—we were not a diverse group.

Beyond Senior Staff, my relationship with Gail was critical. She was a new board chair who wanted to make her own mark. And she, more than anyone, was invested in my success. At first she would call me at least once a week and push me, kindly but firmly, with a shotgun spray of tough questions. I would have answers to a few and would promise to be back to her on the others. Next call, same thing, and I was off on a new scavenger hunt. I recognized this as an excellent way for me to learn fast, but perhaps not the way for me to establish my authority with the trustees. I was not leading the board, as the president should. Years later I would look back at the goals I presented to the board that first year. I titled them "Klapper-Walsh priorities," as if we were co-presidents, she in the senior position. This was a rookie mistake and far from the only one. Gail and I became very good friends over time and I have always been grateful for her faith in me.

"Sometimes you're a poet and sometimes a social scientist," Will said one day in the midst of a Senior Staff meeting. I was pushing him for more refined data on the budget. "We like the poet better." The social scientist was the one who was holding her staff's feet to the fire. What they didn't know was that I was determined to walk the fire myself. My goal was to lead a high-performing team whose members were honest with each other and able to learn together. To signal that, I decided to be open with them about the steps I was taking to bring myself up to speed. This made some of them uncomfortable, especially the two Nan loyalists who were unsure about me anyway.

"You need an Ernie Sargent," Will said to me at the end of one of our private meetings in October. "When Nan had a problem," he explained, she called the college's outside counsel to discuss it in confidence. I asked him where to find an Ernie Sargent. He suggested a management consultant, Rod Napier.

"He's an acquired taste. You may not like him. But he's good at build-ing executive teams." I called Rod right away and arranged to meet him. He had a straightforward quality that I liked and an understanding of how hard it is to lead successfully. Plus he brought a humility that the slick Arnold Zenker sorely lacked. Self-knowledge was important to him, and to me, that and a willingness to go out on a limb. You might not suc-ceed but at least you'd know you tried. I was put off, however, by Rod's tough macho side.

"You have to pledge to do this," he said to me, "whatever it takes," and pressed his two wrists together crosswise as though taking a blood oath. I wouldn't be doing that. But he did appeal to the part of me that wanted to be open to the truth, come what may, to face unpleasant realities, if necessary. All my life I'd written in journals, often in an effort to learn from mistakes. If I could be hard on myself—harder than anyone else— maybe I could make myself tough enough to withstand the worst I would have to endure.

Two years earlier, my Harvard colleague, Rima Rudd, had challenged this ancient pattern of mine. We were having lunch in a sunny atrium at the medical school. I was rehashing a minor mistake I'd made in the class we'd just co-taught.

"You know," Rima mused, "it's as though you have two conflicting theories of motivation. One is for your students. You inspire and encour-age them. You see and evoke their best. But when *you* make a mistake, you haul out the whip and chain. Surely both pedagogies aren't equally effective. What's the double standard all about?" Now the work with Rod was raising that question again. Even as I was attracted to him as a poten-tial co-conspirator in my stern self-improvement project, I was leery of the extent to which he seemed to see a leader as a courageous hero, self-reliant and larger than life. I hadn't yet worked out to my satisfaction all the distortions of that patriarchal model. But I was certain I didn't want to try to lead in that lonely way. I needed to round up a posse to join me in my exploits. That's where the fun would be, and where we could begin to have an impact.

I had an opportunity to fill a vacancy for a special assistant to the pres-ident and director of affirmative action. The incumbent was recruited away to Spelman College the year before I arrived. She was the only minority member of Senior Staff. Everyone told me I should replace her. She did too when I met with her at Nan's inauguration. The consensus was that we should conduct a national search run by a broadly representative campus committee of faculty and staff with support from a professional search firm. The position carried a lot of symbolic and substantive freight on a campus that was scrambling to diversify peacefully.

I selected two co-chairs for the search committee. They were well known, widely respected, and trusted by campus minority groups. I asked them to draft a charge for their committee and to propose members, which they did—a large committee representing all imaginable constituencies. I negotiated a few changes and sent the revised materials to Senior Staff for reactions. Will came to see me.

"I'm worried," he said.

When Will was worried, which was often, I became worried too.

"You're giving up the one position that is yours to fill. You need your own people and now this job is going to be owned by the community at large." We were both conscious of constraints on staff hiring. Shortly before she left, Nan drew from the endowment for a voluntary retirement program to shrink the administration. In our only meeting during the transition, she told me not to let the staff grow again. Will was responsible for holding that line.

Advocates for a stronger role for the affirmative action officer, including the committee co-chairs, insisted that the position should report to the president and be a member of Senior Staff, but should no longer include responsibilities as a special assistant to the president. Affirmative action, they contended, was a full-time job, one best not encumbered by divided loyalties. They had a reasonable point, but I was beginning to see the need for a true special assistant to me, a strategist who could handle complex assignments, quickly develop a sophisticated picture of all sides of an issue, and give me a menu of options.

"You really need this person," Will said and shook his head. I agreed but saw no way to wrest the affirmative action position back from the constituencies that were intent on controlling it. When Peter saw that I needed help he offered, as a stopgap, a member of his staff. Her strength was event planning, and she became fully immersed in coordinating the committee planning my inauguration. I still didn't have my assistant; those were not her skills.

The search for the affirmative action position went on all year. In my office, when the committee came to deliver their slate of the top three candidates, it was obvious they had a strong preference.

"If you are serious about affirmative action," Selwyn Cudjoe, chair of Africana studies, challenged, "you will pick our top contender." I checked her references and could tell she would be strong medicine for Wellesley. But we had unresolved racial issues and needed to make progress. I hired her.

What I hadn't anticipated was how combative she would be, how harshly she would judge the college's racial climate, and the contempt she would show for past efforts to improve it. Senior Staff meetings became tense and defensive. She berated everyone, including me. This was not workable, not at all constructive. She departed with a hefty severance package and I cobbled together a temporary arrangement to carry the work forward. But this had been a drubbing.

Walter Cabot's question during the presidential search was echoing in my mind: "How are you at picking people?" Not great so far, Walter. I'd hired and fired the affirmative action officer who came out of the complicated search over which I'd lost control. Peter's event planner ably helped manage my inauguration but lacked the skills of the executive assistant I was ever more certain I needed, soon.

So I took a risk. I enlisted five colleagues from the faculty and staff to join me as a search committee in a peculiar hiring process. These were adventuresome people I admired, and I hoped they wouldn't find the experiment too weird. Rod Napier had pitched an approach to interviewing that he assured me would greatly increase the odds of getting the right person. I was still on the fence about Rod, but I needed to get this one right and his approach sounded promising. He called it the "Power Interview."

And so, with my small but intrepid search committee, I crafted simulations of five situations I would want my executive assistant to handle well. We would role-play them during five finalist interviews, with one or two of my co-conspirators taking up roles in each of the scenarios. The others would observe and assess how each candidate performed. We also designed a final scenario that would be the ultimate test. Facing the candidate, with the observers across the room from us, I would describe three things about me that might trip up the new assistant in this role, then ask the candidates to follow suit with things about them that I might find challenging at first. My plan was to lead with candor and self-awareness and see what I got back.

I was completely honest. First, I said, I'd been doing both jobs and it was going to take me some adjusting to give up the parts that came most naturally in favor of those that didn't. Second, people pushed my buttons when I looked indecisive. But when I made hasty decisions, I sent confusing signals. I needed a partner who would help me be more deliberate, responsive, and consistent. Third, I was trying too hard to do everything and please everyone. I was not saying no enough. I was determined to become more guarded and circumspect, but it was an ongoing effort. The good news, I ended, was that I was aware of these deficits, was working on them, and did have compensating strengths.

I will always remember how brilliantly Patricia Byrne responded to this eccentric gambit from a potential new boss who laid her insecurities on the table and asked to be met there. I soon forgot how the other four candidates moved through all five scenarios, especially the last one. Pat had already served two presidents and knew the executive assistant job better than I did. She knew both jobs better, really, the assistant's and the president's. She was self-aware and wise, quick and strikingly insightful, with an easy manner and an Irish sense of humor. I felt seen and met by her in this one encounter.

My concern was that we wouldn't persuade her to accept a job so like those she had already done. As one of her "truths" she admitted that she was undecided. But our offbeat interview must have convinced her that this job could be different. A week later she accepted my offer.

In retrospect we all agreed that the interview made emotional demands that bordered on excessive. And yet it brought me a truly unique partner with whom to advance my own leadership. I would promote Pat within two years to a larger role, my chief of staff, and soon thereafter to vice president of administration and planning. I never found a hurdle she did not clear.

Beyond her manifold talents, Pat was the right choice for me in this vital advisory role because she was a woman. Before my return to Wellesley, my mentors and close colleagues had been as often men as women: Bill Bicknell, Ralph Hingson, Dick Egdahl, Sol Levine, Parker Palmer. It hadn't escaped my notice that my career had often been advanced by powerful men, including my husband, who saw promise in me before I had claimed it. Barnard and Planned Parenthood, on the other hand, were two organizations, like Wellesley, dedicated to breaking down barriers to women's empowerment; both had women in prominent leadership roles who were sophisticated about their use of power. We talked and read about power a lot in those heady days. At Harvard, I'd synthesized the literature on gender and power for our flagship book on *Society and Health*. Yet when I arrived at Wellesley I was still working out for myself how I wanted to deploy the considerable—if at times confusing—authority inherent in my new role. I found in Pat Byrne a close woman partner who was tough, incisive, no-nonsense. She had clear boundaries, high standards, and unshakable, deep values; was efficient and effective in every situation; and also had a big heart and a natural spiritual inclination. I would come to see Pat as an existence proof of the alternative I was looking for to the male model of leadership.

Right away, I put Pat in charge of the leadership development program I had launched. A total of fifty middle managers were participating, together with all members of Senior Staff. I had asked each of them to select members of their divisions whom they thought would benefit. I knew I wanted to strengthen the Wellesley administration, in part so they could hold their own in collaborations with faculty. I'd commissioned Rod to lead the training program with his wife, Julie. I myself was participating fully to imprint a presidential imprimatur on the program and reinforce the message that I wanted my presidency to be about *learning*: everyone's learning, not least, my own. I wanted us to wade into difficult situations with open minds and hearts, with an ear tuned to competing voices. We would need new skills if we were to do that well and I saw the training program as a small start, a public enactment of a longer-term goal. Senior Staff members humored their new boss and went with the idea, some grudgingly. I was way out on a limb with this too. Rod was not exactly Wellesley's cup of tea.

And the program was intense. That was part of what made me believe it could make a difference. It required four three-day sessions off campus at a retreat center, spaced six weeks apart. There were cases and practical exercises on group process, meeting design, supervision, transforming conflict. We learned techniques for organizational diagnosis with simple but clever tools for collecting and using data. This part, my favorite, tapped into my proclivities as a social scientist, and drew on my Kellogg dive into leadership studies.

As soon as Pat was on board, I asked her to keep an ear to the ground for me, to monitor how it was going. She picked up mixed reviews.

"Well," she said, "I'm hearing appreciation from quite a few that the college is investing in their professional development. That's new to them. And many like to be working in new ways with colleagues across departments and divisions. A few of the more adventurous are really excited by Rod's unusual tools and hands-on exercises." This all came as a relief to me. But, Pat went on, others weren't so sure. Some were finding it arduous, intimidating, even, a few said, invasive.

In public, Rod received nothing but praise for his attention to everyone's needs. From the outset, he said explicitly that the goal was *not* to force anyone to change, but simply to offer participants fresh data on their behavior. Our intention was to free participants to make informed choices about the impact they wanted to have. Pat and I continued watching, and decided that the program was bringing the administration together in common purpose and was improving the quality of our meetings, our planning, and our collaboration. It was also teaching me lessons about organizational resistance to discomfort and change, lessons that underscored for me the managerial skills I would still need to add to my repertoire.

With Pat as my partner, I could plainly see that I had been investing way too much of my energy in a narrow slice of my new job, the uber-manager role I was learning on the fly. I delegated more and more of the operational work to Pat. We did have our conflicts at the beginning, generally over habits that I had predicted, during the interview, would irritate her.

"It's as if you are driving a huge garbage truck, careening along College Road," she told me one day. "You are picking up bags of trash and piling them so high that they're tumbling off the back. All the things people want you to fix. You never say no. And I am running along behind you, picking up the fallen bags."

I never forgot that image. It came to mind every time I came to her with an unexpected new delegation. This happened less and less often, once I was alert to the burden I placed on her when I took on impossible tasks. I'd been ambivalent about the power inherent in the president's role, uneasy about when and how to deploy it, when and how to articulate boundaries that I could not or would not cross. The time spent forming a working alliance with Pat helped me sharpen and resolve those questions.

With Pat's partnership I could concentrate on the things only the president could do: speak for the institution, work with the board chair and the trustees, support and supervise the academic deans, discern what was up with the students and in the student life division, keep an eye on the alumnae office. It was for me to connect with major donors, lead the Senior Staff team and, through them, faculty and staff at every level and in every precinct of the college. I listened and learned and refined my vision for the future. All the while I worked to become more adept at leading myself.

Another colleague who saw me in this labor was Victor Kazanjian. He reported to the dean of students and had a dotted line into the president. The year before I arrived, he was hired as dean of an innovative multifaith program. He created and oversaw a student multifaith council, supervised thirteen part-time chaplains, and served as the chaplain at all-college events. Together he and I took up the concern that was raised with me during the search about same-sex commitment ceremonies, and quietly welcomed them in our chapel as a matter of college policy.

Victor had fought hard for his access to the president when he was hired and made sure to show up on my calendar for a private meeting every other week. When I was new he brought me encouraging perspectives on my leadership, like a scout into the hinterlands collecting bits of evidence. His gentle support was a refreshing counterpoint to Rod's pull-up-your-socks approach and an antidote to the self-admonishments that dominated the journals I still kept, albeit sporadically now.

I had written in journals off and on my whole life. Over time I came to consider them a makeshift spiritual practice, a form of contemplation that provided space to still the rancorous chatter inside my head. I used them to find my way back to a center that felt solid and true. It took me time to arrive at this view of what they were. Often, they had an edge. I turned to them when I was feeling inept, a perfectionist making humiliating mistakes, a rookie playing in the major leagues under klieg lights, groping in the dark for the wherewithal I would need to learn what I considered the cardinal law of good leadership: how to become a *trustworthy* leader, first, and foremost, of myself.

In my second academic year as president, Victor and I both addressed the annual plenary meeting of a group of alumnae members of Wellesley's Business Leadership Council, the BLC. Victor spoke in the evening on 'Wholeness, Not Perfection'. He encouraged this accomplished group of roughly fifty dynamic and successful businesswomen, most my contemporaries, to ask themselves whether they had their priorities right. Were they taking adequate care of their souls, attending to their friendships and their families, the noninstrumental relationships that had nourished and sustained them, made them who they were? If the answer was no, Victor said, it mattered.

Inspired by Victor's words, I enumerated in my talk the next morning some of the ways his question mattered to me. "Is it possible to lead well without taking time out regularly to renew and replenish, read and reflect? And if we believe we can remain effective with no time for Victor's 'wholeness,' we are still left with the question of what sort of message we want to convey to younger women. By assuming the mantle of leadership, we've traded glass ceilings for glass houses into which everyone can peer for a glimpse of how it's truly going for us in there. So it matters what we're *doing* in there, as we blaze new trails, but equally who we are *being* in these demanding, competitive, crazy lives that we've chosen or had thrust upon us. It matters because, as we used to taunt LBJ in our youth, 'the whole world is watching.'

"The world is watching our generation of feminist trailblazers to see if we can do it better. While we spend intellectual and emotional capital we've amassed over decades. The reserves are pouring outward with few new deposits to trickle back in. Such are the demands of leadership," I said. "Or at least the demands of the solo, macho, controlling models of leadership we're trying to transcend. The question is whether we can dismantle the competitive structures we've inherited. Can we invent new ones that are healthier and more humane?"

Not easily. I was sure of that. I did not see my posse mounting up briskly to follow me over any cliffs. In November, the BLC was back for their annual meeting. Their planning committee requested that I pick up the theme Victor and I introduced the previous year. They wanted more from me about what I was *doing* to maintain a semblance of balance in my demanding job. Uh oh. They had called my bluff.

The request reminded me that I had not honored Parker Palmer's charge to keep my poetry alive, so I wrote a speech that took off from an early essay and a favorite writing of his, "Leading from Within." Leaders tend to do violence when they "live a divided life," Parker wrote, their inner selves disconnected from who they are in the world. Leaders have particular power to cast shadow or light over others, which is why their inner conditions matter.

I laid out and illustrated simple practices I tried to sustain by devoting time and attention to them. Time to nurture my identity and integrity, to resist the projections of others, and stay grounded in who I am, what I bring, what's mine to give. Time every day for a short period of reflective solitude, whether in a morning run around the lake, or a journal entry to work something out, or a poem to read or write at the end of the day, or a meditation.

Time for friends—old and new—with whom I could be calm, courageous, and authentic. I sought out feedback for myself and tried to offer it skillfully to others. I tried to be conscious of how I affected others, to minimize damage in each interaction, and to make amends when I saw I'd failed. I tried to take in affirmations when they came my way, to feel the relief and grace of reciprocal connections and mutual support, to feel the gratitude that I knew as profoundly nourishing.

I attended to the cycles of life, cycles of growth and consolidation, of celebration, mourning, loss. To acknowledge parts of me that were falling away even as I approached new paths toward growth. Finally, I tried to be my own good teacher—challenging, caring, inspiring. One who listens for what is being spoken, and for what remains unspeakable. A teacher who asks questions that invite self-awareness and strikes a balance between support and challenge.

When I finished, Amalie Kass, a senior trustee and a medical historian I revered, rushed up to me. I sensed in her a combination of agitation and excitement.

"That was amazing! I don't know how you did it. I could never have been so *open* with this group, so painfully honest." I thanked her, and quelled an impression that she might have thought I'd crossed a line, exposed too many of my insecurities, given my power away.

The next day the BLC broke into small groups to discuss themes from my talk. I heard later that they spoke with a candor they hadn't achieved before and plumbed new depths in one another. Still later, I published the talk I gave that day in a volume of essays on leadership collected by the Drucker Foundation. That laid to rest my initial worries about being too personal or self-revealing. I continued to experiment with practices that enabled me to be open and authentic. The key, I discovered, was to reveal insecurities only after I'd managed, in private, to make my peace with them. It was best not to present myself while in the throes of self-doubt—that made people uneasy—but rather, after the fact, to offer vivid and funny stories of difficult moments and how they had felt at the time. I could offer as lessons for others the stories of how these incidents had affected me before I was able to let go of them and laugh at myself, before I had found the wherewithal to lighten up.

Four months after the BLC meeting Victor told me he had been working with Dick Nodell, one of the outside facilitators that day. Dick was helping him sort out tensions in his dual reporting role, accountable to both the dean of students and the president. Victor asked me to participate in a three-way meeting as the final step in the consultation. I agreed.

We met for lunch in the President's House. Dick was a big bear-sized man with a deep voice that was disarmingly gentle. I liked the tone and precision of the discussion, and, as dessert and coffee were served, he turned to me with an easy smile.

"How are you enjoying the job? Do you mind if I ask?" I didn't. He had mentioned that he was standing in the back of the room when I gave the revealing BLC talk. I commented about the work with Rod and some of the challenges I was facing. I didn't go into much detail, but was more frank than I might otherwise have been because his manner reminded me of the spiritual forays during my Kellogg Fellowship.

"It doesn't have to be so hard," he replied simply after I'd finished, a comment I found intriguing but didn't pursue. Our time was up, and I went on about my day. I thought of the comment, off and on over the next few months, when I found myself in one scrape or another. I knew I could trust Victor's judgment and my own instincts, and I recalled Dick's thoughtful demeanor that day over lunch. So one day I called him to explore the idea of working together. He came across as markedly different from the conventional management consultant, as a true intellectual with a large spirit. He was more like Parker than Rod. He said he'd encourage me to develop the practice of "looking at everything that happens as meaningful, and perhaps even enjoyable." That sounded good to me.

I wanted to pay him out of my own pocket, but he insisted that a contract between us had to be "clean and out in the open." Otherwise, it would be based on a false premise that would compromise our working alliance.

"The structure of our agreement has to recognize what you need as legitimate," he insisted. "You need to be clear about that." I felt certain that some women at the college would be horrified to see me turn to a man for advice and that some faculty would disapprove of my spending the college's money on outside management consultants, whose intelligence, expertise and "corporate values" they disdained. I hired Dick for a six-month trial period, during which it became obvious to me that working with this unorthodox thinker would make me more effective for Wellesley. As a woman, I was intent on developing my own authentic leadership. As the leader of a women's college, I was chary of yielding my autonomy to a man, or even appearing to do so. In the work with Dick, I regularly asked myself what was his and what was mine, and how the two of us—in an evolving and collaborative partnership—could invent an approach to leadership that would be uniquely—even joyfully—my own. It revolved around robust partnerships as basic units of organization.

Much later I asked Dick what prompted him to ask how I was doing when we first met.

"Watching you give that talk," he said, his wife, Kate, and he "saw you call people to a different way of being, to a radical change that you advocate and embody. Your leadership is based on emotional power, on a vision that comes from your heart. People see that and they also *feel* it. It's those feelings that you stir up that attach to you if you're not careful. I knew then that you'd need the armament to deflect those emotional reactions."

I continued to work with Dick throughout my presidency, as a consultant to me and to individual members of my Senior Staff, and as a facilitator of Senior Staff retreats. I was his first higher education client and, in the years that followed, he became a sought-after consultant to presidents of dozens of colleges and universities across the country.

8

THE PERMANENT PEOPLE

Chris's scientific collaborator and our close friend, Jeremy Knowles, was the new dean of Harvard's Faculty of Arts and Sciences. A British biochemist in the catbird seat, Jeremy was delighted and amused to hear of my new job.

"Good luck," he said. "The word on the street is that the Wellesley faculty is ungovernable."

"Really? Worse than your famously confident collection of curmudgeons?"

"Yes," he replied, and we both chuckled, commiserating. We knew about faculty power. First, they have a lot of it. Second, they dedicate much of it to competition within their own departments, divisions, and disciplines. Local turf wars over space, money, faculty slots, student enrollments, influence, recognition—parking even, famously—skirmishes that tend to produce collateral damage and cause headaches for the administration. But, third—and this is the nub of it—at the hint of a threat to their autonomy, a fragmented faculty can congeal into a collective juggernaut united against the administration. They can bring down a president. Quickly. Public humiliation followed by symbolic defenestration.

I took Jeremy's comment to refer to explicit levers of power that might trip me up—the formal rules of the game at Wellesley. My new faculty had a strong grip on those, and I knew from the outset that I would have to master the rules, early and thoroughly. So I spent a lot of time in the opening years of my presidency with the person who knew them as well as anyone on campus: the dean of the college, Nancy Kolodny, the chief academic officer. I learned everything I could from her. I also asked myself repeatedly what I could bring that would be distinctive. How could I lead the faculty, not just defend myself against them? The dean was *of* the faculty. She could lead them on my behalf with my delegated author-ity. But I would have to lead the dean and the faculty if I was to have an impact. Working out those details would take some time. I would not be able to call myself the true leader of the institution until I did. I knew this to be true. I saw it as one of my first and toughest challenges.

In the meantime, Wellesley faculty had already demonstrated to me that along with their formal power codified in the articles of government, they also had more than their share of informal, or tacit, power. They knew where bodies were buried. They had invisible networks of personal relationships with each other and with individual trustees and alumnae they taught through the years. They had connections with long-time administrators who shared their notions about how the place should—and should *not*—be run, with donors, and with outside scholars, outside critics, journalists. They had their current students too, those taking their classes or majoring in their departments. These were all key constituen-cies of the college that could cripple presidents if rumors raged out of control. Few presidents survived a faculty's formal vote of no confidence, an extreme case and mercifully rare.

But short of that, I'd already concluded, I would neither enjoy the job, nor thrive in it, if I didn't win over at least some of the faculty. I'd crossed over to the place we would sometimes modify with the word "bloat," the administration. Now I was not just of it; I *was* it. I walked around campus with a bullseye on my back.

Warning arrows grazed my ears even before I'd moved in. Chris and I first made the move from Newton part way to our fancy new home. We were placed temporarily in off-campus faculty housing, a small furnished apartment to squat in, with our dog Magellan. This freed the President's House for a hasty round of renovations. The trustee building committee, Gail explained, angled for years to get into the house and take care of deferred maintenance. A transition was the perfect opportunity to tackle it. But we'd better be careful, Gail warned.

"The faculty will crucify you if they see you literally feathering your own nest even before you arrive." She appointed a trustee committee to serve as a buffer. An early signal that working with the faculty would be anything but straightforward. Nancy suggested that before we made any changes to the house, I had best check with Peter Fergusson, a senior professor in the art history department.

"He is the self-appointed guardian of the historic integrity of the campus," she explained, "and will make your life miserable if you don't seek his counsel." I called him to describe what we had in mind. He cut me off.

"Oh, don't worry, Diana, they've ruined that house already."

Peter was just warming up. A few weeks later he and a senior architecture professor showed up on my calendar to lead me on a tour of the campus as they saw it. They instructed me on the campus's evolution as an expression of competing ideals of individuals and groups held in dynamic tension. These were influenced by prevailing fashions, and sometimes defied them. They moved through periods of persistence and vigilance, but then the occasional crisis. We were approaching a choke point, they concluded. Cars were everywhere. Formerly beautiful views were now mediated through glass and chrome. I had "an obligation to posterity," they warned, as the steward of an American campus known as one of the most beautiful anywhere.

Four months previously my office had been in a high rise with its back turned to a run-down inner-city block. It opened in the other direction on the vast medical school quadrangle and hospital complexes densely packed across that part of the city. If someone had suggested to me then that I'd be worrying about Wellesley's landscape and grounds, I'd have called them crazy. But these two senior professors were here to make themselves perfectly clear. I was on the verge of doing irreparable harm and I had an obligation: to posterity? to them? They were watching me.

I needed to get to know more faculty. I decided to tour the academic departments and demonstrate that I planned to be accessible, a leader who walks around. Jane set up a series of visits spaced through the year. The language departments welcomed me warmly with sumptuous spreads of foods representing their cultures, and with music. They told stories and jokes and became my friends. The biologists toured me through their laboratories and explained posters of their students' projects. From Chris I knew this world; I knew what mattered to them. The political scientists worked to impress on me the leadership roles they played throughout the college, and their global reach.

The economists wanted me to appreciate their high enrollments. Wellesley's economics department could hold its own with many at top universities, they insisted. They presented me with data on faculty laurels and graduates' track records. At the end, in a few private minutes, the economics chair advised me to be sure to "display" my knowledge. Had I been displaying my ignorance? I'd never thought of knowledge as an ornament, and I wondered what judgment of me his advice might betray. No English professor had told me, as a major decades ago, that the knowledge I gained of literature was for show. I shrugged it off. I was learning to steel myself against barbs from the faculty.

The visits to chemistry and English were the most loaded for me. A chemistry eminence approaching retirement had been my instructor, just starting, when I was a student. In the knowing glances we exchanged, I inferred that my secret was safe with her; I had barely squeaked through a chemistry course in the first semester of my freshman year. In English, my major advisor was still there too, also preparing to retire. Much revered I learned now. All I remembered of our interactions was that he instructed me to take his course, seventeenth-century poetry and prose exclusive of Milton. I didn't love that poetry, never studied Milton, and later wished I had. Mostly these echoes of the past reminded me how far I'd come, how fortunate I was to be back in this role where I could write forward my personal history of how this college enriched my life.

On the evening before my meeting with the psychology department, Jane sent me home with a loose-leaf notebook they'd compiled for me. Bios of every faculty member, each with a headshot. I arrived for the visit to find them seated around a table. The chair handed me an alphabetized pile of name tags and challenged me to label each member correctly.

"Good try," I laughed, and handed the pile back. I told them I knew the story of the job candidate who was asked to open the window, not knowing it was nailed down. I was not falling for that trick. My relationship with that department was pure pleasure after that, even when they had their occasional conflicts.

On my visits I asked faculty to tell me about their work as scholars and teachers. What brought them joy? I saw a few cringe. Well, then, satisfaction? Later I would push gently beyond their comfort zones. I would use words that, after my Kellogg experience, rolled more easily off my tongue: joy, gratitude, even love. For now they were comfortable with my questions about contributions their departments made to the whole. How is *this* department different? What do you add? They gave me mostly predictable answers. And one universal response that came forth loud and clear.

"We don't know what those colleagues are doing over there, but over *here* what *we* do is teach our students how to think." I liked that and quoted it in my travels out to alumnae across the generations. That's what Wellesley did for us.

When I visited sociology, I was careful not to let on that I never took any of their courses. And then studied a lot of medical sociology in graduate school. Nevertheless, their Parthian shot came across as a dare.

"Thanks for taking this time with us," an associate professor said. "Good of you to make the rounds of the departments. But the real test of your leadership will be whether you return." I said I would come back, and, in the meantime, would invite small groups of faculty to dinners at the President's House to explore how we might improve the student experience.

My most regular contact with the world of the faculty occurred in the weekly meetings of the committee on faculty appointments, CFA. It was a standing committee of Academic Council, formally established in the college's bylaws and articles of government, the rules I was learning to use. The president had one vote, of eight. Six tenured faculty members were elected by their peers for three-year terms. The president and dean were permanent members. Service on CFA was prestigious for faculty, I was told; I could tell it was demanding. The Wellesley rules were unusual in that they made no provision for the president to arrange a second review of a case that had been close, or contested. Any influence I exercised would have to take place within the committee's deliberations.

The decisions could be agonizing and unpopular. They left lasting imprints on individual careers, on departments and the content of the curriculum, and, in aggregate, on the quality and stature of the Wellesley faculty as a body. Every department had a committee that prepared cases for reappointments and promotions, the R&P committee. Comprising all of the department's tenured professors, the R&P was led by the chair and made recommendations to CFA. I was learning all of this on the fly, as I hadn't been involved in formal governance at BU or Harvard. Anyway, this Wellesley system had its own quirks, as Jeremy had warned me.

In meticulous detail, CFA reviewed, then accepted or rejected the R&P recommendation. Special scrutiny was applied to tenure decisions which committed the college to cover the junior faculty member's salary and benefits through thick and thin for another forty-plus years. The size of the faculty was capped, leaving no room to create a new slot to meet a need for an emerging field of study. The student body was changing rapidly, as was scholarly knowledge. We needed to diversify our faculty; we could ill afford to tenure it up.

Here, then, was another of my obligations to posterity. This one I felt acutely. Among the most enduring measures of my success in the presidency would be whether, on my watch, we enhanced or at least sustained the overall quality of the faculty. I knew how hard it would be for R&P committees and the CFA—and for me—to deny tenure to a colleague who for six or seven years had come up through the ranks as a young member of our community. This I knew from friends denied tenure at BU, MIT and Harvard, from the depth of their bitterness, anger, humiliation, their sense of betrayal.

Every Tuesday for two to three hours the CFA met in the dean's office just down the corridor from my suite in Green Hall. The dean presided over the meetings in a wooden armchair at one end of a long wooden table. I sat at the other end, in another insignia armchair. Everyone in the room had served on the committee multiple times. Except me. As we dug into the cases, I monitored what role I wanted to play. Committee members tried to draw me in as a regular member with responsibilities no different from theirs. This struck me as wrong and I resisted, which I could tell confused them. But I needed time to understand how the committee operated and how to claim my authority as one member. The dean was in charge. This committee had sat all last year as my predecessor completed her twelfth year, in the groove by then.

Most candidates for promotion had strong records of teaching, scholarship, and service, the three criteria on which we judged them. Many had accomplished more in one of the three areas, but some more than cleared all three bars. Those were the cases that inspired me; they made me proud to be at Wellesley. The one or two cases that were dicey consumed most of our time. They vexed me, and called for all the skills I was working to hone in real time.

A few years into my presidency we were hung up on one such candidate. Her scholarly record was slender—only three published papers, all in obscure specialty journals, and a hodgepodge of unconventional work in film, multimedia, art. These were the cases that soaked up CFA time. Usually they involved younger scholars eager to open emerging fields and new epistemologies, to challenge the canon. They tended to be opaque to members of the CFA, most of whom were elected principally from the canonical disciplines that carried the most prestige in our faculty. The outside letters for these candidates often came across as advocacy from the outskirts of established disciplines.

The R&P's documentation in this case was inadequate. We summoned the committee and pressed members at length on what quality standards they would have us apply to this scholarship that was intentionally transgressive. How might the candidate's career unfold and mature over a lifetime? What judgments and projections were her colleagues prepared to stand behind? The R&P, adamant in its support of the case, was in disarray as a weak department that seemed not to have mentored her with useful advice as she was moving up through the ranks. This clouded the picture even more. Had the college given her a fair chance to succeed? We questioned members of the R&P individually. When we met alone with the chair, I said we needed her committee to bring us stronger evidence so that we could get to the truth. Her reply took my breath away.

"We don't believe in *truth*," she exclaimed. "That's why you are not hearing us. It's relative. Everything is." I got nowhere in my effort to anchor this postmodern conversation in a practical reality. We were obliged to make an administrative decision that would stand rational scrutiny. I realized that the CFA would have to parse this case out on our own.

We spent more hours during which the dean and our CFA colleagues were beyond diligent. I listened to the deliberations, paying close attention and stepping in with a question when I sensed a view or voice taking over. When fatigue seemed to be nudging us toward a premature compromise, I made sure we dwelt in the uncertainty for as long as was fruitful. I held a space for divergent perspectives, for marginal voices to arise and be heard. This underscored for me a strong counter to the department chair's brief against truth. There was a truth in dialogue faithfully practiced. It had integrity. I developed confidence in the CFA's *practice*. Individual decisions might not always be right when viewed in retrospect. But they would be principled. They would be true. And I developed confidence in my ability to help lead the deliberations in that direction.

Because this particular department had so badly managed its case, we made the unusual decision to give their candidate another year to prove herself. The next year her portfolio was stronger, and we voted to tenure her. I heard later that instead of agreeing to teach the survey courses that would be responsive to requests from minority students, she opted to teach specialty courses with small enrollments. I was irritated. So, was our decision a mistake? It was impossible to know for sure in the long sweep of her career. We could not know the future. The dean and I did make plans to strengthen the role of the academic department chair.

My weeks were filled with meetings of committees chaired by faculty. This was an instance of Wellesley's particular take on the "shared governance" prized at leading academic institutions. Trustees formally delegated the responsibility for the educational program to the president and, through her, to the faculty. Student input came through their college government. I thought I was familiar with this set up from my college years when I was a CG officer, but found it notably different in how assertive this new generation of students was. They were better organized, more savvy, and far less patient or deferential than we were in the mid-'60s.

All of this governance came under the umbrella of the Academic Council. The president presided over its monthly meetings. From what I heard in the early days, the meetings sounded something like theater of the absurd. One evening in October of my first year I took a stroll alone through the Academic Council chamber a floor above my office. It had a musty air and the feel of a miniature British Parliament. There were tiered bleachers for members to sit, facing one another across a massive wooden table that ran the length of the hall. The top rows rested against walls of mahogany wainscoting. Windows at both sides and on one end of the long chamber were recessed in gabled dormers. The plastered walls above the wainscoting tilted inward toward each other as if to hold a lid on the proceedings within. I tried to visualize myself presiding there. Margaret Thatcher? No, surely not the Iron Lady. Queen Elizabeth? Hardly. Then who *would* this antiquated structure make of me, I wondered.

Soon I had made sense of the Academic Council's twenty-plus committees. I had a seat on all of them. Fortunately, I was expected to show up regularly only for the critical ones—and for the others only at critical moments. I was represented at the important ones by members of my Senior Staff, who kept me informed. Even so, as I dashed from one meeting to another in the first year, I was conscious of a constant scrutiny that made claims on me. People would project onto me the president who would serve their particular needs, for good or ill. Sometimes it seemed the college didn't want a president, as though it could run on autopilot, content with a leader who was nothing more than a life-size cardboard cutout. At other times, it seemed they wanted a leader who was omnipresent and omnipotent, who would catalyze every committee meeting, legitimate every event, render every decision, validate everyone's worth. As though nothing of meaning could happen until she arrived—and anointed it.

I was learning to see these projections for what they were, thought forms in the minds of others that would hook my ego and perhaps trip me up—*if* I allowed them to. I was the only one who could regulate my own responses, and I was becoming more adept at the inner work of leadership. It was my task to corral the contentious committees arguing inside *my* mind. To tame my inner voices. To lead from within.

The merit review committee, an extension of CFA, met every spring to assess their colleagues' performance for salary increases. Every tenured professor came up for review every third year. As president, I sat with the committee through its deliberations and was free afterwards to accept or adjust its recommendations, which were far less freighted than the tenure cases. But faculty were understandably sensitive to judgments from their peers.

In the spring of 2007, my final year in office, the merit committee recommended that a narcissistic and chronically disgruntled faculty member receive less than the full merit bonus for the three-year cycle. His work had suffered, his colleagues concluded, because he'd been so busy picking fights. No surprise there; the CFA had seen this coming years earlier when we tenured him. We had debated for days what to make of his abrasive personality—whether his character defects justified a denial—and, in the end, decided they should not. Over the years it was clear to me that his contributions as a teacher and scholar probably did compensate for the chip on his shoulder, but only barely. I concurred with the merit committee's salary recommendation.

It was my task to write letters to notify faculty of their merit awards. In each case I chose to emphasize positive things the committee saw, and specified the amount of the increase. My incoming mail during that time was plentiful and uplifting as I was preparing to depart, filled with well wishes for the future. And then came along a message dripping with venom: a threat to sully my reputation and thwart the higher ambitions this aggrieved professor imagined I must harbor. How he planned to accomplish that he didn't specify.

As it happened, I had a quick dinner that evening with Allison, who had been invited to Boston to lecture at MGH. I showed her the email. "Ugh," she said. "Truly vile. Just delete it, Mom." I did, then and there. My wise daughter has always been better than I at holding boundaries.

As I became more sure-footed in leading the faculty, I began to speak openly about problems I saw in their culture. As much as I admired and enjoyed almost all of them, treasured quite a few, and valued their dedication to their students and the college, we had too many bystanders concealed along roadsides lobbing grenades, and too few brave souls willing to venture out and clear away dangerous debris accumulating in plain view. In my weekly meetings with the deans I heard of faculty issues that exasperated them. Departments in melt down, individuals on a rampage, territorial disputes. A whole series of ongoing melodramas, some more public than others, many sticky or stuck. More than a few landed in my lap.

The academic deans were protective of the faculty, guarded about their foibles and internal squabbles. Other members of Senior Staff brought me *their* issues with faculty who made unreasonable demands of administrators. I was offended to hear the faculty grouse about "administrative bloat" because it hit hard-working staff as a slap in the face.

One incident ricocheted across the campus, carried on knowing looks among staff. A project director convened a small committee for advice on furnishings and fittings for a renovated classroom building. She included a faculty member known for uncompromising aesthetic taste. Best to bring a potential critic inside the tent. As the final decisions were being ratified, the faculty member was not getting her way. She exploded.

"The permanent people should decide!" The ace in the hole, and an affront to all on campus without the protection of lifetime employment. I was not surprised to see the administration tiptoe around the faculty as though passing a hibernating beast no one dared disturb for fear of being mauled. Individual faculty members ran the gamut from delightful and helpful to hostile and morose. Most were admirable in most respects, except when provoked. Not different from any other group. But I saw the faculty as a constituency being watched, coddled, and handled by staff at all levels with enormous investments of energy and studied restraint. And this thinly masked what I took to be an undercurrent of fear, tinged with resentment.

I saw this not only at Wellesley but, to one degree or another, throughout higher education. In retrospect I realized that it happened at Harvard and BU where I was safely situated on the faculty side of the fence. I saw it at Amherst, from my vantage point as a trustee, and on frequent visits to other campuses. I wanted to do what I could to bolster the confidence and skills of the staff—my senior team and the people who reported to them.

Faculty were proudly independent, sometimes defiantly so. Few would be led. And if they were hard on the administration, they could be even rougher on a member of their own herd who raised a head in a gesture of leadership. This I witnessed early in my presidency when I mediated a nasty fight over an experimental program I found exciting. It addressed a concern I was already picking up: a widely felt yearning for a more robust and satisfying intellectual community at Wellesley. Usually it was described as a deficit, a sense that the "the quality of intellectual life" was not where we wanted it to be, not where it used to be in some idealized past. We had become so fragmented and distractible—and yet so riveted on instrumental tasks—that we seldom made time to explore ideas for pure pleasure. I heard the critique first from faculty, but students expressed their own version of it.

"Wellesley is a very academic place," one said, "but not particularly intellectual. We have high standards for sure. Everyone works hard to meet them. But it's dutiful, not delightful. A forced march, not a free flight." I guessed this one was a poet. Her critique resonated with my recollections of my student days.

So I was glad to hear that Dean Kolodny had convened a handpicked group of faculty she admired to design a creative new course under the radar during the summer. When faculty returned to campus that fall—my inaugural year—some who hadn't been invited to the retreat challenged the legitimacy of the *ad hoc* design group. Who were these people and what special standing did they have? Wasn't the curriculum the purview of the faculty *as a whole*? Did the dean have the authority, they wanted to know, to constitute her own committee to rethink the curriculum with her?

I very much liked the work they had done. I wanted to see more of it. They were designing a new introductory course to be taught by a team of ten to twelve faculty, all from different departments. Entering first-year students would be given a complex problem to study from various disciplinary perspectives. The faculty were developing and debating topics like Origins: how different cultures have imagined the origins of the universe, of human and animal life, of artistic and musical expression, of social and political structures. Others, including The Question of Progress; Identities and Distinctiveness; Colonialism, Racism, Nationalism; Global Limits. Students would live together in a dormitory cluster and have a shared learning experience in their living spaces that would extend to the classroom and beyond, into labs and field trips and team projects.

Biologists and chemists, anthropologists, economists and political scientists, and faculty in languages and literature, music and art history were reading books together, giving seminars to one another, arguing with conviction about how best to present complex concepts to incoming college students. Intellectual sparks were flying, and friendships were being forged. The esprit within the group was radiating out across the campus.

I loved watching this unfold. It reminded me of BU's interdisciplinary University Professors Program where I did my PhD, the place where

I found my grounding as an intellectual. In 1962, as a freshman entering college, I might or might not have signed up for the experimental
program. But the person I was now would jump at the chance to begin
my undergraduate experience in the company of this group of inventive
faculty who were pooling their knowledge, teaching one another, swap-
ping out the roles of expert and amateur. They were leveling hierarchies
and taking risks as they stepped out beyond the limits of their personal
mastery. And they engaged this work in a spirit of fun and discovery,
mutual support and collaboration. All in search of more fulfilling ways
to welcome a new generation of incoming students into an intellectual
community. It was thrilling for me to see.

But I watched in dismay as all this ferment became too much for faculty on the outside looking in. Rather than admit to feeling left out, they
couched their doubts in pedagogic philosophy and governance policy.
Isn't it too much to ask incoming students to make sense of interdisciplinary work when they haven't yet been introduced to the disciplines?
Shouldn't they be learning close reading before they take on broad conceptual problems? And anyway, why was the experiment not thoroughly
debated in Academic Council? Who authorized the dean and her rump
group to go off and redesign the first-year experience? These were not
inappropriate questions, I would note and often say. But let's not let them
derail what is obviously an energizing exploration.

Despite the controversy, the deans pressed on, and their group designed
a pilot program which they offered the next year on a voluntary basis to
100 members of the incoming first year class. It came as no surprise that
this radically new approach had some kinks, and when, at the end of the
first semester, a quarter of the enrollees opted out of the second semester,
the critics moved in for the kill.

The course continued through the second year for which it was funded.
At the end, an evaluation concluded that it did meet its primary goal, did
"build an inquiring, exciting, and reflective intellectual community." The
experiment did not survive, though, without sufficient faculty support,
and the bitterness lingered for years. What began as a shot of adrena-
line—a magnet for faculty creativity and collaboration—deteriorated
into misunderstandings and hurt feelings all around. An old Russian
fable circulated among the program faculty, the tale of the peasant who

is so distressed to discover his neighbor has a cow that all he wants is for the neighbor's cow to die. No matter if, instead, he could have a cow of his own.

I was discouraged. A group of faculty innovators had taken a detour from their normal work and taken a chance. They invested their best thinking into it, with a sense of shared responsibility, and tasted the pleasures of creative collaboration and mutual accountability—qualities I was eager to foster and reward. I invited the course's faculty to dinner to express my support.

They felt judged and misunderstood in a climate filled with "negativity and mistrust." Rumors had circulated furiously. So had unfair criticism. Some of the objections reflected honest intellectual disagreement, they granted, but even those were distorted by misperceptions and partial information.

I took this in but knew from my conversations with opponents of the innovation that they too felt victimized. Their motives had been impugned, they complained. Their serious reservations had been trivialized and dismissed. I began to see signs of a general pattern I was coming to recognize. When faculty found themselves stuck in internecine conflict, they became uncomfortable.

I was learning how to hold my differences with faculty members, to stay in my role, to avoid letting them take my power away. And to do this with a light touch. No big deal. This is how it is. I'm over here being the president. You're over there having a fight. What are you going to do about it? I was also aware that every interaction I had with members of the faculty sent ripples out into the larger system. Ripples that, if skillfully placed, might begin to melt a situation that had seemed impossibly frozen.

Toward the end of the dinner, we discussed a memo the course faculty planned to send out to the whole Academic Council.

"You're going out on a limb," I said over dessert. "I want to be out there with you. I value the work you've done. This could be an opportunity to provoke a deeper dialogue on questions of real consequence for Wellesley's future. I hope we can catalyze that."

In my cover memo, I expressed gratitude for the work this group had done and acknowledged thoughtful arguments on both sides. Then

I raised the broader question that arose out of the controversy: What can we do to create an atmosphere at Wellesley that is more welcoming of innovation, more conducive of risk taking, more forgiving of the inevitable mistakes that accompany any new endeavor, and, indeed, any real learning?

Then I arranged a meeting in my office between the dean and one of the most vocal critics of her project. Two people I admired were at odds with each other. Two friends of over twenty years who were different in many surface ways but similar in deeper ones, most notably in the constancy with which each of them lived a life of principle. Both were dedicated citizens of the college, faculty leaders of their generation who were leaving a lasting stamp. It felt a bit like pastoral work I was about to try, maybe therapy. Neither of which I was qualified to practice. Neither of which they had asked me for. But it pained me to see each of them so wounded by the other. I asked how it felt to be stuck in this stalemate.

"You've put your heart and soul into this project for the past three years," I said to the dean. "It must be beyond painful to feel it has cost you this important friendship." A tear rolled down her cheek. The dean was not one to show emotion. The professor looked shaken. The impasse was broken, although much work lay ahead to mend the relationship. And I sat there, grateful for these two fine people, glad for the chance to be the peacemaker I wanted to be.

Academic culture is known for picking ideas apart. Critical thinking and skepticism are the coin of the realm. When skepticism devolves to cynicism, or criticism to contempt, an acrid brew of belligerence and disengagement can poison morale. I wanted to encourage "connective and responsible accountability for one another and our common purposes." Veiled language to couch my words in the early years. I was meeting many gifted faculty members who were devoting their lives to the college and hoped to bring them together in collaborations and pockets of mutual support.

I began to pay attention to covert resistance to change. People would fight among each other, play "get the leader," fall into despair, huddle in the victim box. Occasionally they rallied together to talk of staging a coup. Some voices of opposition were crafty and hard to recognize.

Others were blustery and hard to oppose. Most were cloaked intellectually but rooted in emotion. They came at me indirectly.

"Fasten your seatbelt, boss." My vice president for resource development was brandishing a copy of the Spring 1995 issue of *Wellesley*, the alumnae magazine. The cover featured a dazzling shot of the campus in springtime, flowering trees around Paramecium Pond, lily pad blossoms on the water's surface, reflecting a sky which—of course—was Wellesley blue.

Nice photo, I nearly said, but then my eye lit on the tagline a few inches from the bottom. "Wellesley's Vanishing Landscape," it read. What??!

The magazine was widely read. I opened to the cover story. It was long. The author was an alumna I'd not yet met, an architectural historian. Was she channeling the art history professors who had put me on notice? I was sure she had spoken to them; maybe was speaking *for* them. We were *destroying* our beautiful campus, she wrote, with distressing photos to drive home her case. Five pages into the piece, the long-time editor of the magazine, who I now guessed was also in cahoots with the professors, had boxed an extract quotation in eye-catching red and black italics, designed to capture the reader who might flip past the piece.

"I don't think there is an alumna who doesn't put the beauty of the campus at the top of her priority list." Well, *this* alumna didn't, I muttered to myself. The article closed with the rhetorical admonition from Olmsted Jr. in his 1902 letter to Caroline Hazard, Wellesley's fifth president, the quotation that had been the capstone of my campus tour:

"Wellesley College has in its grounds a peculiar endowment, and, with the endowment, it seems to me, a peculiar obligation to posterity."

The article unleashed a tsunami of reproachful letters that overflowed my inbox for months. I was now fated to become a champion of campus renewal. The landscape, in the end, would become one signature of my presidency. We would produce a new campus master plan, remediate a toxic waste site, and transform the western end of the campus with a cluster of projects in a neglected quadrant we renamed "Alumnae Valley." But for now I had in this artful end run by the art professor and self-designated guardian of the campus an edifying example of the latent power of the permanent people.

9

THE INBOX EXERCISE

Harambee House sits behind Clapp Library. It was converted in 1970 to a cultural gathering space when the college began to increase its number of African American students. As I entered, I saw maybe 100 young women gathered in the spacious living room, sitting on sofas and chairs, on the arms of chairs, and all over the floor. All were members of Ethos, Wellesley's organization for students of African descent. I was the only white person in the room. I made my way to the front, careful not to step on hands or feet. There was a chair waiting for me. The hot seat, in my very first year as president.

"What is your job?" a student asked. "What is it you are supposed to be doing here?" I replied that I had come to discuss a letter I had sent to the alumnae.

"Who is the 'we' in this letter you've written?" another student interjected. "If you think you are speaking for us when you say, 'We are profoundly disturbed and saddened by Professor Martin's new book,' you've got that wrong."

"Your 'we' is not us!" Another picked up the standard. "Who said you could say these things?" I explained that the trustees had authorized me to speak on behalf of the college.

Everyone avoided eye contact with me as I talked. I was not speaking to the heart of the questions that I sensed the whole group had prepared in advance. Now several told me they had studied with Professor Martin, were mentored and encouraged by him. What right did I have to send a letter to all the alumnae criticizing a book he had just written?

"No one on this whole faculty has seen me and appreciated and encouraged me the way he has," another student said. "Have you even met him?" from another side of the room. I had not.

"How can you judge him without even talking to him?"

"The book speaks for itself," I said. I didn't add that the deans felt sure I'd only incur his wrath if I tried to engage him, perhaps escalate the conflict. The lawyers, too, had advised against a meeting. I did say that all of us were here at Wellesley to learn, that I did not begin to have all the answers, and had called this meeting because I wanted to understand their perspectives.

We talked at cross-purposes for an hour. I did not penetrate their wall of rage even for a second. I left, shaken. One of the qualities the college had sought in their new president was the ability to calm racial conflicts and narrow racial divides. This was not an auspicious start.

It wasn't that I had seen this coming, this harrowing student meeting. If I had, I might have averted it. But the crisis, the slow-motion train wreck, had shown up in my very first meeting with the presidential search committee. And again during my campus visits.

I hadn't met with Martin, true, but I'd been fully briefed by the trustees and by Dean Kolodny. He was a professor of Africana studies who arrived at Wellesley in 1973 with a British law degree, a doctorate in African history and a scholarly reputation as an expert in the life and work of the Jamaican political activist Marcus Garvey. Tenured in 1975 and promoted four years later to full professor, he chaired his department for a time and had recently been succeeded by fellow Trinidadian, Selwyn Cudjoe.

What I mostly heard about Martin were his repeated racial grievances against the college. And then, only last spring, there had been a blow up in Academic Council after a senior professor of classics, Mary Lefkowitz, took the floor to challenge him about his views on Afrocentrism. He responded with such a tirade that over 200 members of the faculty voted to censure him for his verbal attack of a colleague. It was rare for the faculty to coalesce to this degree, and rarer still to reprimand a tenured full professor.

I heard too about Martin's teaching, about a text on his syllabus, *The Secret Relationship Between Blacks and Jews*. The spring before I arrived as president, three student members of Hillel noticed the book on sale in the college bookstore. It was on the required reading list for his survey course in African American history. Published anonymously in 1991 by the Nation of Islam, the book was a notorious anti-Semitic polemic that wove ancient conspiracy theories into a false argument that Jews played a disproportionate role in the trans-Atlantic slave trade.

The students went to see Dean Kolodny about the book, and soon she was under heavy pressure from outside the college for Wellesley to condemn it. President Keohane, after consulting her Senior Staff, sent a simple brochure to all the college's "alumnae and friends." It included a terse statement that denounced the book and upheld the principle of academic freedom. The low-key brochure, they hoped, would spare the college's reputation. I was surely on the mailing list but missed the brochure, and I was not alone. The strategy worked. Things settled down. Professor Martin was on sabbatical, away from the campus.

But now there was news of a new book, written by Martin himself during his sabbatical. The dean had a copy of a Nation of Islam newsletter with a display ad for his new book. *The Jewish Onslaught: Despatches from the Wellesley Battlefront.* Tony was not a member of the Nation of Islam, as far as she knew, but was in a symbiotic relationship with this group, led by Louis Farrakhan, that was sowing discord at the City College of New York and other universities.

This book would raise our controversy to a whole new level, Nancy was certain. This "Jewish onslaught" would be his distorted rendition of the response at Wellesley last year to his teaching *The Secret Relationship.* It was one thing for a professor to teach in the privacy of his classroom from a controversial book; any text could be taught responsibly if placed in context. But this new book, in Tony Martin's own words, would surely expose his personal beliefs and cast doubt on how he was teaching this vile text in his course. And it would drag Wellesley College through the mud. I asked Nancy to get me a copy of his book as soon as it came out. We would read it and then discuss what to do.

Seminars for new leaders often begin with the "inbox exercise." You're given a pile of stuff—phone messages, letters, emails, news clips—and a few minutes to sort through them for the ticking time bomb, the item that requires your immediate attention. Surely this nasty book would be it. My first big test.

Nancy brought me reams of material to read on academic freedom: origins, precepts, subtleties, and threats to it that were rising on a number of campuses.

"Why don't you call some of your contacts at Harvard and see what they advise," she suggested at one of the many early meetings we ended with the dispiriting question, what were we going to do when "Tony's book" came out? I went full-bore into inquiry mode, consulting others who had been through similar situations and had more experience and expertise than I had.

I called Neil Rudenstine and told him what I knew about the forthcoming book.

"Your first decision will be whether or not to comment on it at all," he said. "You don't want to do that lightly or you'll be constantly called on to referee faculty disputes." This one, he observed, might contain "the seeds of its own destruction" if we could just leave it to self-destruct.

A few days later, I hosted Henry Louis Gates, Jr., Harvard's distinguished chair of Afro-American studies. In 1992 he had published an op-ed in the *New York Times*, noting a rise of anti-Semitism in the African American community and exposing misinformation in *The Secret Relationship*. We were seated in the living room of the President's House. He acknowledged the obvious, that Wellesley and its new president were in a scrape. This with wry sympathy.

"Just be careful not to turn a second-rate bigot into a First Amendment martyr," Skip cautioned and counseled strongly against taking any sort of disciplinary *action*, a piece of advice I heard repeatedly in subsequent conversations with experts across a broad spectrum.

"If you go after Martin's tenure," he warned, "you will lose the moral high ground and the support of faculty, here and around the country. The book will be forgotten, and you will be the issue, a threat to academic freedom, one of the academy's deepest values."

Leaders of the principal Jewish advocacy organizations in Boston, meanwhile, were in close touch with Jewish faculty on our campus, and with each other. Through Nancy, they sent me an ultimatum, before I heard anything directly from any of them. If I did not condemn Tony's book, forcefully and quickly, they would make their own public statement. This would heighten the conflict for sure. And it was no idle threat. This we knew from last year when leaders of Boston chapters of four national Jewish organizations issued a joint press release when they heard that *The Secret Relationship* was being taught in a Wellesley course.

A senior political scientist, Joel Krieger, made an appointment to see me and introduce himself. An expert in global governance and an erudite proponent of multiculturalism, he came to me as co-chair, with a staff member, of the standing committee of Academic Council known as CARD: the Committee Against Racism and Discrimination. He knew the book was coming, saw trouble brewing and wanted to help. He volunteered to draft a statement of principle on "how to communicate in a diverse community." I accepted the offer and circulated CARD's two pages to everyone on campus. It didn't mention the pending book but laid out aspirations and principles we might invoke if needed. I doubted it would be a magic bullet but was grateful for Joel's initiative and the support of his committee that seemed to have ample standing on campus.

Meanwhile, I met weekly with my Senior Staff. I was considering the costs and benefits of a range of responses: from stony silence to various levels of condemnation. I was the only one new to the situation; everyone on the team I had inherited was an active participant last year in efforts to manage the earlier skirmish on Tony's "battlefront." The main lesson they learned was the importance of a rapid response, to protect our autonomy to make our own decisions rather than allow organizations outside our community to force our hand.

I decided we would not be silent. I hadn't seen the book, but I had seen previews under the title "Blacks and Jews at Wellesley News." "Broadsides" Tony called these self-published diatribes he distributed on campus. I asked Laurel, who had been actively involved last year, to take a first pass at a statement on the book. Then I began to rework it.

At the November meeting of the board's executive committee, I reported all of this and gave this small group of trustees my draft statement and a one-page sequence of proposed steps. The committee supported both and we agreed to wait for the book's release before moving ahead.

A few weeks later, Nancy brought me a copy of the book's cover. My heart sank. The back cover convinced me that it would be at least as bad as we feared. "The Jews have made a hell of a mistake this time," said the final and most prominent of four endorsements. This was attributed to an individual with no affiliation listed, nor any we could find. Below it an unnamed "Correspondent from Washington DC" commented: "Would that your baying detractors, Dr. Martin, could emulate your sterling performance. We regard you as the last faint glimmer of hope for this immoral, amoral and decadent society." Alongside Tony's photo at the top was a preview of the argument to come and this conclusion: "With rare insight and biting wit, Martin replies to his detractors and offers a historian's analysis of the escalating Jewish onslaught against Black people."

On Thursday, December 2, we received a copy of *The Jewish Onslaught*, self-published by Professor Martin's "TM Press." I instructed my informal team to read the book and told them we would reconvene later, then, at Nancy's suggestion, called her contacts at the Boston chapters of the Anti-Defamation League and the American Jewish Committee. I wanted them to hold their fire while we planned our response. I was miffed to hear that they had copies of the book before we did. They made it very plain to me, this time directly, that they were under pressure from their constituencies and would have to respond if I delayed "too long," measured in days. I tried to suppress my irritation at their ultimatum and did not point out that their pressure on me seemed to affirm Professor Martin's basic thesis that he was a victim last year of forces outside the college.

Then I went home to read Tony's book, hardly a mental exertion. It was a scant 80 pages of text that mostly rehashed and garnished accusations he had already published in his "broadsides." Another fifty-plus pages consisted of unsigned letters of sympathy for his grievances. It wasn't much of a book, but there was enough in it to send chills down my spine. Not only did it amplify Tony's imagined hurts, laced through with innuendo and stereotype, but it also lobbed racial and religious slurs at individual members of the Wellesley faculty, administration, and even students—his many enemies and tormentors, so he saw it, on and off our campus. Tony labeled his colleague, Selwyn Cudjoe, a "house Negro" for having sided with the administration. Skip Gates was "America's most notorious Judeophile." He reserved most of his venom, though, for members of the Wellesley community, especially faculty he made a point to identify as "the Jew . . ." followed by her or his name. I knew I would have to respond to these hateful writings.

That Friday I flew to Atlanta and kept reworking the draft of my statement. As it happened, I had set aside the weekend for an annual reunion with my group of Kellogg Fellows, who listened to my story and offered support. The most heartening counsel came during a visit with Johnnetta Cole, president of Spelman College, the top historically Black college for women and a nationally respected educator. I reviewed the situation with my "Sister President" for over an hour in the gracious parlor of the Spelman president's house. She affirmed my view that the book had crossed a line and that I was going to have to say so. She felt certain that Black intellectuals would sympathize with the decision. I took comfort in this assessment from a peer who spoke with authority both for her extended community of scholars and for Wellesley College, as a trustee.

When I returned to my office on Monday for the advisory group meeting, I read aloud the two-page draft I'd been massaging. Joel wanted to refine the paragraph that spelled out what about this book made it unacceptable, and I asked him to go ahead. We debated whether or not to use the word "anti-Semitic" and I agreed with his position that we should not resort to labels, which objectified individuals, since they were a primary device that made the book so abhorrent.

Instead, we framed our concerns in more analytic terms that would apply in all situations. We said that because of its "recurrent and gratuitous use of racial and religious identification of individuals," *The Jewish Onslaught* "crosses the line from simply unpopular or controversial argument to unnecessarily disrespectful and deeply divisive speech that must be countered, however strong the temptation not to dignify it with a response." How widely we should disseminate the response and in what form remained open questions. Peter Ramsey ardently believed that the notice should go to our entire alumnae network.

"They deserve to hear this directly from you," he insisted. "This is going to shake them up and they should not hear it second hand." Others felt that distributing the message so widely would stir a hornets' nest.

"We need to reach Jewish and Black alumnae for sure," an alum argued, "because they're likely to hear about this whether we inform them or not. But other alums all over the country won't have a clue what you're talking about, and this letter will just worry them and ignite a huge fire." If we sent something out to everyone, she felt, we should soften its impact by embedding it in a mailing with other, unrelated materials. This was the strategy the team had adopted last spring.

In the end, I decided to send a letter alone in an envelope, over my signature, to every living alumna of the college, across the country and around the world. In it I reaffirmed the right of every member of the Wellesley College community to express his or her opinions without fear of reprisal. And I condemned the content of *The Jewish Onslaught* as "antithetical to honest communication and thoughtful argument." I said it "violated basic principles that nourish and sustain this academic community: norms of civil discourse, standards of scholarly integrity, and aspirations for freedom and justice." And I spelled out as concretely as I could the ways in which it violated our values.

As carefully as we had thought about the strategy behind the message, we did not fully anticipate the response we would provoke by mailing nearly 40,000 letters conveying frightful news. For months, my office responded to the mountains of return mail. We received letters and calls and email messages expressing support and appreciation for the letter. But many alumnae wrote to say they were deeply distressed. Some were confused, angry, disappointed in the college. Nearly all of the critical mail insisted that we hadn't gone far enough, that we ought to discipline or fire this professor, and that we were wrong to frame the issue in terms of academic freedom when he was teaching lies. Isn't that the equivalent of teaching the Earth is flat? How could I permit this to go on at Wellesley?

I was asking myself similar questions and was faced with the uncomfortable reality that my authority and degrees of freedom were circumscribed. As I traveled for the college over the next four years at least, I was often asked whether a white professor teaching hateful things about African Americans would be tolerated in the same way. I was pretty sure the answer was no. Influential Jewish alumnae—or, more often, their husbands—would take me aside to say that the college should take a stand and begin proceedings to remove Professor Martin's tenure. I explained that this would only give him a louder megaphone and more book sales. Already he was attracting large audiences and was sought after on the lecture circuit.

My office staff tried to buffer me from the anonymous hate mail directed at me personally. It came mostly from strangers, we inferred. I was called anti-Semite, racist, incompetent, war monger, naive tool of forces beyond my ken, architect of my institution's demise. "A fish rots first from the head," said one unsigned note, written by hand in childish block letters.

I heard directly from only a few members of our faculty, but Nancy told me many were discussing my letter and gathering in small clusters in their offices and departments to decide what, if anything, they should do. I was told that in previous years Tony had supporters among the faculty, but no one was speaking up for him now that this venomous book was out. A senior faculty member who was on the committee that had voted his tenure years ago sought me out one day to express her regret and disbelief.

"This has been keeping me up at night," she said and shook her head. "There wasn't any evidence back then that he harbored these prejudices."

Black faculty and staff, for the most part, quietly supported my letter or remained silent, but I knew that they were torn and troubled by what was happening. Selwyn, now chair of Africana studies, had taken a strong stand last year against Tony's teaching *The Secret Relationship* and now began speaking out against *The Jewish Onslaught*.

Martin had alienated most of the faculty by now, or isolated and silenced whatever latent support he may have had. But he still had vocal admirers among a group of loyal students who believed he had been misunderstood and singled out for harsher treatment than was justified, or fair. To some he was a hero, a courageous and tireless advocate of Black empowerment in a racist institution, a racist country, a racist world. This was the perspective I heard loud and clear during my meeting at Harambee House. I thought I was there to tell them how I wrote my letter, and why. They were there to tell me that I had it wrong.

I spent a fitful night after the Ethos meeting and woke up the next morning clear that if I had it to do over again, I would have gone to Harambee House with the letter in hand *before* it went out, not after. The students would probably have been every bit as exercised about the content of my message, but at least I would have shown my respect for their justified interest. I resolved that from then on, whenever I felt called to issue a public statement that might be objectionable, I would make it a practice to check in ahead of time with students and others most directly affected. And I was determined to earn back the trust of Ethos. That was going to take time, I had no doubt.

Meanwhile, I discovered, the Jewish advocacy groups were still unsatisfied. I ended up on the phone early one morning with the heads of the Boston offices of the Anti-Defamation League (ADL), The American Jewish Congress, the American Jewish Committee, and the Jewish Community Relations Council (JCRC). I was taken aback when the regional director of the ADL, Leonard Zakim, called my letter "unacceptable" and "tepid," because I chose not to use the term "anti-Semitic."

Years later, I came upon a blow-by-blow description of the phone conversation and the surrounding events. I found it on the web in a book called *The Death of American Antisemitism*. To my chagrin, I learned there that the JCRC director who orchestrated the conference call—intended as a peace overture—was fired a few days after I reported to my New York trustees how violated I felt by it. All I knew at the time was that no one was satisfied, and that their "unified approach to the Wellesley problem" felt coercive, rigid, and unhelpful.

Fortunately, as I would learn, the natural rhythms of the college calendar tended to redirect the ebb and flow of emotional upheavals. We were headed into exam week and then winter break, so the focus moved away from Professor Martin's book as students and faculty burrowed into the end-of-semester foothills. As all-consuming as this conflict had felt, I, with my fledgling administration, had many other challenges to manage. With luck, I said to myself, maybe we had put *The Jewish Onslaught* on a back burner.

Nope. The respite was short-lived. Second semester opened to a flurry of media attention at the end of January Wintersession. In early February, the *New York Times* described our predicament in a news story with a photograph of the college's distinctive bell tower placed, in the New England editions, next to an unrelated article on Minister Louis Farrakhan. A subliminal message that he had his eye on us? The next week, the college featured prominently in the *Boston Globe*, first in an editorial, then, the next day, on the op-ed page, a contribution by Professor Cudjoe condemning Professor Martin's book. Stories ran in national newsmagazines and on network television. The *alma mater* of the First Lady of the United States was the site of a frightening rift between Blacks and Jews in America, and an exemplar of hate speech on university campuses. Alumnae wanted their college back. I did too.

But another important player in the controversy, Professor Mary Lefkowitz, was now offering talks at alumnae clubs and other venues across the country. Telling the story from her vantage point, she was as invested in it as was Martin, and her involvement—as much as his—kept the spotlight on the college. She had already crossed swords with Martin in Academic Council and she was not going to allow the college, her *alma mater*, to put this issue on a back burner.

A formidable intellect and a powerful and appreciated presence at the college, she was a scholar immersed in the philosophical and cultural foundations laid by ancient Greeks and Romans. She took special umbrage at Martin's embrace of Afrocentrism, a movement bent on rewriting world history through the lenses of colonialism and slavery, racism and imperialism. Afrocentrists faulted Western historians for ignoring or discrediting the intellectual, cultural and artistic contributions of Black Africans and their descendants. Tony's antagonist was now investing her energy in a detailed critique of specific false claims in what she was branding his shabby revisionist history. I did not know then that in decades to follow, this debate would be grounded in robust and compelling scholarship that would move it beyond the angry and hollow polemic that characterized Martin's approach. What I knew now was that we were mired in the mud.

I appreciated Mary's years of devotion to the college and was basing my actions in part on critiques consistent with her views. At the same time, I could see why some of her faculty colleagues who wanted to quell the conflict—as I did—wished she would moderate the battle she saw herself fighting against ignorance and intolerance. She was vigorously stirring animus against Martin. The college was paying a heavy price for her determination to turn her scholarly eye, as Martin had done in his clumsy way, to the Wellesley "war" they were perpetuating. I found myself muttering the African proverb, when bull elephants fight, the grass always loses.

We owed it to ourselves and to our students, I repeated often through the crisis, to meet the conceptual challenges embedded in the controversy. My problem was that the controversy was such a Rorschach test that everyone I consulted had different notions about the learning we ought to extract from it. Some wanted us to organize courses or symposia on the origins of modern slavery and the conditions that produce it. Others had felt strongly for a long time that we weren't providing our students the intellectual and interpersonal tools they needed to resolve their differences. They believed a better understanding of the causes, effects, and manifestations of racial and religious intolerance might augment students' skills. Still others thought the answer was more exposure to the history of US civil rights and liberation movements. Behind some of the differences were unspoken territorial disputes among departments, especially in the social science disciplines, each of which could claim special expertise in issues of race and class and power. Added to this were tensions between the faculty and the staff over who was ultimately responsible for student life.

Meanwhile, from the standpoint of the many cultural groups on campus, a new president's interest in supporting new educational programs came as a mouth-watering invitation to foreground their favorite sidelined agendas. Why limit the focus to Blacks and Jews? What about bias against other ethnic and racial groups? What about homophobia, lesbian and gay rights? What about social class? After a few chaotic meetings it dawned on me that I was making a tactical error. I needed to step back and see my role as a facilitator and champion of others who wanted to take initiative. Did I really think I could cobble together a unified program that would come out of the President's Office? I had colleagues whose work this was and should support them in it.

Leaders in the faculty were mobilizing to do what they could. In February two senior professors, a historian and a sociologist, circulated a petition condemning the personal attacks and the anti-Semitic rhetoric in *The Jewish Onslaught*. It was signed ultimately by 124 of their colleagues, just over half the faculty, with tenured faculty strongly represented. The document carried moral weight. The History Department then conceived an even more potent sanction. Martin's courses had been cross listed for departmental credit in both Africana studies and history. After careful debate, the historians voted to eliminate all of his offerings from the roster of courses that would count for credit toward a history major. Their reasoning, the chairman wrote, was that Professor Martin's approaches to historical material as evidenced in his book were "inconsistent with those of a professional historian and incompatible with our own view of pedagogy in history."

These moves by the faculty provided a story I could carry out to the alumnae. It comforted these audiences to hear that we had a strategy that seemed to be working. And it was a relief to me that the faculty supplied me with stories to take on the road: initiatives that expressed my commitment to make of this mess a learning experience. Not as a hollow slogan but as a serious effort to identify and address important gaps in our understanding. This was imperative for me, no matter what else happened. It was why I took the job, because I knew we were not perfect, and I trusted we could learn.

The strategy was simple. We would expose what we saw as reckless and harmful in Tony Martin's writings, isolate him and diminish his impact on campus and, I hoped eventually, in wider academic circles. We would counter his divisive rhetoric with educational initiatives. Individual professors who taught in subject areas that shed light on the controversy found ways to work lessons from it into courses they were teaching. Two young faculty members, a male sociologist and a female art historian, teamed up to design and offer a new course on propaganda and persuasion.

The college had many endowed funds for faculty and students to tap if they wanted to organize lectures and cultural events, and those funds fed an entrepreneurial tendency at Wellesley to let a thousand flowers bloom. The faculty lecture policy committee, responsible for allocating these funds, selected Cornel West, then a professor at Princeton, to deliver the college's most prestigious annual lecture. Known in part for his interest in promoting dialogue between Blacks and Jews, West called for what he termed "audacious hope" in a world whose hostile cleavages seemed to be deepening, a world, he said, in which economic and social inequities had become commonplace and taken for granted. To heal the wounds in our society, he said, we needed to address deep structural injustices, an analysis that resonated with my roots in public health. A month later, former US Surgeon General, Jocelyn Elders, MD, brought a similar message to our campus, on behalf of the nation's minority children.

The most dramatic healing event occurred the following fall, in November 1994, when Elie Wiesel came to speak at the invitation of student leaders of Hillel. I was with the student who had brought me this dream of hers the previous spring. She saw it through with determination and, with a committee that invited Professor Wiesel, lined up twenty-four departmental and organizational co-sponsors, and spread the word. Our largest auditorium was fuller than I could remember it, alive with anticipation. She and I escorted our guest out onto the stage. The hall fell totally silent. We made brief introductions, and our guest walked slowly to the podium. Wiesel stood there, expressionless, as the applause died down. His deeply creased face was a familiar symbol of sorrow and transcendence, but his presence was much more than that in this collective silence. He sighed and drew a deep breath, leaned forward into the microphone.

"I know why I am here."

He paused again. The crowd held itself in total stillness as if the slightest movement would break a sacred connection. Then he began his lecture, and after those first six words, made no further reference to the controversy that was tearing our campus apart. Instead he gave us stories that honored how hard it is, how heartbreaking, how unlikely to work in every way possible to "build a moral society," yet how urgent it is that each of us do so.

"We all know," he said, "that there are no victors in wars, that the people only lose, that everyone loses. How can we build a moral society when we know how fragile the structure of our survival is? Indifference to evil is evil and sometimes worse than evil. The opposite of love is not hate, but indifference. There is no alternative to humanity except humanity. A community striving to be moral," he taught us that evening, "lives in dialogue, honors the humanity of all of its members, and recognizes that any one of us can at times wear the mantle of learner, teacher, witness."

We left the auditorium that night, I felt, on our way to becoming a healthier community. I spent another restless night in the President's House, wondering where I would find the courage and the leadership cunning to enact Elie Wiesel's vision for Wellesley. When a noisy squadron of Canadian geese out on the lake announced the approach of dawn, I still had more questions than answers. Could we really parry hate-mongering by investing in making peace? If I could resist the seduction of throwing my energy into opposing the haters, might that undermine their ability to set the terms of engagement? Would this help break the fruitless cycles of blaming and name-calling? Could I craft the tools to lead the college on beyond this debilitating pattern that I now saw had been recurring for some time?

My best hope, it seemed to me, resided in the higher values of peace and human dignity Elie Wiesel so fully embodied for us that night. And they were the values I knew had called me back to my *alma mater* to see if I could fashion myself into the leader it needed now. I hoped I would weather the storms if I could remain focused on the possibility of an educational community that protects individual freedom, expects personal responsibility and somehow manages to foster an overriding concern for the learning and wellbeing of everyone here.

"Be careful," John Clarkeson would say to me a few years later when I began talking to him in those terms. "Culture is notoriously resistant to change." John was CEO of the Boston Consulting Group and had just joined our board. He had asked me the question I heard often in the early years of my presidency.

"When it's all over and you look back on your time here as president, what do you hope you'll be remembered for?" We were having the first of our early morning meetings in the breakfast room at the front of the President's House, the sun streaming in through the wide bay window.

"I love this place," I said to John. "It made me who I am. I love so much of what it stands for, everything, really . . . But there are some things about the culture that have long troubled me. Habits I believe are holding the college back—perfectionism, an air of constant judgment, a fear of making mistakes. A harshness to the criticism. I'd like to see that change. I think it impedes learning."

And then John's caution.

Outside the bay window, the sprinklers were spraying lazy, tall arcs of water along a broad expanse of rolling lawn framed by an enormous pair of sprawling 200-year-old trees, an oak and a copper beech. I noticed how hard it was to see from the breakfast room that each of those dramatic trees was completely wired together, inwardly, every one of its thick branches attached by sturdy cables to another of its own branches, or to its trunk. Surely this was a metaphor. As our campus community was splintering into subgroups, we were attaching guy-wires to try to stabilize a center. But I would be kidding myself if I saw these as permanent solutions. There would be no denying the hard work we still had to face.

10

TWO LEADERS, TWO TIGHTROPES

As soon as I arrived on the job at Wellesley, I picked up the gauntlet Nancy had dropped at my feet during the presidential search. She explained to me that at the end of the previous year—Nan's final year as president and Nancy's first as dean—the Academic Council had rejected all but a single item in a comprehensive package of curricular innovations developed by a faculty committee. This was two years of work trashed and a stinging repudiation. Nancy was determined to neutralize its impact by leading her faculty in a do-over. The specifics were less important to her than it was to restore her colleagues' confidence that they could reach consensus on what and how Wellesley students ought to learn.

I decided to place the prestige of my office behind the effort. It was risky. I would give away a piece of my power. It was Nancy's project; she was in charge. And if it failed, my fingerprints would be all over it. Soon we were ensnared in a dicey process that became one of the major dramas in my first three years as president. The contentious summer retreat in which Nancy and a few faculty colleagues set out to design a new first-year course was only the first salvo.

The ongoing review became the main event at meetings of the Academic Council. I presided monthly from a raised dais on which I stood. Only I spoke from the elevated platform. Nancy sat beside me on a bench and spoke from a second microphone and lectern on the floor beneath my roost. A clerk typed minutes into a laptop hooked up to an antique recording device that coughed, clicked and chugged. Two guys leapt up on occasion to bellow corrections. They were the parliamentarians, one official, the other large, loud, and self-appointed. The first, a senior political science professor, was on hand to mediate disputes. The second, an elderly professor of religion, provoked them. He protested the slightest deviation from the gospel according to Robert: *Robert's Rules of Order.*

At best, the melodrama was an amusing parody of meaningful democratic discourse, at worst a chaotic display, as Jens Kruse joked one day, of "serial oratory." One-by-one, the usual suspects asked to be recognized, and held forth, making no apparent effort to amplify points already made. Were they even listening to each other? And where was the pedagogic artistry that earned them accolades as classroom teachers?

The dean and I updated the board at every quarterly meeting. The newer trustees were astounded that the process was so cumbersome and all-consuming. Those familiar with faculty politics were not surprised to hear that pockets of hesitation and resistance threatened to derail an airing of differences on what really mattered. Were we going to pull this off? I had my doubts. And if not? I would have to emphasize other sources of success during my first three years in office. I did have quite a few irons in the fire, but a replay of the curricular stalemate I had inherited would have turned it into a spectacular defeat on my watch.

I consulted and coached the deans at our weekly meetings but in a shadow role invisible to other faculty. Indirectly I heard rumblings that "the deans are running the college." This bothered me a lot. But I told myself to be patient, to take the time to learn. How do faculty innovate here? What obstacles do they face? Individual faculty were free to experiment with their courses and did. I could see that they took pride in what they expected of their students, more still in what students could expect of them. I never heard of Wellesley professors who taught for decades from old yellow sheets of coffee-stained lecture notes. I had sat through some of those lectures at BU.

Wellesley's departments hammered out the sequence of courses for a major. The more effective chairs inspired and cajoled their junior and senior faculty to keep the major fresh. But the chairmanship rotated every three years, providing little in the way of leverage, continuity, or accumulated learning on the job.

It was in the committee on curriculum and instruction that faculty exercised ostensible oversight of the academic program. I attended many of those meetings and found them bureaucratic. They seldom raised questions of how programs of study fit together or whether they enabled students to integrate what they were learning. Instead I watched them apply a rubber stamp to individual course proposals. But not until they'd haggled over syntax and punctuation, with occasional veiled struggles over departmental turf. I stopped attending and assigned one of the associate deans to keep me advised.

Changes to the overall curriculum were another matter entirely, rare, and deliberately so. They required formal approval in a two-thirds majority vote of Academic Council, all hands on deck. What worried me was how hard it was for any of us to attest to the coherence of a student's four-year experience. So many pathways were open to them. And how could we rally the faculty to a collective sense of responsibility for the quality of every student's education? We had a value conflict: academic freedom in tension with institutional accountability.

That's why I was backing Nancy's effort to entice the faculty into an engagement she was inventing on the fly. I had faith in her and offered input when she requested it, which was often. I respected her autonomy as the chief academic officer. That was the kind of leader I wanted to be: engaged without imposing control, encouraging and empowering, fostering collaboration. Sure, I would sometimes mutter to myself, nothing but a soup of cliches. In truth, I was feeling my way and noting what I was feeling as raw data that pointed to matters that might warrant my attention. I was making good on my justification to my daughter that the presidency would constitute my scholarship. The dean and her committees soldiered on through that summer of 1995.

But if I thought I had troubles, I had only to glance at my husband's face one cold February night when he arrived home later than usual. He was in the fourth year of his presidency of the Dana-Farber Cancer Institute. He looked as grim as I'd ever seen him.

"I may have to resign over this," he said, his eyes averted.

"What happened?" I asked, but added, "You're not going to lose your job. They love you there." They did; I'd seen him in action. He was leading the place skillfully and was widely respected. Then he told me what he knew so far.

A clerk in the DFCI data archives had stumbled upon a grievous clinical error. Two breast cancer patients in a treatment study were given lethal overdoses of a drug. Four times the prescribed amount. One died two days later, and the other sustained irreversible heart damage. The patient who died was Betsy Lehman, an award-winning health columnist at the *Boston Globe*. She was thirty-nine years old, married with two daughters, seven and three. The mistaken dosage was administered and charted in November and only now had come to light.

As one of the nation's top comprehensive cancer centers, Dana-Farber was renowned for its combination of cutting-edge science and world-class clinical care. In the past, DFCI presidents had been physician-scientists. Chris was a scientist, not a doc. He had no experience, or intuition, or even detailed knowledge of clinical medicine. But he now had on his hands an appalling clinical crisis.

"We are going to tell the truth to everyone who has been harmed by this," he continued. "And then we'll have to turn the place upside down. I've taken full responsibility and of course will continue. I'll lead us through whatever happens for as long as I can be effective. But there may come the day when the best I can offer is to fall on my own sword."

I hugged him, and made no further predictions about how this would play out.

Within days, I could see that Chris had not exaggerated. The regulators descended and documented numerous deficiencies which were widely publicized. Soon both of us were dreading the early morning thwomp of the *Boston Globe* and the *New York Times* when they landed on the portico of the President's House. Nearly every day brought another prominent story to detail new events along with rumors and speculation. The *Globe* staff mourned the loss of their beloved colleague with relentless criticism. The *New York Times* kept the pressure on at the national level.

Chris personally met with the families of the two patients to tell them all he knew. He was the point person for a retinue of high-powered emergency consultants. In constant contact with his board and senior leaders of the Institute, he made sweeping changes. He had no choice but to require several of his senior colleagues to resign. They were valued contributors who had the misfortune to be responsible for systems that failed. I could feel how unbearable it was for all these people to see the hospital they had served with pride being blown apart in a very public degradation ceremony.

From a distance, I watched Chris do all he could to keep spirits up, everyone else's and then, finally, his own. I saw the stress wear on him, grind him down. He worked day and night, was seldom home, was always on the phone, and slept hardly at all. Occasionally we went to the Cape but it was not the same. No golf for Chris with his Falmouth friends. Even I was finding it hard to reach him in his lonely effort just to hold himself and everyone else together.

Peter Ramsey wanted me to pay a summer visit to Kathryn Davis at her home in Maine. I should make it an annual practice, he said, as Nan always had. Kathryn enjoyed entertaining and would welcome me warmly. She was a legendary and generous senior trustee from the class of '28, deeply engaged in world affairs still. She would have dignitaries in to meet me, Peter explained. She was proud of her college and her friendship with its presidents over many years. She had homes also in Tarrytown, New York and Hobe Sound, Florida where she was an illustrious hostess whose dinner guests included national and global movers and shakers, former cabinet ministers, diplomats, public intellectuals, even the occasional former head of state. Mikhail Gorbachev for one. It was vital that I establish a strong relationship with Kathryn; making the summer pilgrimage with my husband was an ideal vehicle for doing that.

Anyway, Peter added, Chris could use a break. It was only three days and Kathryn would gladly arrange a golf date for him. We could drive up Friday afternoon for dinner and head home Sunday after breakfast. We set the date for September 8, 1995.

On the way to Maine in Chris's car, we reviewed the current situation at Dana-Farber. Over the seven intense months since the news broke, they'd completed a massive reorganization and had reformed many of the essential quality control systems. They had more work to do and a reasonably clear roadmap forward. But the media feeding frenzy just wouldn't let up. Dana-Farber had become the poster child for error in medicine, a serious national problem that was elevated by this high-profile Boston tragedy. Public communication in health was one of my areas of expertise, but I didn't pretend to have answers. All I had was sympathy and support.

As we crossed the state line into New Hampshire, Chris raised the question of whether it was time for him to step down, but then changed the subject. He had an audiobook one of his consultants had given him. She coached CEOs under fire, a different sort of professional from those he normally encountered. He couldn't remember who found her, but said he liked her.

Let's listen to it, I suggested, and inserted the tape into his car's cassette player. I was expecting a treatise on risk management or crisis leadership and was surprised instead to hear a familiar voice come through the car radio. It was unmistakably David Whyte, Rick Jackson's neighbor on Bainbridge Island, an Anglo-Irish poet with a lilting voice and a distinctive style of reciting poetry. His latest book, *The Heart Aroused: Poetry and the Preservation of the Soul in Corporate America*, had just become a bestseller and this was the audiobook edition. Chris was never one to listen to audiobooks, and this was not the kind of book he would normally have read. It was more my style. I was glad he'd found a coach who dared use the word "soul," and we both enjoyed the consultant's gift for the rest of the trip up to Northeast Harbor.

The weekend went well. Chris played a round of golf on Saturday morning while Kathryn and I visited a nearby Japanese Garden. That night at a small dinner party, we met Kathryn's neighbor, David Rockefeller, and his houseguests. David was happy to spend the evening with a graduate of The Rockefeller University. Sunday morning, we set off after breakfast for the five-hour drive home. Chris was quiet, preoccupied.

Let's listen to more of your tape, I suggested. Soon we heard David Whyte reciting a poem called "The Journey" by Mary Oliver. A poem I knew by heart from retreats with Parker Palmer. A poem Parker used often as a "third thing," in the "circles of trust" he facilitated.

"One day you finally knew / what you had to do and began," Mary Oliver's poem opened, "though the voices around you kept shouting their bad advice." I glanced over at Chris and saw it had his attention.

As David recited it in his unique style, the mood of the poem penetrated our car, penetrated our lives through the horribly difficult months that had consumed everything Chris had to give. Midway through the poem, the "voices" shifted as stars broke through the clouds and a "new voice" could be heard. This was the turning point of the poem as Parker worked with it, Parker who had introduced me to my own internal voice, one that knew my heart, knew my needs—when I could still hear it. That new voice was "your own," Oliver wrote, and it "kept you company / as you strode deeper and deeper / into the world, / determined to do the only thing you could do—determined to save the only life you could save."

I sensed a stirring in Chris, a letting go. After a long silence he asked me to wind the tape back so we could listen again. We did. And then he told me he was going to resign. As soon as we were home, he would call the chair of the DFCI board, who would notify the whole board. And then he would call the former chair, Dick Smith, to let him know.

"What if Dick tries to dissuade you?" He had been adamant that Chris should stay at the helm up to the bitter end. That it was still Chris's watch.

"I will hold my ground," he replied. Then, with a smile, "When my parents tried to make me eat my vegetables I'd sit at the table for as long as it took. Until they'd gone to bed if necessary. I won't be dissuaded."

We arrived at the President's House and he went to his study and made the calls. Dick did try to talk him out of it. He said Chris's career would be ruined. Chris held his ground. Within minutes he received a call from Dan Tosteson, the medical school dean who had enticed him to leave MIT for HMS. Chris had resigned the HMS department chairmanship when the crisis befell DFCI so he could give it all his attention. An acting chair was in his place. Dan was entreating him to return to be chair now, to resume his leadership at the medical school. Chris said no.

"Why not go back to that?" I asked.

"I've left Mary Oliver's loud voices behind," he said. "I want to hear what some new ones may have to say to me."

Chris returned to the large research laboratory he still led at HMS, the Walsh group. He carved out a small cubicle for himself there. He, who had occupied so much real estate at Harvard that the second-year medical students, two years earlier, made his empire the theme of their annual show.

As Parker Palmer worked with "The Journey," he always asked those in the circle what they made of Oliver's phrase toward the end, "you strode deeper and deeper into the world." Why was that line there? How did it mitigate the closing lines? Eventually someone would see it. This is not a poem of retreat and defeat, or self-indulgence. It is a poem of resilience, power, and transcendence. Word of Chris's decision traveled rapidly. I watched him and hoped that this would mark a new beginning for him. Meanwhile I had my own preoccupations.

Shortly after Chris resigned, Victor Kazanjian appeared in my office for our regular meeting. He asked how we were doing. Naturally, I'd been thinking that something awful could easily happen to me at Wellesley. Tomorrow.

"Yes," Victor replied. "That's true. That's always true. And so, all we can hope is to bring our best to the situation, discern and do what it demands of us, and try to come out of it more whole than we were when we went into it." Those words stayed with me as I watched my husband recover slowly from his ordeal, and wondered what sorts of tests would still litter my path.

My second year at Wellesley I approved a second associate deanship to accelerate the curriculum project that felt like it would take forever. Together, Nancy and I recruited a sociologist and a master teacher, Lee Cuba, for his diplomatic skills and connections to the social scientists and humanists. He enlisted more faculty for the review. Over 160 volunteers came from all ranks and all departments to serve on five task forces.

They worked through that winter and spring. My contribution was to host a series of faculty dinners at the President's House, seven altogether, for a total of forty-seven individuals. They were small groups mixed by discipline, department, length of tenure at the college. I wanted to understand more fully how faculty were thinking, what their issues were, who the visionaries were and where I would find those with an appetite for renewal. Maybe I would influence some of my dinner companions, and create modest ripple effects across campus. I found many constructive voices, and a few expansive thinkers, but was discouraged on occasions when the conversation began with grousing about the students.

"There are students crossing the stage at graduation who don't have thinking and writing skills anywhere near where they should be," one declared. "For whom are we redesigning the curriculum is the question I keep asking myself."

I recognized comments like this as thinly veiled objections to the increased diversity of the student body, the result of a deliberate admissions policy which I strongly supported. I said so and called next on someone I believed would change the tone.

"The real issue is whether we're challenging students enough—or challenging them in the best ways," Ann Velenchik, an economist and master teacher said one evening, and others took up her theme. "Are we encouraging them to take intellectual risks, supporting them in that?"

"We're not such great role models ourselves," an English professor muttered. "But we ought to do a better job of cultivating failure and making it safe for our students." I agreed with her.

"Isn't that an oxymoron?" a social scientist jumped in. "If we make it safe, then *are* they taking risks? Students are far too grade conscious. They personalize everything."

"How do we get students to trust their own views?" a scientist ventured. "How do we transfer the responsibility for learning from faculty to students?" This last question took us into the heart of the matter as I saw it, and I said so. But I did not see it as a one-way transfer, from professor to student. I was looking for a more interactive choreography of self-responsibility and interdependence—the two values I wanted to be sure we modeled for our students.

As the new academic year began, 1995–1996, Lee came back from another summer retreat with a synthesis report of the committee's recommendations. He had done a fine job, and I agreed that it was ready for the deans to distribute. I was determined that we bring this curriculum review to closure by early May. Three years was long enough. I encouraged student leaders to canvass and communicate student sentiment on the faculty proposals. They were eager to help shape the discussion, and they brought an intelligent and measured perspective. The proposed changes would not be in place until after they had graduated, and I liked their spirit of responsibility for the future of their college. They saw the stakes as high. One college government officer told me she wanted to be sure her younger sister would still want to come to Wellesley after the changes were in place.

Through the fall we aired the report with all constituencies and in all the relevant standing committees of Academic Council. The committee on curriculum and instruction and the agenda committee would bring it to Council in the spring for a vote. If it failed, we would have dug ourselves into a deeper hole. We had asked a great deal of our busiest and most dedicated faculty citizens. It was hard to imagine that we would rally them again soon if all this came to naught.

And the board! The trustees waited patiently, offered encouragement, and strained not to step on turf they knew faculty considered sacrosanct. I knew they would be concerned if we didn't pull this off. As they should be. The faculty seemed to be splintered and I was worried that we would never reach a consensus. I was out on a limb, side by side with the three deans. I stayed close to them as they continued to solicit feedback, modified the proposals, mobilized the silent majority, caught the flak, and titrated when to exert pressure and when to pull back. I said at every opportunity that the process had been beneficial, whatever the outcome. I was whistling in the dark, girding against abject failure. I had no Plan B.

We called for the first vote on the curricular proposals in mid-March 1996. The Academic Council chamber was as full as I'd ever seen and felt it, full of people and the frisson of uncertain anticipation. Lee moved that the faculty adopt a new quantitative reasoning (QR) requirement, a proposal from faculty in the sciences and the quantitative social sciences. The goal was to ensure that every Wellesley student would graduate with at least rudimentary mathematical proficiency and would take at least one course that applied numerical and symbolic reasoning to solve problems and analyze data. Those who did not pass an initial screening test would be required to take a new one-semester QR course. We wanted students to be confident citizens in a world of policy and decisions driven by ever more complex data. This proposal so unnerved some math-phobic faculty that they rose and inadvertently added fuel to the proponents' fire.

"I'm just not a numbers person," a Spanish professor began, "and I don't think we should force students to take courses they can't master." Many hands shot up and I called on an eloquent architect of the QR proposal.

"You've just made an air-tight case for the requirement." She said this gently as I trusted she would. "We can *teach* these reasoning skills so that our students won't be closed out of subjects that require a basic facility with numbers. They won't have to define themselves as people who have an inherent deficit." The debate continued and I could see the proponents making inroads. When the moment was right, I called for the vote. Council approved the QR requirement with one "nay" vote. A miracle! Well, no, more like the unpredictable result of a very carefully orchestrated campaign. And gratifying to me, who would have appreciated the QR program had it existed when I was a student.

In April we brought a complex restructuring of the distribution requirements. This was intended to clarify for students selecting courses, and faculty advising them, how to weave their choices into an integrated liberal arts program. The old system required students to select from three departmental groups: A, B, and C.

"That approach contains no useful information," Lee commented as he made the motion. "The proposal will organize distribution requirements into meaningful categories based on the course's content and the reasoning skills it fosters." He explained that the faculty committee argued for months about the new categories and came up with eight, from language and literature to epistemology and cognition. Reaching accord was a major feat of diplomacy and the labels were still being debated as the proposal reached the Council floor.

Lee didn't say but we all knew that underneath the semantics was a hard reality. Any changes to the course requirements created winners and losers in the all-important competition for student enrollments, and for the resources that followed the student numbers. As I managed the give and take, I noticed faculty speaking around the issue of enrollments. They would propose amendments and then argue over parliamentary procedure. Even the two parliamentarians ended up in an altercation, after which we entered a long and rambling sequence of speeches about the category "epistemology and cognition." What was in it, and what was out, and why? Did we need it at all?

I kept one eye on the student section, the CG members who regularly attended council. They rarely spoke up, but I knew they had strong opinions about the curriculum review. I wondered what they made of this wild free-for-all. I saw a student I knew well raise her hand. I was delighted to call on her.

"If the faculty are worried that the students don't know what epistemology means," she said in a strong voice, "I can lay that concern to rest." Then, with just a hint of irony, "We do." She sat down to snapping fingers, a signal of approval from her fellow students. The room erupted in laughter. I called for the vote. The margin was close, but the resolution passed.

In May we took up the final proposal, half-unit courses. This might be a skills-oriented course, or a half-semester option for an experiential learning project. Faculty would be free to choose how they might take advantage of the flexibility. It was more subversive than it sounded because it would open the way for innovation. I was pleased when it passed easily. I called for a vote to adjourn the meeting and gaveled it closed. A cluster of faculty who had worked tirelessly to advance these reforms lingered in the Council chamber rehashing the arguments and kvelling over the result. Every one of their proposals had made it through!

"We should break out the champagne," the chair of the agenda committee exulted.

"No. Scotch," said Lee. He had his own private supply of aged malt scotch in a cupboard in the kitchen of the President's House. We walked over there and broke it out, together with a bottle of champagne. I hate scotch but this was indeed a moment for celebration.

That night I lay in bed and took stock of the three-year journey. Chris had led Dana-Farber through its annus horribilis with authority and integrity. The changes he made would help launch a hospital safety movement. He had reinvented himself again, and I was proud of him.

I had moved beyond my faltering and sometimes inept early efforts to connect with members of the faculty. At the beginning, I had worked too hard to win their affirmation. Now I was able to recognize when I was being set up by the system. When I presented myself as their peer, I would relinquish my power and become lost in a fog of false intimacy that drew me out of my role. From here on, I would be consulting with the faculty, not joining them, not seeking their approval.

My task would be to enfold them into my vision. I would not entreat them to follow me but would be the person who could lead them over into the future. It was as if the family were moving to a new house and my job was simply to see to it that everyone managed their own feelings, chose their own wallpaper, made their own beds. The first three years had been for me a series of experiments in leadership. And now I was maturing into a leader who could be free from a lifelong need to please everyone but myself. On the anvil of the faculty's steely gaze I had begun to hammer out leadership principles that would enable me to find promise and pleasure even in the heat of conflict.

11

THE STUDENT SHADOW

I was forever reminded of the paradox of my power: I had a baffling blend of too much and too little influence over who did what to whom in that tightly knit domain that seemed hyper-reactive to my every whim. It started with the announcement of my appointment to the presidency. I realized then that I needed to be aware of the unintended impact I had, as if my mere presence was the leading edge of a weather front. I saw this pattern at play in my interactions with students, as I watched them challenge authority and unseat easy assumptions, my own included. Or maybe mine, especially.

We had a new art museum. An award-winning showcase by a Spanish architect, Rafael Moneo, his first commission in the United States. I inherited it from Nan, who built it with the trustees: the culmination of her campaign. I dedicated it in my first month on the job. It was magnificent and I endeavored to stop by whenever there was a new exhibition. I often found the galleries mostly empty and worried about what that meant. When I asked students if they had visited it, many drew a blank.

"We thought it was for the trustees and the alums," one responded. "Not for us." An art museum was a foreign, even forbidding place for more than a few of our students, I realized, and made a mental note that we'd have to see to it that this one was more universally enticing. When I carved out time to tour a new show, I was often by myself at the close of a busy day. As soon as I entered the building, I saw the student guards whisper into their walkie-talkies. One day I caught their words.

"The president is on the premises." The alert was relayed from one guard station to the next as I moved through the galleries. Am I a security threat, I wondered with amusement, and what kind of threat to whose security? It sometimes felt as though everyone on the campus carried a walkie-talkie to track the movement of the president-as-mother-superior with eyes in the back of her head.

Another encounter occurred a few weeks later. I was sitting amidst a row of students in the Collins Cinema, part of the newly opened museum complex. We were there for the inaugural film festival and my arrival set off the usual buzz. As we waited for the show to begin, I struck up a conversation with two students who were chatting together to my left.

"How do you like the cinema?" I asked.

"It's great."

"All we lack is popcorn," I offered.

"That's not allowed," the student next to me said, frowning. "There's a rule against eating popcorn here. It's messy."

"Really?" I asked, "I didn't know that. Whose rule is it? Where does it come from?"

"From high up," the other one said.

"High up." I looked at the ceiling. "How high?"

"The very top," she said, with authority.

"The very top," I repeated slowly, accentuating each word. "I guess that would be the president?" She stared at me for a long moment. Was I pulling her leg? Then she returned to her conversation with her friend. I guess she didn't recognize me. Or did she? When I asked around later about this putative rule, no one on my staff could trace its origin; it had spontaneously established itself, with the force of law.

The incident reminded me of the Wellesley of my youth, a labyrinth of unchallenged rules and unspoken expectations, which were relatively familiar for privileged students to negotiate. But they are less so if you come from a place where museums and their cinemas were built for somebody else. How would these students read between the lines?

A few days later, I learned of a Red Cross blood drive in Alumnae Hall and asked Jane to clear my calendar so I could walk over and donate a pint. I would set a good example for all those people watching me. Back in my office I found a student email awaiting me.

"President Walsh," it said. "We noticed you like blood. We think you would enjoy our rugby matches." A schedule was attached. Now this did not remind me of my student years. We didn't play rugby then, nor did we write President Clapp messages about blood. I went to a wild scrum and did my best to guess the rules so I'd know when to cheer. They played in what used to be a pristine meadow that I would have bet had never before seen such mayhem. But I didn't see any blood that day.

Through the eyes of the Wellesley students I met, the world looked very different almost three decades after I was a student. Back in 1969, when I lived in New York, Hillary Rodham, who had arrived at the start of my senior year, delivered her famous commencement speech, the first-ever student address at a Wellesley graduation. When Senator Clinton announced her candidacy for the US presidency in 2007, that speech was quoted again. A *New York Times* article predicted that Barack Obama would make the baby boomers finally "get over themselves" and move beyond "uberboomer" Hillary Rodham Clinton's call in that speech for "a more immediate, ecstatic, and penetrating form of living."

By one definition I just missed the boomer cutoff and Hillary's ecstatic turn. By another, I just made it. Either way, my sensibilities, instincts, and perspectives were indelibly stamped by the cultural turmoil of the late 1960s, just as those of my parents were by the Great Depression and Second World War.

I was curious to learn how feminism had fared at my alma mater in the decades I'd been away. I found enterprising student organizations doing a brisk business selling T-shirts that proclaimed Wellesley was "not a girls' school without men but a women's college without boys." I bought one and quoted the slogan often. Woe unto anyone in those early years of my presidency who slipped and uttered the word "girl." I was reminded of the Doonesbury cartoon series from the '60s that followed Joannie Caucus, the confirmed feminist, through her pregnancy. The day her baby arrived the word went out: "It's a woman—a baby woman!"

Some of the Wellesley students seemed barely more than baby women, trying on identities, searching for the new devotion that would carry them through this day. They'd find a new one for tomorrow. But all of them seemed to know for sure that they would have careers. They took much else for granted, it seemed to me. And their world seemed more distant from my generation's than mine was from my mother's. One night I hosted a reception for the first-year class. I chatted with an animated young woman who was relishing everything about her new college. She gushed about how beautiful the President's House was.

"I'm glad you like it," I said. "We had an interior designer help us spruce it up." I gestured toward the massive Oriental rug on the slate floor in the hallway next to the grandfather's clock.

"Good, I know what I want to be," she said, squaring her shoulders.

"A designer?" She shot me a glance. It was a look of disbelief.

"No! The Wellesley president!" Oops, how retro of me. I laughed off my gaffe. Her ambition far exceeded mine at her age.

Following the heady days of the women's movement I and my feminist friends watched with dismay as successive generations of younger women disavowed the label "feminist." Had the media successfully marginalized our movement as the refuge of aggressive malcontents who hated men and burned their bras? When educated younger women proudly proclaimed themselves "post-feminist," we asked if they believed in equal pay for equal work or sharing the burdens of parenthood. They would look blankly at us and reply with breezy confidence that everything would work itself out for them.

Now I was on the alert for answers to the question I had withheld from the search committee at our first encounter: whether Wellesley's single-sex status would continue to be viable as women's lives changed. This was a question I often asked without, ever, gaining much traction, even toward the end when I led a thorough review of Wellesley's future. All who considered the issue could see no advantage to forsaking the mission that still so successfully defined the college and its essential purpose.

In my early months, the first and most obvious change I saw in the student body was its visible diversity. When I arrived, nearly a quarter of Wellesley students were Asian American. Another 10 to 15 percent identified as African American and/or Latina. Many of these students were first- or second-generation Americans and quite a few were the first in their families to attend college. Wellesley practiced "need blind" admissions, which meant our recruiters could assure applicants that if they had the credentials and were admitted, we would provide financial aid to meet their full need. Aid applications were processed in a separate office after the admission decisions were made. Wellesley and only a handful of other well-endowed colleges could afford to make that guarantee, writing a blank check to the board of admission. More than half of enrolled Wellesley students received financial aid and the diversity of the student body—racial, ethnic, religious, geographic, and socioeconomic—was a strong selling point for recruiting students. Current students impressed on me at every opportunity that they were attracted to Wellesley in large measure because of our diversity.

On a Saturday in early September of my first year, Jane had set me up for a morning with about forty Wellesley senators, juniors and seniors in key roles in college and dorm government. It was 9:00 a.m. and the students looked bleary-eyed. They had invited me to talk to them about leadership.

"Listen," I said, "you don't need to sit through another lecture on a Saturday morning. How about you give me some advice instead?" That perked them up. I broke them into small groups and asked them to brainstorm for fifteen minutes. "Come back to me with two kinds of advice for an incoming president, returning to campus after twenty-seven years away. One of your jobs, I know, is to orient the incoming first-year students. This is a rare chance to orient your president." I asked them to list for me, in order of importance, the things that were essential about Wellesley, things we should all work hard to conserve and maintain, even in a changing world.

"And then take some time and develop a ranked list of the issues we should address," I continued. "I want to hear your best thinking about what we might do together to change Wellesley for the better from the student point of view."

They went off into their groups and came back energized. They talked with enthusiasm about the quality of the educational experience—easy access to faculty, small classes, a rich and varied curriculum, high standards of academic performance, an honor code that is truly honored, and the reciprocal trust that accompanies the honor code, and that suffuses academic life. They talked, too, about a sense of community and mutual support, about feelings of solidarity, about "sisterhood." All of this was music to my ears. The Wellesley I knew. Maybe even better.

Then came the problems they wanted my administration to rectify. The concerns ran the gamut from campus life and the difficulty of meeting men, to stress and the need for more opportunities to let off steam, to political correctness and the feeling that some opinions were unsafe to voice. They said the faculty was nowhere near diverse enough, given the growing diversity of the student body, and they lamented the lack of easy interaction among students of different races and cultural backgrounds. I was moved by their passionate intensity, by their impatience with Wellesley's imperfections. They wanted every student to love the college as they did, and they were alerting me to the hard reality that many minority students were having a hard time here.

I wanted my administration to take these comments seriously. It wasn't immediately obvious how. I would have to improvise strategies to convert conflicts into openings for learning and growth. I would learn from so many students over the years, students like these who were brave and generous enough to open their lives to me.

Every spring I met with the incoming college government president (the CGP) right after the student body elected her, and every fall again at the start of her senior year. One began her term as CGP by inviting me on a tour of "my Wellesley," as she called it. The Wellesley she saw through the lens of a financial aid student who didn't have the means to join others for meals or movies or trips to Boston, much less trips home to DC for Thanksgiving. She took me to her residence hall's dingy basement where she did homework and wrote papers alone on the vintage public computers, sometimes into the night. She couldn't afford a laptop or her own internet hookup in her room upstairs. As we parted, she gave me a new copy of a paperback, *A Hope in the Unseen: An American Odyssey from the Inner City to the Ivy League*. I stayed up most of that night reading it. I should have read it long before. I detected not one scintilla of self-pity in this student leader's education of her president. Nothing but generosity.

A few years later, when I asked another new CGP my stock question—what she hoped to accomplish in the year ahead—I was ready for her version of the list I had heard from her predecessors, a specific set of reforms they wanted to push.

"Maximum happiness," this one replied, simply, sincerely, with no hint of saccharine. The students had elected her CGP after a period of

simmering conflict on campus. Students had rebelled against new policies in the student life division. Maximum happiness sounded good to
me. At orientation she welcomed the incoming class with a story about
the time her mother bought her an expensive set of colored pencils. The
set cost her mother a week's salary. In her telling, the story was about
happiness, pure happiness and promise, and love. She told similar stories to gatherings of prospective students when she spoke to them at
open campus, at family and friends' weekend, and to groups of alumnae.
She set a new tone that seeped into the culture, calmed it. At graduation, she brought me her mom who wanted to express her gratitude to
Wellesley. I did my best to convey what a gift her daughter had been to
us—to me.

Still later, in 2005, another new leader came to see me soon after she
was elected CGP.

"I was just wondering," she started, "did your life totally change as
soon as you were elected president? Even before you assumed office?"
Her friends were treating her differently, she explained. There was an
awkwardness, a distance that felt lonely. "I'm suddenly isolated. I wasn't
ready for this."

I wanted to exclaim to this student: pull up your chair and let me tell
you how dehumanizing it can be! This being a leader. How confusing I
found it when I first walked into this job. My reaction reminded me of
Richard III: "For god's sake let us sit upon the ground and tell sad stories
of the deaths of kings." I restrained myself and instead pulled up a document on my hard drive and printed her a copy. I'd never done that before.

"Becoming Presidential Means . . . to me" was the title. I had written it
for my own use in the early months and added new items as they came
to mind. I referred to it often and revised it for the last time in 1994, after
a visit to Parker Palmer. I'd written him to say I wasn't keeping my poetry
alive, a minor confession, and he invited me to Wisconsin for a weekend
with him and his wife, Sharon, at their Madison home. We walked and
talked in a meandering two-day excavation of my inner experiences so
far as Wellesley's leader. On Sunday morning as I left, Parker offered me a
question I might want to carry back: "I wonder if you can think of your
presidency as your poetry for now?" He had echoed my pledge to my
daughter to make of it my scholarship.

Through my final year as president it was my pleasure to watch this CGP's leadership mature in a successful senior year. She was a natural. Just before commencement she came to my office to say goodbye and pulled out of her backpack the page I'd given her the previous spring. It was covered with notes in several colors of ink. She'd been in dialogue with it all year. And made of it a poem. Years later I would tell this story at the two fundraisers I hosted to support her candidacy for US Congress.

In my fourth year, to prepare a keynote for a professional conference on "student values," I convened a group of about twenty student leaders—mostly house presidents and members of the student multifaith council—to hear their take on the topic. They talked about their efforts to build community, respect differences, model integrity. They told me how much it meant to them to serve a cause larger than themselves. They spoke too of pressures they faced, especially in times of conflict, inspiration they drew from one another, and from the support networks of advisers they could turn to for help. They found it reassuring that "people have been through this before and we can get through it too." They described concretely the communal aspect of their work, how central it was for them. They were eloquent. I was loving this conversation, when about halfway through our hour, a member of the multifaith council raised her hand.

"You have to know that there are lots of people on this campus who feel the opposite of the way we do. First-year students arrive with enthusiasm and a deep desire to become part of the community and we watch them come bounding up the hallway in the dorm and run head-on into the cynicism and alienation of upper-class students."

Well, this I hated to hear, and yet I knew I had to listen, because as sure as I was that we were providing our students a great education, I was concerned that we might be letting them down in important ways. I'd been reading everything I could lay my hands on about trends in higher education. The history and philosophy of liberal education as it emerged in the United States. A growing chorus of critiques of contemporary responses to new pressures. I accepted invitations to give talks and write pieces on these topics to advance my thinking, and thought a lot about what a twenty-first-century education would need to accomplish, given the conditions today's students would be facing in their lives—unprecedented challenges I was coming to believe.

I particularly appreciated the 1997 book, *Cultivating Humanity*, by Martha Nussbaum, a University of Chicago philosopher, who saw the traditional tasks of a liberal education being unseated by rising cultural diversity in the United States, and global connectivity worldwide. For students to learn to be educated citizens in this newly configured world, she wrote, they need capacities of both love and imagination. To develop these, they will have to examine themselves and their own traditions critically, to locate themselves both in—and beyond—their immediate surroundings and affiliations. With "narrative imagination," they can come to understand themselves as humans tied to other humans through bonds of mutual recognition.

These capacities, Nussbaum argued, can best be cultivated in communities whose members engage in public reasoning to resolve disputes and to ascertain truths in pursuit of common goals. We will need citizens willing to re-examine tradition, Nussbaum concluded, if we are to retain a thriving democracy, and this will necessitate that previously excluded citizens have influential and respected voices.

A liberal education should aim to make lives "not just more successful, but more significant," according to Wellesley trustee and Harvard English professor, Jim Kloppenberg. He called for more emphasis on helping students develop the intellectual, ethical, and political tools with which to craft lives in which "inner joy, courage, and endurance are joined with an ideal." Quoting William James, he added that the only way to prepare for such a life—as to live it—is to "back one's ideals with virtuous activity."

This outspoken student leader, in her willingness to raise an awkward truth, had called in the voices from the margins where the buried wisdom tends to reside. In doing so, she had taken us in an entirely new direction. She had unseated our certainties and asked us to sit with the discomfort of what we didn't know—or didn't want to know. It seemed to me a promising step in the right direction.

I had resolved after my enlightenment at Harambee House not to put myself in that position again. I would not enrage a group of students by presenting them with a fait accompli as I had done in December of my first year. The following year, at the summer Senior Staff retreat, I raised the subject of a smoking ban.

"Wellesley is woefully remiss in still permitting indoor cigarette smoking," I said to my team without arousing much in the way of enthusiasm. Of course they knew I was a public health professional who had taught and published on the harms of cigarette smoking and policies to reduce them. "We have a moral obligation," I said. "Or I feel I do, to protect faculty, staff, and students from the well-documented dangers of smoking and secondary smoke inhalation." I gathered from the tepid response that if I wanted to pursue this, I would be on my own. The dean of students expressed serious reservations about this hobby horse of mine, and coaxed me at least to postpone a decision on smoking in the residence halls.

"It's accepted now to ban smoking in places of work," she conceded reluctantly, "but a dorm room is a student's home away from home. They'll see this as a blatant infringement of their personal rights." She told me we needed to do more "groundwork" before banning smoking in the residence halls. I thought she meant months but, in fact, we didn't get back to it for another four years, which drove me nuts. But I didn't think it wise to take on the entire student body without the backing of the student life division.

So for starters I decided to act on smoking in public spaces. I wrote a memo to announce a workplace smoking ban. I was intimately aware of the rationale and the counter arguments and composed a memo to announce my decision. As a former smoker myself—one who developed a tobacco addiction while a Wellesley student—I knew that smokers would find the new policy inconvenient and irritating. I wrote that. And I said that I hoped they would also see in it a genuine concern for their welfare. I also hoped they'd see through the tobacco industry's cynical attempts to portray the anti-smoking movement as coercive, punitive, and sanctimonious. I had Jane send my memo out.

Soon the academic dean let me know that several members of the faculty, confirmed smokers with no intention of quitting, were irritated. But I heard no more from them. They would probably just go on smoking in the privacy of their offices and maybe think twice before lighting up in front of students. Or maybe they would open their windows.

Students were another matter. Within hours of my announcement, the dean of students called to report that students were distraught. I needed to meet with them. I told her they could come the next day at noon to my monthly president's open office hours.

As it happened, I had a first-year student shadowing me all day. A reasonably representative day Jane had selected weeks ago when the student made the appointment. There was nothing confidential on my schedule. The student shadow wanted to see what it might be like to be a college president. All morning she sat with me through a series of innocuous meetings.

When we emerged to see who was waiting for my office hours, Jane told me she'd moved us to the Faculty Common Room down the hall. Students had called all morning to say they were coming to protest the smoking ban. My shadow and I looked down the hall and saw a huge commotion at both entrances. The room was filled to overflowing, and noisy. I felt my body tense as we elbowed through the crowd. Students had rearranged the furniture and placed a seat for me in the center. Ah, the hot seat again. They were packed on sofas and armchairs, on the floor, perched on windowsills, standing three-deep along the edges of the room.

"Does the group have a spokesperson?" I asked. A pause. Apparently not, but a bold warrior charged into the breach.

"I want to express my disgruntlement at your new nonsmoking policy," she said, her voice quivering. "I am a nonsmoker, and I am allergic to smoke. But I don't think this is fair. In the cold weather, I don't think smokers should have to go outside and freeze."

"Okay," I said. "Anyone else? I'd like to hear from as many of you as possible and then I'll offer some general responses." I had a pad of paper and a pen and made a quick note after the first speaker: smoking outside in the cold.

"To take away something so suddenly is unfair," a voice added from the back of the room. "I don't smoke either, but you've made a big mistake. This is college, probably the first home students will have on their own. There should be more democracy, especially in preparation to enter the real world beyond school." Applause and cheers.

"I don't smoke, I don't like smoking," another student scowled, "but this new policy is unnecessarily restrictive. I have never felt exposed to smoke, beyond a whiff in a hallway. Smokers here are courteous and respectful. You want to stigmatize one of the few groups it's still fashionable to cast as outsiders. You'll send them out in front of buildings to puff ignominiously on their cigarettes." More applause and snapping of fingers. I appreciated the drama and eloquence of the arguments, and the humor. I had to work to suppress a smile. I wondered, are there any smokers here?

The next speaker stood up. "I don't eat meat. I haven't for almost eight years. I am living proof that one can live a beautiful, happy and extremely healthy life without eating any dead animals. I hate it when people eat meat around me. We all know that fatty meat is bad for your health. So, why don't you ban meat?" She was building a head of steam, addressing everyone in the room and she was far from done.

"I have to say—and I am an ex-smoker, and ex-smokers tend to hate smoking more than other people do—I am sick and tired of you and your administration making decisions for us. We live here. We work here, and we pay way too much money to have some person in a position of power tell us—as legal adults!—what we can do to our bodies if we want to. I'm glad I'm graduating, before some watchdog committee can tell me what to major in and how to dress!" Her voice trembled.

"You say you care about our health," a calmer voice jumped in. "But if you take away our cigarettes—and I do smoke—then we'll just have to take up an even worse habit."

"Like what?" I couldn't resist asking. She had to think for a moment. Then said triumphantly:

"We'll shave our heads!"

"It'll grow back." I allowed myself a smile. "The linings of your lungs won't." I made a few more comments about why and how I made the decision and thanked them for taking the trouble to speak to me directly. My memo had triggered a long string of angry comments on the electronic conferences, and I told them I had read them all.

"I especially appreciate your willingness to confront me face-to-face," I said. "I'm not going to reverse the policy, but I do hear your objections. I'll keep them in mind as other issues arise." They shuffled out of the room, muttering and looking morose. After the room had cleared, my shadow looked at me as if I had just emerged muddied and bloodied from a truly violent rugby scrum.

"How did that feel?"

"Not great. Still want to be a president?" She looked down at the floor.

"I'm not so sure."

Just then one of the students—a vocal participant in the torrent of invective—peered around the door and asked if she could come back in. I assumed she had left something behind.

"I came back to make sure you're okay," she said, stepping into the room. "We were kind of rough on you. I hope we didn't hurt your feelings." It was as though she'd been sent back as an emissary to demonstrate, for me and my some-day successor, a fundamental lesson about positional power. I would tell myself repeatedly when I was under fire, and would forget nearly as often, that it was seldom about me personally; it was generally about the office.

These feisty students—with their energy and wit and youthful certainty, and a touching sensitivity—constantly reinforced my desire to develop a style of leading that was principled and consistent. I thought of my student shadow that day as a proxy for the many students who paid close attention to what the president said and did, how I carried myself. At the same time I envisioned her as a shadow of my former self, the dutiful student leader, the idealistic public health professional.

The issue of when and how to consult students was tricky. I'd already reneged on my pledge to check in with them before I made a consequential decision. But when I failed to rouse Senior Staff on this smoking ban, I was on my own to come up with a process for that decision. This one was not as clean and clear as it should have been, I said to my shadow.

As a sociologist I'd studied power, but I had to admit that I was ambivalent about wielding it. I thought of myself as a gentle person, a peacemaker at heart, who succeeded by being tenacious and gracious, by working hard and staying the course. At Wellesley I was challenged to reconcile at least two competing tendencies within myself: the forbearance of the sensitive diplomat and the ferocity of the resolute achiever. I wanted to bring them together into a unity. I experimented with the various constituencies to find the correct balances. It was the students—smart and stubborn—who directly challenged me to put my skills and beliefs to the test. I watched them channel their aggression and ideals—their creative ferment—into the formation of provisional adult selves. I loved that world of theirs. Loved them in it. Even when they weren't so sure they liked themselves. Maybe especially then. And they, in their struggles, provoked me to pose a question that I asked of myself and spoke about to many of my colleagues in higher education. How can we be the leaders we will need our students to become?

12

TURN OF THE MILLENNIUM

My seventh year in the presidency was a rough one, maybe my hardest yet. I was up late groping for the right words to prepare the trustees for their upcoming meeting. I wanted them to have my balanced and honest assessment of the unrest of which we had all been painfully aware, the clashes between student groups and my administration. We'd been enduring a rash of flare-ups in the division of student life. This task had my mind in the jaws of a vise as we approached the closing of the academic year. It was not over yet. Not even close. Spring was always a mountain to climb, the air thinning, the peak receding, boots chafing, burdens far heavier than they felt in August when we packed for the expedition, eager to be on our way.

Now it was May, and the campus was in full flower, but I was in no mood to savor its beauty. Every ounce of energy I had left was concentrated in the finale: my closing meeting with the trustees followed by commencement and reunion. And then? I would escape with my husband back to the Cape for a whole week. Chris was running his lab, traveling as a consultant and involved in biotech startups. Dana-Farber was behind him, but he seemed a little tired, down, maybe even depressed. On the Cape, I would keep an eye on him. We would read poems together over breakfast and he would play golf with his friends. I would take morning runs and, later, lose myself in the rhythms of the ocean, the forgiveness of the sky, the soaring of the osprey, the simplicity of the afternoon farm stand and impromptu meals with friends. And at dusk, out in my kayak, I would follow the trail on the water laid by the setting sun, alone with my thoughts.

For now, there was only to soldier on.

I set my alarm for 5:00 a.m. and checked my email one last time before heading for bed. Chris had been asleep for hours while I'd been in my study drafting the end-of-year memos and polishing speeches I had written last weekend. Tomorrow the Amherst trustees would meet. I'd speed-read their board book in the two-hour drive, with John at the wheel, hoping that would be time enough for me to be prepared. I would bring them what I had to spare.

The email was a curious one, from Chris to his doctor and copied to me. I skimmed it fast, then read it again. He had sent it at 4:00 this afternoon with the heading "Making an Appointment."

"Hi Mark," Chris had written. Mark Aronson had been Chris's internist for twenty or more years, the sought-after doctors' doctor my friend Tom Delbanco had recommended when I confided in him my growing concern about Chris's risk for heart disease. There is no one better than Mark, Tom had assured me. "I don't know which email address is current, so I am trying both. I would like to schedule an appointment to see you as it has been some time since our last consult. (We did connect briefly as I was getting over influenza in January)."

Ah, the January influenza. It marked the midpoint of the tough year. Chis was miserable with flu for weeks, including on New Year's Eve, which he spent in bed. I drove alone that night to a party at the Silbeys'—our close friends now living in the Back Bay—made a brief appearance, then sped back to Wellesley on a deserted turnpike to be with Chris by midnight. But he was asleep. So much for the turn of the millennium.

"The main reason I wanted to check in has been that I have felt particularly fatigued for the past couple of weeks and if I walk up three flights of stairs to my office about a third of the time in this month I have a brief tight feeling in the chest which resolves in about a minute. Occasionally, I have a little tingle down the left arm." Chris went on to say that it couldn't be too alarming if he was able to play golf the previous week, and asked to make an appointment.

I thought about forwarding the email to Allison, in medical school at Harvard, but decided that if Chris wanted her to have it, he would have copied her. He didn't sound worried, and I could always count on him for worst-case scenarios. Defensive pessimism was his role in our marriage. As the optimist I was not overly concerned, relieved maybe that Mark had the information and would know what to do. For just a fleeting moment I did pick up in my gut a coil of terror I could feel Chris straining to hold at bay.

My early alarm didn't wake him, but my hairdryer did. I apologized, whispered goodbye, and told him to go back to sleep. John was out front in the car and we drove, through the dark, west toward Amherst. Sitting in the front seat as usual, I plowed through the board book but missed our normal conversation, which we both enjoyed.

Right on time for the first session, he dropped me at Alumni House, where the trustees met, and delivered my bag to the Lord Jeffery Inn where we stayed overnight. The first two committee meetings felt lackluster to me, hardly worth the effort I'd made to arrive on time. Next up was a plenary session with the faculty resources committee, which the academic dean had neglected to tell me I would lead as chair of the instruction committee. Mildly irritated, I muddled through and saved a little time for calls back to Wellesley before the finance committee was to meet.

When the meetings were over around 3:00 I returned to the Lord Jeff for the evening. I'd planned all along to skip the ceremonial stuff that I thought of as "a busman's holiday," an old phrase picked up from my mother. Amherst would be celebrating a campaign gift over dinner at the president's house. They didn't need me as a passenger on that bus. And I needed the time for my memos for my board.

I settled into my room and my writing when Chris called, around 5:00. He'd been in meetings all day and just checked his office voicemail before going home to pick up Magellan and drive to the Cape. Our plan was that he would have dinner with Elaine and her husband at their Cape house on Friday night, and John would drive me down from Amherst on Saturday after the meetings. We had a reservation for four on Saturday night at the Chart Room, a popular restaurant on the water.

Chris was calling with a change of plans: he was on his way to Beth Israel Hospital, instead of the Cape. As soon as Mark saw the email, he had left a voice message instructing Chris to go straight to the hospital, where he would be waiting to meet him. Chris didn't know whether he'd be admitted, and promised to call me when he knew more. I left a message for John alerting him to the possibility that I would need him to come right back out and get me, but I didn't really expect it to play out this way. I went back to writing the memo, which became its own unfolding drama. Chris called again an hour later to say he'd been admitted, and that Mark had chided him that "email is not for chest pain." He sounded worried, so I decided to come back, and he didn't tell me not to.

I was restless in the car riding back, but not frightened. I worked fitfully on the memos, struggling with a new laptop on which I had somehow managed to lose much of the writing I'd done while waiting for John.

Back at Wellesley, I thanked John and drove myself to the hospital, arriving at around 10:00 p.m. Chris was being observed fairly aggressively, with an IV of heparin and heart monitors on his chest and legs. He seemed okay, but subdued and worried. I stood by the side of his bed looking down at him and felt myself unable to connect across an expanse of awkwardness and fear. I was exhausted and he encouraged me to go home, which I did, a little concerned but still not terribly so. He was in good hands, I told myself, and the last thing he needed of me was to feed his anxiety.

Saturday brought a few voice- and email messages from Amherst expressing concern. No one at Wellesley knew yet what had happened. I had called Elaine from Amherst Friday night to cancel our weekend plans. She checked in by phone on Saturday but wasn't overly worried. As president of Boston Medical Center, she knew emergencies. And she cared—deeply. We often joked that she was Chris's second wife. He liked the joke; so did I. The friendship ran that deep. Her calm helped staunch my fear.

In the morning I worked on the two memos, one to the whole Wellesley board summarizing the year and one to the small compensation committee. The writing had become a kind of obsession, an effort Dick referred to later as my "Second Inaugural." He had encouraged me for weeks to look on the closing events of this hard year as my opportunity to deliver a decisive message about the meaning of it all and where we were coming out. I was dubious that I'd find worthy words. The pressure was on.

I was pressed for time to pick up Allison at her Boston apartment on our way to the BI. She was on the night float and was due at Mass General at 7:00 p.m. to work through the night. She and I sat with Chris then went for a quick pizza. Allison was reassuring, glad her dad was in the hospital being watched. She was sure that "something real" was going on with his heart, but optimistic that it would be easily repaired. Her hunch was that he'd need a cardiac catheterization and a stent or two. Her calm was as calming as Elaine's was, and I registered for the first time that our roles were reversing. Chris laughed often about the time when she was little and asked, "Dad, when I get big will you get small?" It was starting to happen.

On Sunday morning, I worked on the trustee memos and sent them to Pat, without any mention of what was going on with Chris. She responded quickly, counseling that the one informing the small committee about where I stood with student life was too negative. I replied in a return email about Chris's situation. She called to offer sympathy and support, and suggested ways we could clear my calendar on Monday and Tuesday.

I spent the afternoon with Chris. He was in the east section of the BI/Deaconess; he was adamant that he didn't want to go to the west campus. I didn't ask why but assumed it was a residue of his Dana-Farber days. A not-so-subtle reminder that the internecine politics of Harvard's teaching hospitals were among the stressors that had taken a toll on him during the most punishing five years of his life. Those DFCI years put a strain on his heart, I said to myself now, and recalled a cartoon portrait presented to him at a party as he was leaving. Up to his neck in a sand trap swinging at a buried ball, his face was wan and ashen.

We talked about surface things. I spoke lightly of my Amherst meeting and the ongoing saga in student life. He'd heard more than enough on both topics already. He was worried that his further tests—the ones so far had all been negative—would either reveal nothing, when he knew something was wrong, or would reveal something serious. He seemed unsure which outcome he dreaded more.

The blood tests for enzymes indicative of a heart attack all came back negative, which was good. Chris's first book was a textbook on *Enzymatic Reaction Mechanisms*. As a biomedical scientist he studied human systems; as a nonphysician, though, Allison had impressed on me, he knew more about what could go wrong in a body than about what could be fixed. She was on her way to becoming an oncologist and told me over and over how grateful I should be that this was heart disease, not cancer.

"The cardiologists fix stuff, Mom," she kept saying to me. "They intervene and they repair and you're good to go. It's mechanical." I was crying a little when we were alone together, but not in front of Chris. Or anyone else, except Elaine.

On Monday morning Chris underwent an exercise stress test. The results were not awful. The interventionist who ran the cardiac catheterization lab came up and spent time with us. He had a swagger designed to instill confidence and implied that he would be able to fix anything he might find. Cheerily he ran us through an inventory of his instruments of torture. Jerry Kolodny, the husband of Nancy, my first academic dean, had read the films from the stress EKG and came up to say hello. He, too, was relaxed. All the signals were pointing to a straightforward procedure in the cath lab the next day.

On Tuesday morning, I was in the office, awaiting word from the cath lab. Instead the call came from Mark, his voice tense. The angiogram revealed a much more serious problem than anyone anticipated. The left main ventricle was 90-percent occluded and other arteries were blocked. We were in an emergency now. Chris was scheduled for open heart surgery—a coronary artery bypass operation—first thing tomorrow morning. Later, Chris would describe his experience in the cath lab, fully present and observing the cardiologists' monitors. The tone was confident and upbeat until it wasn't. First an icy silence and then the only hopeful thing left to say: "You're a good candidate for surgery."

"He is bummed out," Mark went on to tell me, and sounded concerned at the depth of Chris's distress. I dropped everything and raced to the hospital where I was greeted by the smooth cardiologist. He too expressed surprise at how hard the news hit Chris. What did they expect? I was barely keeping myself together. My husband of thirty-four years was facing life-threatening surgery. His heart would be removed from his chest. It sounded like an ancient curse. Five hours or more on a mechanical life-support system.

Mark met me at the hospital elevator to take me up to see Chris. I was lost in a fog of terror, not knowing what to do. We were alone in the elevator, and I was trying to be brave.

"Mark," I started to say, "we are so lucky we found you all those years ago to be Chris's doctor; I'm so grateful to you." The words had barely left my mouth when Mark replied.

"We'll have to wait and see, Diana."

The door of the elevator opened.

I woke at 5:00 a.m. and began to gather things to distract me while Chris had his operation. I imagined, foolishly, that I would pass the time working and fussed with the new laptop on which I couldn't seem to load any files. Defeated, I stuffed too much stuff into a big briefcase, rushed downstairs, threw some food into Magellan's bowl and jumped into the college's car to drive myself to the BI. I was there by 6:15.

I found Chris sitting up in bed, looking OK. Not too scared.

I told him that Allison saw this as such a disaster averted, that she wasn't as shaken as I was. I stopped myself. Chris was not the only one monitoring his vital signs; I was on the emotional channel. He had spoken to Elaine the day before, too soon after the dire verdict, and he confessed the conversation had almost made him cry. Since then it was as though he'd installed a "no sympathy" sign on his door, and another on his chest. No visitors. No sympathy. No sentiment. I swallowed my memories of the many times when Allison, growing up, was hurt or hurting, and I was absorbing her pain, meeting her in it. Chris would implore me not to "make her cry." This was no time to disarm him. Not while we were both peering into a chasm of terror.

We sat in silence a while longer and then, as if reading my mind, "This is who I am," Chris said gently.

"Yes," I replied, "and you are wonderful."

His way had carried him a long way, I reminded myself. There might come a time when he would be ready to let down his guard. And I would be here.

Gradually the small room filled with hospital staff, each with a role to play in preparing the patient for his trip to the OR. To one fell the task of ejecting the wife. I kissed Chris on the forehead, kept my tears in check, and promised I'd be here all day, awaiting his return. My kindly companion directed me to the family waiting room.

During the wait I was in a stupor. I never touched the bulging briefcase I had packed before dawn. There would be no Lucky Strikes in this era of smoke-free hospitals. Not that I would have known what to do with one. Victor showed up unexpectedly in his pastoral capacity and I appreciated his company. He left after a couple of hours and soon after, the confident surgeon swept in to report that he had done his work well, as promised. The procedure went smoothly with every prospect of a full recovery.

I was just absorbing the relief of that news when a nurse arrived to escort me to the recovery room. As we walked, she offered a gentle warning that I would not like what I was about to see. She was right. I was horrified. Chris was in no condition to communicate. He had tubes coming out of him everywhere. I sat with him for a while then touched my lips gingerly on his forehead and said I'd be back early in the morning.

Back home I composed and sent an email to a long list of friends, his and mine. In a message I addressed to "Dear Friends of Chris Walsh," I told the story of Chris's sheepishness at first for causing a stir, the ambiguous exercise stress test followed by the serious problem revealed in the cardiac cath lab. And, this morning, the coronary artery bypass—five new grafts in all, including one to the left main ventricle, which was 90% occluded.

"We have been told a dozen times today," I wrote, "that we are incredibly lucky that he is alive. Luckier still that his heart is pumping beautifully. Chris doesn't feel all that lucky at the moment. He looks like he was run over by a train. But we are counting our blessings. We came very close to losing him. I've got lots of support here so don't worry about me," I added. "Wellesley's Commencement is this Friday; how's that for timing?"

One of the recipients was Chris's younger sister, Kathy, who called to offer help. Kathy was an R.N. and a lawyer, living in Lexington, Kentucky, and working for the VA in a job she could handle remotely. I checked with Chris, and we eagerly accepted. Kathy made plans to arrive a day or two after his return home.

During the hospital stay, I drove the thirteen miles from Wellesley two or three times a day, rushing back to campus for the functions I couldn't miss: the trustee meetings, the seniors' baccalaureate service and their graduation. If all went well, Chris would be home before thousands of alumnae arrived on campus next Friday for their reunions.

By now my closest colleagues were in the loop, but word of our situation hadn't spread much farther. The seniors would have noted my absence at their breakfast on the morning of Chris's operation. I was scheduled the next day to open their baccalaureate service, a popular event that drew most of the seniors and their guests from all over the world.

I spent much of that day with the trustees, leading them through the last of the year's quarterly meetings. Vicki Herget, completing her first year as Gail's successor, was a treasured friend who also, on behalf of the board, was responsible for gauging whether the president was able to function. She could see how spent I was and I could feel her support. We sat together at the baccalaureate, in the front row of Wellesley's historic Houghton Chapel, a space in which I had participated in more deeply moving gatherings than I could begin to count. Victor delivered the invocation then called me up for the president's welcome.

I climbed the seven steps to the chancel and stepped onto the small stool Victor had placed for me there. We'd laughed about the news photo of Queen Elizabeth at a rostrum that obscured every part of her except the top of her hat. The first time I spoke from this dais, Victor had brought a step stool from home, the one his son, Kyle, stood on to brush his teeth.

Whenever I spoke publicly, I took a deep breath and paused to survey the audience, scanning the faces, making micro-connections. I stood now, my hands on the rims of the pulpit, for an elongated moment, inhaling the energy that floated up into the rafters of the cavernous cross-shaped chapel. I exhaled and said to the seniors that I was sorry to have missed them yesterday. I congratulated the award recipients and welcomed the guests.

"My thoughts were with you," I said, "and I know yours were with me. I felt your concern and support, and I thank you." I wasn't sure I could maintain my composure to say anything more about what I was feeling, but felt I owed more to the seniors, to the intimacy of the four years we had spent together.

I went on, "I needed to be near my husband as he underwent life-threatening surgery. And you needed to see me making that choice to be with him. You'll be confronted in your lives with choices that test your priorities, your values, your heart's desire."

"Sitting in a hospital waiting room for five hours was excruciating," I said. "And now, I find my own heart opened in a welter of feelings: sadness, fear, pain, gratitude, and awe." In that spirit of tenderhearted-ness, I invited the seniors to ask themselves what it might be like to go through the next several days, and then through the rest of their lives, meeting the tests of what they cared most about with their own hearts widely exposed, whatever the risk, so that the choices they made would be life-affirming.

I took my seat and was, again, lost in an emotional fog through most of the service. Vicki had her eye on me. But when the organ blasted the opening notes of our traditional recessional, "Ode to Joy," I was called out of myself, as though Beethoven was thundering: Let the healing begin.

The next day brought commencement under the big white tent. I opened this ceremony with a reference to the week I'd just had, "a brief word," I said, about "how my day intersects with your joyful day, the one we are here to celebrate."

"I woke up early this morning and called the ICU," I said, and I felt the silence under the tent deepen. "The report was encouraging. I opened my email and found many warm and caring words, as I had heard the day before. I am grateful for the support. I put on the T-shirt from the rainy day four years ago when you, the class of 2000, first arrived on campus, and went on my morning run. I thought about you seniors and your guests, about what you must be thinking and feeling, each of you having your own experience." I added, "One of the beauties and wonders of this community we have assembled under this big white tent is how diverse it is—along so many dimensions."

A previous commencement speaker, Oprah Winfrey, told an earlier senior class that "God whispers to you but if you don't listen, she shouts." I quoted her and added that "each of us has our own sense of how spirit enters our lives, but being so close myself, this day, to a pretty loud mes-sage from somewhere, I want to open a silent space in this huge tent, just for a moment, and invite each of you to reflect on what this journey has meant to you. Your gratitude, your sorrows, your uncertainties, and your love. Let's just hold that together for a moment and then we will move on."

Pamela Daniels, a beloved class dean who was retiring, gave a magnificent speech and I reinforced her messages in my annual president's charge to the seniors. It was a beautiful commencement. When I returned to the office, I found emails and notes from faculty and staff expressing concern about Chris's health, but mostly commenting on the emotional connections they had felt under the tent that day. The note from Selwyn Cudjoe spoke for many. Selwyn had been chair of Africana studies during the eruption over Tony Martin's book. He had walked a narrow path in those days, between an administration that was censuring his colleague for writings of which he, too, disapproved and the sentiment in communities of color that the line I had drawn was harsher than it needed to be. Selwyn's note said this:

Dear Diana:

I was saddened to hear about your husband's illness. A literal hush was heard in the silence that accompanied your announcement. You must know that there was a profound sense of sadness. And then you went on to give the greatest speech of your life. It was not only a charge to our graduates. It was a charge to all of us to go forward in the world and serve those who come into our paths. I suspect it had even more impact on me in that it fortified my desire to go forth and speak my truth regardless of the consequences. I will find another opportunity to thank you for your efforts. But you are a good and wonderful person who exemplifies so much that is human; so much that is love. In your own quiet and unassuming manner, you are a bundle of dynamite. I suspect that it takes moments such as these to release the power of your emotional fusion: the transformation of Chapman 235 to Walsh 238 (I am trying to remember some of my physics that I learned thirty years ago.) . . .

In this time of need and a certain amount of sadness, know that you are loved and cared for by many.

In respect, appreciation and love, Selwyn

Emotional fusion. My friend, Parker Palmer, wrote about his bouts of depression. Hearts do break, he taught; that comes with being human. But when they break, they can shatter and send lethal shards in every direction, or they can break open to let in light and love. I delivered no second inaugural to end the challenging year. But something real had shifted, first in my tiny nuclear family and then out across the community I was leading and trying to heal.

Commencement the following year was on June 2, 2001. Allison was married that afternoon in the Houghton Chapel. Victor officiated. We hosted a large reception in a tent on the President's Lawn. She married a beautiful man, our beloved son-in-law, "beautiful inside and out," Chris said in his toast. In another toast, Thomas's best man and identical twin, George, told the story of their arrival from Bangalore, India, to Princeton for college, leaving everything they knew behind. He toasted his mother for letting them go, knowing that they would probably never return to India to live. The four Kurian brothers and their children were at the wedding, the two little nieces as flower girls along with my niece, Meaghan.

That Chris was there to walk Allison down the aisle of the Wellesley chapel was our family's ode to joy.

13

OUT OF THE BLUE

I was in my office, sealed off from the outside world well into an early-morning session with Dick Nodell, our weekly call. I was whining to Dick, the only person to whom I could whine with impunity. I'd been a magnet for messy problems as the new academic year began. I felt like the boss in the *Harvard Business Review* article whose employees came in with monkeys that clung to their legs, climbed up their arms, scratched them on the head, nibbled on their ears. The boss's task was to avoid being left with any of the pesky primates and to offload some of hers on to the departing subordinate. But now my time to whine was up.

I headed to the front of our suite to check in with Jane. She always raised my spirits. Jane had a miniature television set by her desk that I'd never seen turned on. But it was on now and had a small clutch of people staring at it. Just then I heard a collective gasp. I watched for the first time—in real time at 9:30 a.m.—an image I would see in an endless loop over days and months and years ahead, an image I would never expunge from my mind or heart.

September 11, 2001.

The second of two commercial airliners had just crashed into New York's World Trade Center. People streamed into the office from divisions and departments all over the building. The vice presidents and deans were here—my Senior Staff. My new assistant, Kate Salop, standing in the doorway, reported that the dean of admission was stranded in California on a recruiting trip.

I turned to my chief of staff. Smart, strategic, pragmatic and always firmly grounded, Pat was the person to turn to in a storm. A circle formed around her in a rapid-fire brainstorming session as she named specific steps we should take. But I was suddenly aware within myself of an urgent need to slow everything down.

I took a deep breath and asked the group to return in forty-five minutes when we would begin to develop a plan. Then I went into my office and called Chris. He was safe and believed Allison must be too. His thoughts were with me. How was I holding up? It must be chaos. It was, I replied, but I had my team and they were rallying. I took solace in the sound of his voice, as I always had.

Back for our first meeting, we moved into the conference room. I scanned the oblong mahogany table with my colleagues now arranged around it and paused to make eye contact with each one. All were deeply shaken, eleven women and men who were going to be my core group for as long as needed, my Senior Staff and two others I had asked to join us. We would meet frequently, and on short notice, I told them, to handle whatever arose. We would meet hourly through today and most likely tomorrow.

Ideas flew. I was feeling the weight of responsibility and then a subtle shift from me to we, a visceral sense that was also conceptual, a shift in consciousness. With a loosening of the grip of fear I sensed the social field around us slow into a state of flow. It was as if a thin curtain had opened to reveal, in the words of the poet Wendell Berry, that "what we need is here."

My first announcement went out on every channel at 10:21 a.m. It declared a state of emergency, canceled all classes and events, discouraged any travel. I urged students not to leave campus and to go to their residence halls where members of the student life division would meet them. We asked faculty and staff, if able, to stop by the dorms, too. We were setting up systems of communication and support, I added, and would stay in touch.

At the end, for me, was the most important point. "Please do not jump to hasty conclusions about who is responsible for the attacks or what they mean. It will take time to sort that out. Please try not to panic. Our prayers go out to all who have been injured or killed and to all who are in harm's way." That was all. Eight lines.

I was aware that the people I had asked for help were dealing with their own fear, the safety of their own families, their own heartache. I doubted that many faculty and staff, other than student life professionals, would report to the dorms. I made a mental note to cut everyone some slack, not least myself.

I made a few more calls, including one to Victor, then drafted a second message. Kate posted it on the Community online conference at 11:50 a.m. It referred to a preliminary plan, noted that Houghton Chapel would be open all day, with prayers for peace offered on the half hour. "The most important thing all of us can do now is to support and comfort one another," I said in conclusion.

I'd spoken by phone with Vicki and told her I would call her again later. While I composed a brief email message to the board, a call came in from David Spina, CEO of the State Street Corporation. He was stuck in Toronto, on a business trip, and reaching out to his board, the corporation's nine outside directors, to schedule an emergency meeting. He wanted me to know that the firm had mounted a heroic—and, so far, successful—effort to keep the nation's financial trading systems running. Several of its massive computer operations were transferred to emergency back-up sites around the country. Those were operating smoothly.

I commended him and suggested that he keep in mind employees from Middle Eastern countries who might be subjected to scapegoating. I also asked him to think about longer-term implications for the corporation. The nation's financial systems—the core of State Street's business—were targeted. What might that portend for the future of the economy—and the company?

By early afternoon I took a quick break to call Chris again. I was comforted that he'd reached Allison.

"She's at Mass General," he said, "on emergency alert since the first strike, ready for victims to be airlifted from New York." I almost never bothered Allison at work but wanted to hear her voice, just for a minute. I had her paged and said I doubted she had time to talk.

"We're still standing by," she said, "but haven't seen even one victim." She and her colleagues were coming to terms with the prospect that they would not see survivors. I was touched by the mix of disbelief and despair in my daughter's voice. As much as she wished she could help, reality was sinking in. There was nothing much she could do. I told her we all felt that, in our own spheres. Helpless and confused.

After multiple tries, I got through to my sister, Sally, in her office some ten miles from ground zero, on the Upper West Side. Barnard had canceled classes, Sally told me, but the city's transportation systems were in chaos, and cell phone service was mostly down. She was seeing many people who'd walked for miles—exhausted, dazed, disoriented—looking for loved ones. Everyone felt like a target. No one felt safe. And there wouldn't be candlelight vigils on the Barnard campus that night.

The Wellesley student life division was hearing from parents of students who were Muslim or of Middle Eastern or South Asian heritage. They wanted our assurances that we would protect their daughters from harassment and danger on campus, and keep them safe later when they ventured into the greater Boston area. I instructed the dean of students, with the chief of police, to connect with these students, hear their concerns, offer safety tips, and let us know what we could do for them. The IT group had already ordered special cell phones they were programming with emergency numbers for students to take when they traveled off campus. IT had also opened landlines in the residence halls for free long-distance calling to fill gaps in cell service. They streamed CNN to desktop computers and common areas for all who wanted to follow breaking news.

An impromptu roll call of sorts appeared spontaneously on the alumnae association website. Recent graduates in New York and Washington posted names of Wellesley friends they knew to be safe, and they solicited news of others. More and more names appeared, from more and more alums, hundreds by the afternoon. A week later, the list had grown to nearly 10,000.

The three academic deans raised a question much on my mind: what was our role as an educational institution? We owed the campus—and the nation—our best effort to understand the worldviews of the attackers and to imagine what the attacks might unleash. As a cosmopolitan community, Wellesley's students, faculty, and staff came from more than seventy-five countries and every major religious and ethnic group. We had faculty experts in relevant fields, and they participated in worldwide networks with scholars in their disciplines.

At this point, though, our concerns were more pragmatic. Victor consulted his multifaith team for thoughts on spiritual support. The chaplains and student representatives of thirteen faith traditions planned two outdoor vigils on Severance Green, at the center of the campus. They also scrapped their original design for the special service, Flower Sunday, scheduled in less than a week.

I called Chris to tell him about the vigil that night and was touched to hear that he would be there to support me. In the afternoon, with the dean of students, I made the rounds of the residence hall complexes, where we offered what assurances we could and answered questions. I grabbed a quick bite at the Bates cafeteria and then headed back for the vigil. I'd always loved the walk from the new dorms to the academic heart of the campus. I lived in Bates my sophomore and junior years—half of my college career—and made the passage hundreds of times. Alone, with friends, in every season, in every mood I walked down the sloping path from the three-dorm complex, crossed the meadow in front of the Science Center, and felt my eyes drawn to Galen Stone Tower, 200 feet high. It rose up out of Green Hall and was the very essence of Collegiate Gothic. This is college, it said. *I'm* at college, I would think. A great college. How lucky I am.

The carillon in Stone Tower started to peal. It carried me back to the fall of 1963, thirty-eight years earlier, the date November 22. President Kennedy had been shot. The vice president, LBJ, had been sworn in. My political science professor instructed our class to go back to our dorms. I was a sophomore, rattled and confused as were all my friends. Speechless, we were glued to the TV on our floor until late afternoon when an "all house" announcement instructed us to come down to the main living room. My friends and I crowded onto sofas, chairs and the floor. President Clapp stood at the front of the room. She wanted us to know that the nation would survive the blow, as shocking as it was. I was glad she had come, but could feel the tension in her body. It undermined the reassurance she meant her words to convey.

Now people were streaming in from all directions to fill the open meadow. Hundreds of students were sitting on the grass with their candles lit. It was a beautiful fall night, the air still, only the murmur of muted voices floating across the green. The sky was as deeply black now as it had been impossibly blue all day. The mood was somber but, more than that, it was sacred—the candles, the boundless sky, all of us were open, needing nothing more than connection.

Victor led a moment of silence, followed by a prayer, then, quietly, yielded the microphone to me with a simple "President Walsh."

"An act of terror is intended to destroy the foundations of coherence and meaning," I said, "but in this place we can summon compassion and mutual support. We can move through the uninvited tides of emotional reactions—fear, rage, grief, disbelief—and allow them to move through us so that we can in time move on. There will come a time—and soon—for us to try to make sense of what has happened. In all its complexity. The scholarship of multiple disciplines is what unites us in this place of learning. The effort to make meaning of chaos is our duty and our trust."

Then the carillon started up again with melodies that stirred memories of every kind of elation and sorrow that had visited this college community over its 125-year history. I was undone by the sounds. Chris walked up to the platform and took me by the hand. It had been the longest day, one none of us would ever forget.

Up early the next morning, I was leaving for the office when the phone rang. It was Jane, and her voice braced me. She had news she wanted me to have before I left home. She struggled for composure, and then:

"Rahma died in the crash, with Micky. And the baby."

Rahma Salie and her husband, Micky, were on the American Airlines flight from Logan Airport bound for Los Angeles. She had worked in the President's Office all four of her student years. Rahma was a beacon of light and we loved her dearly. When she started dating Micky, she was reluctant to tell her parents. He was not a Muslim, she was, and her family expected to arrange her marriage. But soon the whole family had fallen for Micky. He and Rahma were married in the Wellesley Chapel. She was 28 when she died; Micky was 32. They were en route to the wedding of a Wellesley friend. Rahma was pregnant with their first child, due soon.

When I arrived in the office, the air was thick with sorrow. I called Rahma's parents who ran a bakery in Newton. Their daughter loved Wellesley, they said through their tears. Could we arrange a memorial in our chapel? Of course. I offered the President's House for a reception. I called

Victor, who had officiated at Rahma's wedding, and he agreed to oversee the arrangements for the following weekend.

Victor and I joined Rahma's family and hundreds of mourners from all over the world in our chapel. In the raw agony of this senseless rupture of all that was right and good, it was hard at the time to see the service in its larger context. But it was a brief moment when our local Wellesley tragedy knit strangers together. Muslims, Christians, Jews, Hindus, people of many faiths and of none, gathered in a profound ritual of grief, we were as one.

Over the next few days we began to deal with the repercussions of the event, both the immediate effects on our campus and community, and how Wellesley could marshal its resources to respond. The FBI had contacted our chief of police for access to student records from our summer school. Two years earlier we had started it for our own students, and others. To my amazement, I now learned that two nieces of Osama bin Laden had taken our courses last summer. My senior team was divided about how to respond. Some raised concerns about personal rights and civil liberties. Should we—the administration—allow ourselves to be enlisted as agents of the government? Others could not imagine hesitating to cooperate with a government investigation of a terrorist attack on our nation. We would insist on a subpoena, of course, but that did not obviate the civil rights concern. We were hung up—or I was anyway—on how realistic it was to think that Wellesley could find a new way of responding to violence. If liberty was going to fall victim to security, then the United States might, in effect, sacrifice democracy in a gesture to save it. That was the big picture.

A more immediate concern was that the agents were considering interviews of faculty and staff who were on campus last summer, those who might have had contact with their persons of interest. On this we were unanimous. We did not want federal agents loose on the campus asking questions and stoking fear. In the end, after the agents scoured our student records in the company of three members of our team, they determined that there was nothing in the files to justify further investigation. We were off the hook.

"God help us if we find out that we've been harboring anyone responsible for these acts," a colleague muttered a few days later at a national
meeting of college and university presidents. I breathed a private sigh of
relief, and did not mention our near miss with the FBI.

I asked the deans to assemble a group of faculty for their thoughts on
what of substance the college might bring to the crisis. These were professors from a dozen departments, intellectual leaders all doing research
relevant to the terrorist attack.

"We have an opportunity to think in a whole new way about the
twenty-first century and American empire," a religion professor said,
going for the big picture. A historian raised questions about "how we witness," and cited her studies in Rwanda as a reminder to listen to people
for whom terror was not new. Another historian worried about "the con-
catenation of events," and how that would affect our ability to address
fear about an uncertain future, about things that have not happened. A
German professor found terrifying the assumption of a national consensus behind a violent response. She wanted us to throw ourselves into the
public discourse.

Had this attack shattered my illusions, my Panglossian liberal world-
view in which the moral arc of the universe does bend—eventually,
anyway—toward justice?. I believed in social progress rooted in reason
and research, in the possibility that we, in this microcosm I was leading,
could cultivate places for all of us to congregate in peace, and mutual
regard. Where would I come out of this abrupt attack that had breached
so much I had taken for granted? An English professor, a pacifist who
studied Thoreau, touched a raw nerve in me when he said he was repulsed
by "the kill-the-bastards talk on our online conferences." Me too. But it
was my job to make space for the full range of conflicting views.

Then came the slow baritone of a Nigerian philosopher and poet. "We
ought to be very engaged in supporting the Muslim students. And we
should *not* pin this on US support for Israel. This is not the time for that."
I mentioned a number of steps my team was taking to reach out to the
Muslim community. We were focused on that. But I didn't pick up right
then on the significance of his warning about Israel. I later came to wish
I had.

From another historian especially close to Muslim students came a caution I did take to heart. "We must *not* ask them to speak *for* Islam." She studied Somalia and Sudan. "And if they criticize the US, we must *not* assume that they approve of what's happened." She was fighting a losing battle, she started to say, as her voice and eyes lowered, "managing my anger." She and I had been exchanging emails over several days about her concerns for Muslim students and I thanked her publicly now for her care, and acknowledged how painful it had to be for them—and for her.

Flower Sunday, Wellesley's oldest tradition, is held on the second Sunday of every academic year. In recent times it had become a centerpiece of the college's revitalized religious and spiritual life program. This year it was five days after 9/11.

Young alumnae living up and down the east coast had traveled back to campus for the weekend. I just needed to be here, they said to me, needed to reconnect with friends and faculty, find some solace, begin to make sense of what had happened. Many threw their arms around me in a full-body hug. Quite a few were crying.

The chapel filled rapidly, this place of peace to which some of us had retreated for moments of respite over the last four days. Wellesley's drumming group, Yanvalou, issued the call to service with the rhythms of Africa. Victor opened, a commanding presence in his vestments. I followed with a few words about our purpose and ended with a Vaclav Havel poem. "It is I who must begin," it opened, and closed. "Whether all is truly lost or not depends entirely on whether or not I am lost." The service was a tapestry of ancient and modern threads, holy and secular, and ended with the organist pulling out all the stops for our customary recessional, "Ode to Joy." I lingered a while on the steps to take the measure of the students. Most headed off in small groups, looking carefree, at least for now. I breathed a sigh of relief.

At the regular meeting of administrative directors I opened with a moment of silence, a pause I'd never asked of this pragmatic group, some 100 mid-level to senior managers, three-quarters women, from units all across the campus. I thanked them for keeping the college going and said I wanted to hear their thoughts—what has been the worst of it for you, and what do you need now to begin the healing? They spoke of tensions between regular obligations and new, unprecedented, demands, of tensions between work and home, focus and distraction, time standing still and yet racing out of control, surges of fear, then feeling flattened. I knew this as a conscientious group, serious almost to a fault. But now they were telling me they didn't want to be here. They felt detached, dissociated. Their question was how to progress to a new normal. What might that look like?

Many spoke of small kindnesses they extended to students who seemed lost, and kindnesses students extended to them, or to fellow students. Waves of what someone called "parental energy" coursed through the room. Many expressed special concern for students of color, lest they be blamed or shamed. Koko, an elderly member of the resources staff, offered her personal story as a Wellesley student at the outbreak of World War II, a young Japanese immigrant. The college prevented her being shipped to an internment camp. Her words conveyed everything we needed to hear right then, I said when she finished.

What of our fundraising campaign? David Blinder and Lynn Miles, who led the campaign, had contacted our volunteers in New York City to take their emotional temperature. Two-thirds said we should carry on with our plans and upcoming meetings. We would skip the fall annual giving appeal and replace it with a letter from me. The campaign leadership committee chose to move ahead with their scheduled meeting—many passing through Logan Airport, still eerily shuttered. We shortened the meeting and devoted one morning to a conversation I led about what had and hadn't changed for our campaign. I offered my thoughts and invited theirs on how to address the incongruity of running a major campaign on the heels of a national tragedy, and in an economic downturn.

Susan Vogt, our new vice president for finance, brought news of the budgetary impact of the attacks: the unanticipated changes in enrollment, with cancellations of junior year abroad and students unable to travel home for fall break. There would be pressures on our operating budget, and on budgets of parents and students suffering post-9/11 financial reversals. Already a few had filed for financial leaves of absence. The ramifications of this calamity would continue to affect the college for years.

At a Senior Staff meeting in those first weeks someone raised the issue of flags. There weren't many flying over campus, which was "interpreted to have meaning." In the suburbs that surrounded the college, American flags were on display everywhere, in front of all but one or two houses in most neighborhoods. My office had been fielding student requests that we install more flagpoles and fly more American flags but I had held off out of deference to international students and my own belief that this was a time for us as Americans to recognize the world. More than a few faculty and students had been posting comments on the electronic conferences critical of knee-jerk jingoism and veiled militarism. Others had countered with heartfelt expressions of their patriotism. There would be some bitter disagreements, I was sure. In this volatile mix we hadn't decided yet what, if anything, to do about flags. My inclination was to age the problem for a while.

But I sensed something deeper. Was another gap opening within my senior team, like the one days earlier about the FBI visit? This one cut across a new axis. Had our educational responsibilities changed in this newly ruptured world? As divisions among the faculty became more pronounced, I was hearing a range of opinion among Senior Staff about messages the college should and should not try to convey to students, faculty, others.

The academic deans advocated a decentralized, organic approach, which sounded right to me. A multiplicity of voices and choices, not any kind of institutional response purporting to speak for the college as a whole. They'd been conversing with faculty about what had been happening in classrooms. How were faculty taking up the new reality? Some, meeting their first classes after the attack, delivered prepared remarks. Others opted to stick with what they knew, their course material, and avoided commentary altogether. There was no right or wrong approach, the deans felt. And I did too. They had heard from some students who wanted faculty to discuss the attacks in class, and from others who preferred that the classroom remain a refuge.

We wanted to move on—or I did—but my team wasn't ready to follow me.

"We have to find a middle ground," said one.

"There is no middle ground," insisted another.

"It's all middle ground," said a third, exasperated.

"We need separate and integrated processes," added our process expert, Pat, "to contain both the emotional responses and the intellectual questions. Our challenge is to *keep it* complicated." Pat had a gift for holding complexity with curiosity about what it might in time reveal. Well-designed processes can offer grounding amid multiple and competing allegiances—to country, to religion, to conflicting values. Above all, I said in summary, we must ensure that our campus remains a place where people can disagree. Many intellectual, moral, and emotional questions will continue to flow out of this crisis, questions related to patriotism, civil liberties, human rights. What constitutes just war? What conditions are necessary to sustain civil discourse?

Some of these questions were taken up at a seminar offered by three of our faculty who volunteered to offer students some context for making sense of what they were hearing and, at the same time, to model how to discuss controversial issues with intellectual rigor, mutual respect, and integrity. I encouraged the effort and attended.

The first speaker, a sociologist, positioned himself as a lonely conservative willing to stand up to reflexive liberals. He invoked George Orwell to classify himself as a patriot in a defensive response to this attack. We must not excuse mass murder by blaming US government policies, he concluded, "the basis of any morality is to hold individuals responsible for their actions."

The second, a young philosopher, distinguished between a rational "exchange system" and a "spectacle system" that followed a logic of excess, was nothing but surface, conveyed many meanings, and none, demanded only our attention, and was all about performance. The 9/11 strike unleashed the spectacle system, he argued, and disabled the mass media's search for truth. I was fascinated by this concept of spectacle as a weapon of terror. It rang true to me and boded ill, I thought, for the role of a free and responsible press as a pillar of democracy.

Next up, a junior faculty member, also in philosophy, asked how we should assume responsibility for something that happened *to* us. When we are responsible not *for* it but *in the face of* it? We begin by trying to understand it, he answered. It was an act against three kinds of order:

global capitalism (the World Trade Center), state legitimation of violence (the Pentagon), and Western liberal democracy (the White House). An attack on "legitimacy itself," designed to "snuff out the very legitimacy of our existence," leaves us to ask whether we have acted responsibly toward "the values that confer our legitimacy, now tragically exposed." What have we been doing in the name of freedom and dignity?

In the margin of my notes I flagged this part of the talk. "These are our questions," I wrote. It is for the academy to pursue self-knowledge, to come to terms with our flawed understanding, to ask sincerely what we as a nation have become.

Already, across the country, any impulse to look honestly at provocations underlying the attack was being branded unpatriotic. I'd heard rumors of an "enemies list" of academic scholars being labeled unpatriotic in their pursuit of exactly these questions we were asking. Keeping the academy open for a free exchange of ideas was going to be ever more challenging, I scrawled at the bottom of the page. And never more vital.

Through many conversations, in the weeks following, with faculty and administrators, I was reminded of how different my role was. Many spoke of feeling detached, disoriented, but if anything, the crisis had riveted my focus, centered my energy, heightened my sense of responsibility to every member of Wellesley's extended community. I felt responsible *to* our history and *for* our future. I was moved again and again, by the vulnerability my colleagues revealed to each other and to me. If we could continue being this honest and open, I was convinced, we would emerge stronger and clearer about the values we wanted to preserve and about what, concretely, made those values so important to us.

Faculty, students, staff, I'd been meeting with many groups, young alumnae back over the weekend for Flower Sunday, alumnae volunteers across the country and the years. They were standing by to get back to work for the college. The trustees, with whom I was in constant contact, were eager to help us move forward with confidence. They were aware— all of them—that we were doing something distinctive here. We were trying to reserve judgment, insist on respect, listen for larger meanings and for the unanswered questions that had a claim on our attention now. As these and other themes interacted in the crucible of multiple conversations, they had begun to crystalize a way forward for the college.

Despite all our best intentions there was one aspect that did become a full-blown conflict. It came to my attention that we had scheduled a college-wide event on Yom Kippur, just days after the terror attack. It was a dumb mistake, but the harm was done. The grievance escalated and was read as further evidence of our disregard for the Jewish community. It became clear to me now—and too late—that I should have reached out to the Jewish community with reassurances right after 9/11. As I did to the Muslims.

Relations between the two groups deteriorated. I held multiple meetings with Victor and the college rabbi. Also with representatives of Hillel, including distraught students and a cordial and constructive group of six women faculty leaders who were Jews and had always, without fanfare, made it a point to support Hillel. They were a small but tightly knit group, a model of mutual support.

We worked things out and developed stronger policies to honor religious holidays, but not before we'd stirred old antagonisms from *The Jewish Onslaught*, in particular my choice not to use the label anti-Semitism in my censure of Martin's book. I would not be forgiven by a senior professor of history, a male and a Zionist who had his own history of bitter resentment of what he perceived as Wellesley's chronic anti-Semitism. He came after me with a vengeance, denouncing me in public as *the* anti-Semite. That stung. Of course I couldn't defend myself with the cliché that most of my friends were Jewish, true though it was. It grieved me to have failed the Jewish community at a time of conflict and pain in the Middle East. I would try to make amends as best I could.

Wellesley faculty organized a number of successful public events touching on roots and ramifications of the terrorist attacks. Some featured scholarship within their departments or in dialogue across disciplines, some with outside scholars. An anthropology professor who spent a sabbatical year in Afghanistan brought in an Afghani speaker, Ashraf Ghani, from Johns Hopkins University. In 2014, Ghani would replace Hamid Karzai as president of Afghanistan. For now he was introduced to us as a friend, a distinguished anthropologist and one of the most prominent Afghani professionals in the United States.

Professor Ghani traced his country's history from the time the Soviet Empire ended in Afghanistan and the whole world turned its back. Warning strongly against the temptation to equate Islam with extremism and terrorism, he reminded us that one billion of the world's people were Muslim. Americans knew almost nothing, he said, of a history that went back 1,400 years, of a religion that through its history had been extremely tolerant, of a country, a former crossroads of exchange and ideas during the robust silk trade, that was one of the few societies in the world never colonized.

In our two hours the professor filled in some lacunae, but left us—or me for one—humbled by my ignorance of this remote world. I exited the lecture hall, and sensed that others did too, determined to lift up the complexity of questions being flattened by our nation's primitive reactions. I was encouraged to see the academic deans' organic approach to excavating the lessons of 9/11 proving itself. The faculty were convening voices to offer our small community deeper insight.

A few days later I flew to Indianapolis to speak at a conference for university and college trustees. Sponsored by a national higher education organization that specialized in governance, they had invited Parker Palmer to lead it and he had asked me to join him with a president's perspective. When Parker opened his talk with the assertion that "unconsciousness is a form of violence," I thought of our Afghani guest, and our many efforts to come to terms with responsibilities imposed on us by the terrorist attacks. "We need disciplines to hold others in our consciousness," Parker continued, and distinguished an institution from a community. Institutions are instrumental. They have their own goals. If I give myself to it, my love to it, it does not love me back. A community is a continual act of forgiveness—of ourselves, and one another. Leaders can create hospitable spaces for that forgiveness, he concluded. Or not. Few see it as part of their role. He turned to me as a president who did.

He was right, I did see my role in that broader way. I told the story of our attempts to respond to the learning demands the terrorist attacks

Chris and Diana with First Lady Hillary Rodham Clinton and President Clinton, at a White House reception for Hillary's thirtieth reunion class, June 1999. Courtesy William J. Clinton Presidential Library. Photographer unknown.

With Phillip, the regal springer spaniel acquired during Allison's "dog therapy." Photographed by Richard Howard.

With Tony Wang and Lulu Chow Wang '66, in front of the Lulu Chow Wang Campus Center, in Alumnae Valley, after the dedication ceremony, Fall 2005. Courtesy Wellesley College. Photographer unknown.

With Madeleine Korbel Albright '59, during Diana's final commencement ceremony in the big white tent, June 2007. Photographed by Richard Howard.

With Kathryn Wasserman Davis '28, and Lulu Chow Wang '66. Three "bold" Wellesley women, 2010. Courtesy Lulu Wang. Photographer unknown.

Gardener Sean with his grandmother, 2011.

With His Holiness the Dalai Lama, at his personal residence in Dharamsala, India, for the Mind and Life XXVII dialogue, November 2013. Courtesy Mind and Life. Photographer unknown.

At the Broad Institute's tenth anniversary celebration, 2014. From left: Eric Lander, president of the Broad Institute; Eli and Edythe Broad, founders; DCW, chair of the board; Drew Faust, president of Harvard University; L. Rafael Reif, president of MIT; and David Baltimore, chair of the Broad Institute Board of Scientific Counselors and president emeritus of the California Institute of Technology. Courtesy Broad Institute. Photographed by Kelly Davidson.

had made on us, how we saw ourselves in this altered context. We were women who were in conversation with the men in our community, Americans who were in conversation with many of our number from other parts of the world, a campus surrounded by a town with values different from ours. We were a community with as many differences as we had commonalities, I said. And we had our conflicts. I was determined that we learn from these.

14

TESTS OF LEADERSHIP

"What's this?" Chris walked through the side door into the President's House with a grin on his face and a bag from The Gifted Hand, the upscale shop in the center of town where we went when we wanted to splurge on someone special. Inside was a large box wrapped in blues and greens, my favorite colors.

"It's not my birthday."

This was back in June of 1999.

"A milestone marker. Open it." It was a black and white paper lamp shaped like a smiling dog. "His name is George," Chris said, and pointed to the tag.

"Cute. But why?"

"You've outlasted Ruth Adams," he said. "The shortest presidency in the history of the college."

In the early years, when my spirits sagged, we invented that meager goal: just don't be the shortest hitter, outrun that ultimate ignominy. Was I ever that insecure? Well, yes, on bad days. They were infrequent. Most days were good, and they were getting better. George would accompany us through a series of moves in the years to follow, the decades of expansion and then contraction of our living quarters and our lives. All the way to California in the 2020s where he continued to laugh with us.

I moved into the middle years of the presidency with confidence. I had a framework for "trustworthy leadership" that I wrote and spoke about. Five commitments I believed would help me remain worthy of trust. I lived them as best I could and they steadied me. Item three on the list was to value differences—of opinion, perspective, and world-view—as a crucial part of life and learning. I saw this as an ethical imperative and a measure of respect for others. But also as a unique creative resource. I had learned to listen for the voices from the margins that carried the buried wisdom that could unseat my self-deceptions.

The post-George years brought ferment from those voices; on occasion they provoked me to doubt myself. But the periods of tension were over-shadowed by a procession of notable successes. I and my many partners would look back with pride on the blueprint we created for the future of the college, the funds we raised to secure it, and the rapidity with which we advanced our best ideas—many transformative ideas. In my mind it was always "we," I and my partners, never I alone. It was the partnerships that made the successes possible, made them meaningful, infused them with energy and fun.

In the end, we would take pride in our diversity too, and what we made of it, the strides we took toward greater equity, even knowing it as a work in progress. It was my heaviest lift, one I experienced as a constant concern. Wellesley was among the most diverse colleges in the country. Finding talented women of color had allowed the college to survive the existential threat it faced in the late 1960s when the leading male colleges began to admit women. Diversity was a key factor in our recovery from what could have been a mortal blow to our applicant pool. Even as we celebrated our diversity as a major source of strength—and it was—I was confronted often with the question of what more our diversity demanded of us, of Wellesley and other historically white institutions approach-ing another millennium in America. We were opening a new century in which the nation would shift to a minority-majority society. Why did we so often find ourselves in deadlock, unsure that we were rising to the challenge fast enough?

Wellesley shared this struggle with other American institutions whose founding myths and moral understandings of race and ethnicity had, in the past, been as ambiguous, blinkered, even shameful, as were those of the nation as a whole. This reality was being underscored in new lines of scholarship that were rewriting the nation's history. Rooted in the Progres-sive Movement, Wellesley's political center swung back and forth through the years, but the college was focused now on equal opportunity and social justice. That was part of what had called me back to my alma mater.

Back to Wellesley, a strong and wealthy institution with a proud past that blended high standards of intellectual striving with an abiding ethic of service. We attracted idealistic students who came to us looking for the knowledge and wisdom they would need to be leaders in a changing world of porous boundaries, hybrid identities, and shrinking natural resources. I wanted us to support them in forging out of their differences the skills they would need in such a world.

From my earliest days in the presidency I experienced our multiculturalism as a balancing act. It forced us to face hard truths about where we were falling short. Our students of color required that of us, and so did those who brought us other forms of diversity: LGBTQ+, social class, culture, religion. These students were backed by many white student allies. And by faculty and staff of color, together with whites among their ranks who also championed multicultural goals.

The goals were straightforward enough but devilishly difficult in the details. Faculty and staff champions of diversity, less numerous than the students, were essential to progress. They were up against a wall of resistance that was genteel, largely invisible, and quietly implacable. The forces of tradition were intent on upholding values some feared were receding. Like the Wellesley Glacier in Alaska, named for the college in 1899 by the Harriman exploratory commission, and melting away.

I convened working groups and asked them to gather more data. I asked for fresh approaches and commissioned new reports. I found faculty leaders to take on this work and funds to bring in outside consultants, outside speakers, and encouraged my team to reach out to peer schools and create collaborations. We hired new faculty. I delivered speeches and wrote wordy memos I'm not convinced anyone read. I threw all these familiar tactics at mutating challenges. The world itself was changing, and, with it, expectations. We put out fires. Then, as if carrying a votive candle to a vigil in the dark, we would trip over a branch and ignite a new conflagration.

So I was not surprised when yet another large student coalition raised provocative questions about how we were delivering on our promise to become an inclusive multicultural community, one that saw and valued all its members. Not so well, they concluded. I was saddened, though, and determined to keep their questions alive. Not because Wellesley had unusual problems but because we had unusual opportunities. Obligations was not too strong a word.

An area that demanded my attention, I decided, was the division of student life. Parts of it seemed to operate through an underground web of connections, preferences, and entitlements. I saw this as an unhealthy breeding ground for unspoken judgments and implicit bias. In one of the division's departments we unearthed a backlog of student complaints that pointed to acts of perceived discrimination. Some hadn't been followed up. Microaggressions, we might have called them, but the term was not yet in vogue. To address the pattern would require a cultural shift, I knew. For starters I would need more diversity in my leadership team. And all of us would need more experience with ambiguity, discomfort and conflict. We were searching for a new dean of students at the time and I instructed the search consultant to bring us a strong pool of women of color.

Following a national search led by a campus-wide committee, I brought in a new dean from a smaller, lesser-known college. The campus reaction to my choice was swift and severe. This is not who we are; not who we want. She is not sophisticated, not polished enough for us. I heard versions of this from students and staff as they undermined her authority. We had seen leadership qualities in her during the search, but I watched this barrage of criticism shake her confidence. I hoped she could rally, and set out to do all I could to help her succeed. It would be a steep uphill climb with boulders raining down on us for a full four years until I had to admit defeat.

That first fall, as usual, the CFA met weekly to conduct tenure reviews. Just before winter break, we always released the results to candidates and their department chairs. As luck would have it, in this fall of student discontent, our marginal case was the candidate who could bring needed diversity to the college and the curriculum. The one whose department chair said she didn't believe in truth, and whose scholarly and teaching records were just adequate, if they were. That was for the CFA to decide. After weeks of deliberation, CFA decided they were not.

Word went out. The campus erupted in disbelief. Anger and outrage at the tenure denial fed on itself and rose in a frenzy night after night on the online conferences. It was reading period, then exams, then winter break, the worst possible time to drop a lighted match into a vat of explosive material. But the tenure calendar was fixed; we had no choice. Still, I was unprepared for the response this time, the force of the student coalition that formed overnight. WAAM they called themselves, the Wellesley Asian Action Movement. They went to the college archives to read up on the protest movements of the late '60s, and drew up a broad set of grievances and demands. This was language I hadn't heard since my days at Barnard and Columbia. I was summoned to a meeting of the college government senate where a dozen or so WAAM organizers brought me their ultimatum. It felt like a declaration of war.

The demands included something for everyone on Senior Staff. I assigned each member to a subgroup of students to search for common ground. Andy Shennan, at that time associate dean of the college, took the students' curricular concerns seriously, more so than they did, as we discovered when we polled them to find out who would sign up for the new courses they were demanding. They admitted that, actually, no one in their alliance would. They were busy with their majors and other academic commitments. But these courses *ought* to be in the catalog, they told us. After all, there was a whole *department* of Africana Studies. Andy explained the realities of how change happens in departments and disciplines. Slowly. And suggested they continue a conversation over time. They agreed to drop the curricular demands that had triggered their rebellion. But we were not home yet.

In time the students coalesced around a single unresolved issue on which they were prepared to go to the mat. They wanted a full-time cultural advisor for Asian American students. After all, Ethos had one, the director of Harambee House, celebrating its thirtieth anniversary with its alumnae founders returning to campus. We offered counterproposals, and they rejected every one. They organized a sit-in outside my office, generated a lot of buzz and a torrent of electronic mail. Our discussions continued the following week, with little forward movement. I was standing on two principles. First, my administration would not be drawn into a coercive exchange. We would collaborate, but not under duress. Second, the specific configuration of administrative roles was my responsibility. I wanted to hear about students' unmet needs but I would not cede to them the authority to dictate how the needs would be met. The students continued to insist on a full-time Asian American cultural advisor. Nothing else would do.

The student body was changing rapidly, with proliferating subgroups of students, many with hyphenated identities. All longed to be acknowledged and valued. Equally. As they should. But we could not afford to hire specialized staff, carve and fit out dedicated campus spaces, and expand the faculty and curriculum to meet rising expectations of each of these small groups. Our costs were excessive already, and our budget was unforgiving. Any concession we made would raise the bar again for the next time. We needed different solutions, more flexible structures.

We had a cultural advising network that paid existing college employees for extra hours to counsel students from backgrounds similar to theirs. WAAM was arguing for unique counseling for each subgroup within their coalition, including South Asian, East Asian, Korean, Japanese, mainland Chinese and Taiwanese.

"The pressures we feel, the expectations of our parents, the way we are perceived," were some of the factors their representatives told me about. They brought me tears, rage, and touching personal anecdotes. But I held the reality of other variables that complicated their stories even more. Family circumstances and wealth for example. Gender identity. Religion. There would be no end to these sub-classifications if we were to reify them in policy. That was my chief worry.

I could see their frustration too. But I was not ready to commit new resources that would set more precedents and tie the hands of my successors. That would be irresponsible. I tried to slow things down and invited students to help us look into other ways to meet their needs. But they wouldn't wait. The momentum they'd worked so hard to generate was beginning to dissipate and they were worried. They wanted a victory. They insisted they would gladly collaborate with us *after* they had their full-time advisor. I couldn't help but admire their tenacity.

The week before Spring Break I heard forecasts of an impending hunger strike. Then, on March 5, the popular part-time advisor to Latina students resigned that part of her job in a gesture of solidarity with WAAM. Her announcement was intended to undermine our case that the part-time model was working. It did. A group of Latina students joined the protest

and called themselves SLAM for Sisters Leading Action for Multiculturalism. WAMM-SLAM presented us with a whole new set of demands. Influential faculty and staff sympathized openly with the student activists.
They asked why my administration was being so stubborn, so "stingy
with our huge endowment." They raised doubts about our "institutional
commitment to multiculturalism." This was a proxy for the emotionally-
laden question: Does this college value *me*—*my* heritage, *my* life story, *my*
perspective, *my* people?

SLAM reached all over the country with word of the threatened hunger
strike. I was knee deep in a swamp of outraged email from outside the college. I read in the local papers on Monday, April 2 that the hunger strike
would be launched outside my office the next morning. With Senior Staff
I developed our best counteroffer, one that preserved our administrative
latitude yet gave the students a victory. Members of Senior Staff met with
them off and on all day but the students held firm. Then, just before midnight, they agreed to our final proposal.

The student newspaper, the *Wellesley News*, crowed that the administration had caved in. My position was that we had preserved the flexibility I needed. We would hire two new half-time advisors, one for Latina
students, one for Asian students. The other half of both advisors' time
would be spent reinventing all of our multicultural programs from the
ground up so we would not find ourselves in this position again.

I was heartened to begin the 2000–2001 academic year with a new and
effective management team in the student life division. Yes, we had a
problem, still, with the top leadership and it remained to be seen whether
the dean could succeed. But I believed the struggle had strengthened the
division—and the college—and opened up new avenues of dialogue about
how we could work together across our differences. Maybe the worst was
behind us. Was I kidding myself?

One more push. I prevailed on Sally Merry, an influential professor of
anthropology—a classmate of mine—to lead yet another task force on
student life. We handpicked a roster of constructive faculty, staff, and
student leaders. I asked them to place the recent skirmishes in a wider
context—recent college history interacting with world events—and to lay
out a program of practical, long-term reforms. The committee worked all

year and did a superb job. Whether the students would settle down was another question.

Apparently not. The college government president elected for the 2001–2002 year was a firebrand. In the confusion of the 9/11 terrorist attacks she set out to provoke the president in public. She posted one hostile question after another about changes in student life. Why did we make this change? That one? Who said it was a good idea? What problems did we think we were solving? Had we noticed that we were actually making problems where none had existed? A spectacle for all to watch.

I answered a few of her questions and, after a while, responded with an abrupt post that ended ENOUGH! It was time to hold a boundary. Word came back indirectly from an opinion leader in the English department that if a faculty member had spoken to a student in that tone, she would face serious consequences. No, not likely, I said to myself, but held my tongue.

Chris and I had a welcome break for Thanksgiving with Allison and Thomas in California. She was starting her fellowship in oncology at Stanford. Shortly after I returned to campus, Lee Cuba, now the academic dean, came to see me. I could tell something was on his mind. He began with the suggestion that he and I host a series of conversations at the President's House with faculty who were distressed about the state of student morale. Partway into our meeting I heard him mumble the words "vote of no confidence."

"What?!" I said to Lee and he made light of it. Idle chatter, but I should be aware of it. A no-confidence vote from the faculty was the kiss of death. Things were going from bad to worse. I did host the meetings, five of them, with groups of faculty and explained to them why I had been so intent on supporting this dean of students, the college's highest ranking African American administrator. I saw her thrown back on her heels by a negative response from the day she set foot on campus. I believed she still had the ability to prove herself. In those meetings, though, I began to face the futility of the lonely battle I was fighting. Maybe it was time for me to acknowledge defeat.

A wise trustee, Dozier Gardner, came to my office to suggest that I might be "investing too much presidential capital," his words, in my defense of the dean. "The opportunity cost may be too high." Dozier had seen me doggedly holding the line on a principle. I wanted the dean I hired to have a fair chance at building a successful career at Wellesley. She and I had given our all to an awkward partnership. The four-year effort had flattened us emotionally and taught us hard lessons about the thankless work of trying to move a strong culture. The dean would have to go, I realized. Telling her so was to be one of the harder conversations I would ever have.

Ironically, that painful ending also marked the close of one of the most celebratory years of my presidency, the 125th anniversary of the college, which we commemorated all year long. It began with a spectacular carnival on opening day at the beginning of September 2001—a week before the terrorist attack. A day of service the next Saturday—"A Day to Make a Difference"—engaged thousands of alumnae in volunteer programs across the country and around the globe and launched an annual tradition sponsored by the alumnae association. On April 20–21, 2002, we held a twenty-four-hour symposium in meeting rooms all over the campus featuring hundreds of graduates from across the decades in thematic panel discussions and speeches to showcase alumnae achievement and women's leadership. It was a multi-generational jubilee of women's contributions to the past and their hopes for the future, across every conceivable dimension of difference. In May, as the capstone on the anniversary year, I moderated a panel discussion, at reunion, between Hillary Clinton and Madeleine Albright, our two path-breaking secretaries of state, close friends who graduated ten years apart.

Before commencement, the associate dean of students, Michele Lepore, agreed to step in as acting dean while we mounted a new national search. The two half-time cultural advisors hired on the heels of WAMM-SLAM reported to Michele when they arrived over the summer. They helped lead a committee that redesigned orientation week with a strong new sequence on inclusion and diversity. It brought the whole first-year class together at the same time the following fall, in lieu of pre-orientation programs that had divided the incoming class into racial and ethnic subgroups. This proved to be a big step in the right direction.

A year later, we would look back on WAAM-SLAM as an episode that set the stage for the arrival of a new dean, Kim Goff-Crews, a lawyer, an established leader in student affairs with a track record in developing diversity programs in higher education. In partnership with me and my Senior Staff, she would complete the transformation of the division. And I would come to recognize the years of conflict and confusion in student life as a period when student voices from the margins riveted my attention, and appropriately so. But I was not out of the woods, not yet.

Revolution Studios was setting up an encampment on our campus. It was early October 2002. I had consented to the invasion, which, I had been assured, would be brief and efficient. The sooner they decamped the better, in my view. This was the very least of the priorities I had in mind for what was going to be a busy year.

A year earlier I was approached for permission to film *Mona Lisa Smile*, starring Julia Roberts, on our campus. The movie, set in 1953, brought her character, fresh from a Berkeley PhD, to Wellesley for a coveted one-year teaching post in art history. A "free spirit," her character shook up the seniors' dreams of wearing a ring by spring and crossed swords with the administration and trustees.

It did not escape my notice that the screenwriters were both male. They had spent time in our college archives doing background research, and did get a few things right. They captured the importance Wellesley placed on close mentoring relationships between faculty and students, and the strains on women's roles in the '50s that fed the second-wave feminist revolution in the decades to follow.

When I previewed the screenplay, the license they took with the generation gap seemed a bit much. I saw it as a crude fabrication that denigrated everyone: students as empty-headed socialites, administrators as hidebound prudes, trustees as social snobs. Only Julia was set up to shine. But my opinion was of no account. Our lawyers told me so—our name was in the public domain. That left me with only one choice: where would this movie about our college be filmed? On our campus or in other venues the producers were free to call Wellesley College? Since the beauty of our campus was a major point of pride—and a selling point to prospective students—the choice seemed obvious. Move ahead. And then move on.

Our staff worked hard to foresee and minimize disruptions during the filming. As word went out, I was glad to pick up a buzz of excitement among star-struck students. I was sympathetic, too, with members of the faculty who grumbled about anticipated distractions from their classes. We would try to keep that in check.

I accepted an invitation to tea on the set with the actor, Marian Seldes, cast as the president. She asked about Margaret Clapp who, in 1953, was four years into a presidency she completed at my graduation. I told the actor her script had her character wrong. Clapp had encouraged women to reach for demanding academic careers. The script portrayed her as a guardian of home and hearth. Miss Seldes listened politely, but showed more interest in Clapp's mannerisms than her educational philosophy. A few days later the director invited me to make a cameo appearance in the film. Jane thought I'd have fun. Maybe so, but I had a gut feeling I should keep this circus at arm's length. I declined.

Within days our public affairs director, Mary Ann Hill, was in my office with news about the call for extras. Some 900 or so students and staff had lined up for the casting call; roughly 200 were selected. The studio was aiming for historical accuracy, so their selection criteria were biased against students of color. Mary Ann prevailed on them to offer off-camera positions, "production assistants," mostly to nonwhite students. She said that student leaders were philosophical about the historical constraints on the casting decisions.

But not for long. As soon as the cameras rolled, everything changed. The campus was swept up in the drama of a real-time Hollywood reenactment of our past. The local press ran interviews with extras who bubbled about the thrill of it. The hype sharpened the sting for those confined to the sidelines. The casting invitation had explicitly called for students with skin "not too tan." I hadn't seen that. Good lord! How flat-footed were these people? What century had *they* emerged from?

Our students of color saw it and went to the college archives. They found 12 students of African descent in the Class of '53. From the casting rolls they concluded that only one African American had made the cut as an extra. Students of Asian descent, meanwhile, seemed to be overrepresented. Black students organized a protest: "Too Tan for Mona Lisa Smile." Their leader was the multicultural affairs coordinator, the MAC, an officer of college government.

The MAC was a cabinet position that hadn't existed in my day. We seldom used the term multicultural. Or even diversity. My classmates and

I did want to figure out who we would be in the world, and to base that on a widened canvas of life experiences and opportunities. But many of us had only begun, in our day, to come to terms with unacknowledged social privilege and structural racism. We weren't exactly monocultural back then, but neither were we multicultural. Millennial students now were—courageously, self-consciously, and sometimes militantly so.

I emailed the MAC and invited her to my office with anyone else she thought I should meet. A half dozen students arrived. The MAC opened the conversation and was soon holding back tears. She'd been on the set last night. She'd watched her classmates, her Wellesley sisters, in costume, and instinctively, in character. "They *were* the Wellesley women of 1953," she said, "intriguing and intelligent women flirting with male visitors from Harvard." She, meanwhile, was "slapped with an eerie chill of nonexistence. There was no place there for me." Now she had a new understanding of stories she had heard all her life, stories that had seemed like ancient history.

I apologized and spoke of efforts we were making to ease the blow as best we could: more off-camera jobs, tickets to the Oprah Winfrey Show when the cast was scheduled to appear. We would offer them first to African American students, including the protest leaders.

In agreeing to the terms of the contract, they said, I had made Wellesley party to an act of overt racism. They were right, I admitted. I should have seen this coming. I described the choice I faced, the information I had at the time. There was no discussion of extras. And no hint of selection criteria based on race. I asked them to consider, on the other hand, the constraints on the filmmakers' choices. How should we think about historical accuracy in a work of fiction? How does their exclusion from this filming differ from—and inform—our understanding today of acts of racism fifty years ago?

What it felt like now, they said, was that their college no longer belonged to them. As though the institution had agreed to write them out of Wellesley's story. They worried about our future ability to attract students of color. Through their sadness and rage they constructed a compelling case that much more than their hurt feelings was at stake. Listening, it occurred to me that we could at least try to set the public record straight. I asked whether it would help if I were to write an op-ed piece.

I could try to communicate some of what this incident had underscored for us. What matters at Wellesley, how central racial and ethnic diversity is to us now, all these years later, what a different college we have become—deliberately and through conscious effort. They thought that could help. I drafted the proposed essay and ran it by them.

It reflected the discussions we'd had during and after the filming. How oddly disorienting we found it to be abruptly transported back a half century in time, there to witness the clash of two competing realities. The dramatic changes in the demographic composition of our student body were set against residual racial wounds we continued to carry as an institution in a changing society. Our students were exploring this paradox with courage, sensitivity and sophistication. That was how I ended the op-ed. After it appeared in the *Boston Globe* I received a note from the MAC.

"My meeting with you and your thoughtful presence has made a powerful difference in how I am dealing with the week," she wrote. "I find myself still secured in a place of love . . . and I am glad to have you here with me . . . Wherever Wellesley has come from, I am glad for where we are today and that we are guided by your leadership . . ."

The note remained on my hard drive through many computer upgrades. It retained the power to move me more than twenty years later. A small archival artifact to affirm the possibility of remaining in connection, even as we took a blind leap toward a new level of collective consciousness.

But nothing was ever that simple. Contraction followed expansion. It was only early November, and our most widely trafficked online conferences were alight again with fiery exchanges. A fledgling student organization had invited a speaker to campus, Amiri Baraka, the former LeRoi Jones. Jewish faculty were up in arms about his anti-Semitism. A few were caustic in their criticism of the students who invited him.

It was not that we were unequipped to handle controversial speakers. We had had our share. And we had a process. The Academic Council's lecture policy committee was established some years earlier to bring the review of proposed events under the watchful eye of a committee chaired by a faculty member selected for good judgment and a level head. Something had gone awry this time.

Long strings of posts chastised the committee and my administration. What were we thinking? Why did we approve this event? Critics acknowledged that freedom of speech might have prevented us from blocking it, but surely we could have insisted on a structure to put Baraka's work in context, surrounding him with sober perspectives and scholarly voices. When he had performed a jazz piece that blamed Israel for 9/11, he was poet laureate of New Jersey. Out of the hailstorm of outrage from the Jewish community, the state legislature had dissolved the post. I was appalled to find us back in the morass that nearly sunk me at the beginning of my presidency.

I was a different leader now. I had my own strong team and made sure that we were mobilizing networks of support for students and focusing on safety. It was too late to organize a different event with multiple speakers. I had a commitment on Saturday night and didn't attend Baraka's performance. The next day I was told that about 100 people protested peacefully outside the lecture hall, and did not disrupt his performance. The performance was a polemic to be sure, and grossly offensive to many, but the protest put the audience on notice that anti-Semitism must not be tolerated. On balance it seemed that we might have dodged a bullet.

No such luck. It soon became evident that we were left with two rifts. The first was within the faculty—a replay of the fracas centered around Tony Martin. Individual members of the factions in that fight in 1993 were back at each other's throats. On what authority did this student group bring Baraka to our campus? Who put them up to it? What were they trying to prove? Split politically, the faculty continued to argue their positions online weeks after Baraka had come and gone.

In addition, I was picking up troubling tensions between students and faculty. I saw negative comments from the restricted faculty-staff online conference show up on the community conference for all to see. This provoked some students to defend the student hosts against harsh criticism from some faculty who were calling them irresponsible. Or anti-Semitic. Or, in one post, "evil." Students were online far into the night arguing with each other and choosing sides among faculty.

I made sure the student life team was doing its best to help students who were caught up in the controversy. I wanted them to find common ground where they could take a breath and listen to each other, actually *hear* one another. I spoke to the Hillel and Al Muslimat chaplains, and the cultural advisors. I wanted to hear for myself how students described what they were going through. I found them sophisticated in some ways yet naive in others. Tough and vulnerable at once and, by my lights, admirable. Many of them felt let down by the faculty, let down by the college, let down by me.

The student president of Hillel sent me a blistering email. I asked her to come meet with me. How could the administration have let this get out of hand, she wanted to know? Why didn't I remove that man from her home, Wellesley College?

It didn't get out of hand, I replied, and it wasn't for me to remove him. She pressed on. There's a huge difference between controversial speakers and hateful ones. Baraka has been hiding his anti-Semitism behind anti-Israeli rhetoric since 1980.

But then she linked the talk to the influence of Tony Martin, implying that he might have been behind the invitation. He was poisoning students' minds, she said. She saw his book, *The Jewish Onslaught*, in the rooms of Black students. This hit me hard, tied a knot in my stomach. It had been almost a decade since I had buried that grotesque book. Or thought I had. Now the bile around it had surfaced again in our faculty? Had it been eating away here all along?

I listened to the Hillel president dismiss our efforts at dialogue as tepid and ineffective. She called the student multicultural council a joke. As Hillel's representative, she said, she was the only white member. Students of color accused her of whining. So what *is* anti-Semitism, they would say. Or how come every time I mention Israel, Jewish students act like victims? We need more support, she insisted. We need *your* support. I told her I was meeting that night with the Hillel alumnae board to map out next steps, but she wanted me to organize and host a high-visibility public event. It had to come from me. Directly from my office.

After the student left, I took a deep breath. Regrouped. I'd learned in the heat of the moment to hold my reactions. To pause. That made all the difference. With that—in that pause, in that decision to lean back into my body and reorient myself—I'd learned also to recognize and avoid the traps people laid for me, sometimes unconsciously, in their expectations, projections, and judgments about what constitutes effective leadership.

The Hillel president's demand that nothing short of an edict from on high would solve her problem had become familiar to me by now.

But it was not just *her* demand. The faculty were split in factions again, and up in arms. They sent me signals about what I had to do to win *their* approval. They made me, personally, the focus of attention, which—if successful—would divert me and my leadership team from the goals we were advancing in the college. We were instituting changes that, if successful, would intrude on those who might prefer to carry on as they had been doing. This was the implicit threat my team—any leadership team worth its salt—represented to the status quo.

To avoid these traps, I'd learned to read emotional upheavals as local weather squalls brewing within the college. I came to see them as evidence of forward movement, as dust storms that marked flare-ups of resistance to change. And then I tried to interpret them in the context of my long-term goals, held clearly in mind. My goals in this case related to diversity and community-building. I and the academic deans were making demands on the faculty to pay more attention to minority achievement. We'd led two recent retreats with the trustees on this topic, the second, just last month, in consultation with academic department chairs. Beyond that, we were focused this year on grade inflation, which was a hot button. So was the review of the honor code, no longer working as well as it should in the new multicultural era. Oh, and yes, as if that was not enough, we were threatening to take everyone's money away, or so it felt to many. We were pushing an all-out effort across the college to slow the growth in our operating expenses. As we pursued these goals, outside incursions—a movie filming, a controversial speaker—tied us temporarily in knots.

In the middle of storms like this, I had learned to focus sharply on my role and my task. I would ask myself, when I was feeling pressed, what do *I* need to be doing here to be useful, effective, constructive? How much of what I'm experiencing now is not my work to do? How much of it is the work of others who are resisting change? How can I redirect them toward more constructive work and deflect their ploys to cut off my sources of power?

For the time being, I was in temporary damage control. I began the familiar series of discussions about a public statement to distance the college from Baraka's anti-Semitism. The ADL was waiting to see it come out. It helped that the offender was not a tenured member of our faculty this time. It didn't hurt that I was conscious now of traps I wanted to avoid. Another one that often snared me in my early years was to dig too deeply into the content of an issue when there were others whose job it was to staff me on it. I knew I should reserve presidential attention—the unique currency of the office—for those instances when I was literally the last resort. My issue was that I was a sucker for the intellectual juice of vexing problems, whether mine to solve or not. People could see that in me. They saw a flashing red button they could push. I struggled to resist but this Baraka conflict was juicy. It tripped questions about free speech and hate speech and stereotype, about truths and untruths, about power and privilege and which groups did and did not have access to money to underwrite campus events.

There were deeper questions too about politics and art and what con- stituted artistic freedom. Pat Berman, chair of the art history department, came to see me. I liked her tremendously. Young with a lively mind and a great sense of humor, she was a distinguished scholar. She had been talk- ing to students who asked her for advice about the Black Arts Movement and how to think about the contributions it made. For her troubles she was now being pilloried by faculty colleagues.

"I can't believe I am the face of anti-Semitism at Wellesley College," she sighed. I couldn't either. She had been one of the faculty members who came forward during the Martin affair to co-teach a popular course on propaganda and persuasion. It was one of the responses that helped bail me out. I cited it often in those days when I was on the road visit- ing alumnae. It served as reassuring evidence that the faculty were doing their job to heal the wound, taking up the educational challenges embed- ded in the nasty controversy we were trying to put behind us.

That night, at home, I drafted a brief public statement from the college and returned early the next morning to my conference room with a large group of student leaders. I'd invited those I expected would have a stake in what my statement said—a lesson learned from the Ethos meeting in my first year.

I opened this one with a few words about leadership. How easy it is to become isolated, beleaguered, split off from your natural allies when tempers flare. To feel dehumanized. It happened to me at times, I said. I had called them here in the hope that we as a leadership group could stay in contact. I had a draft statement and my plan was to read it and invite their comments. We would not edit it line by line. But I did want to hear their reactions before sending it out. I read it all the way through.

"You're going to alienate a lot of people!" The Ethos president was first to respond. She and others objected to specific passages, phrases, words. They questioned my emphasis. The African American leaders were looking for more support from me for their decision to bring Baraka to campus, more affirmation of his work as a voice that expressed some of their reality.

I was troubled that they felt the need to bring such a hateful voice to campus. I said this more than once. It wasn't the anger that interested them, they insisted. It was the empowerment. He sees our struggle and affirms it. They took issue with a lukewarm comment in my draft affirming aspects of Baraka's work to admire. They wanted me to name specific contributions. We went back and forth and then I insisted I had gone as far as I could. I turned the tables. What did they admire in his work? Blank looks. I held the silence. This was a telling moment. No one in the room was expressing much concrete admiration for this man's art. The silence became awkward.

One of the Ethos leaders broke the tension. She didn't understand all the fuss about anti-Semitism and hinted in a convoluted way that Jews had disproportionate influence on campus. This allegation set off alarms in my head. The bogus Tony Martin complaint. That was simply not true, I said.

Then I returned to her other comment: you say you don't get anti-Semitism. So tell me this. Does the inability of many white people to fully understand racism make it any less real? Silence. I felt a stiffening in the room. Whose side is she on? We thought she was with us. I took a breath and looked for signs on the students' faces that the question had penetrated as fully as I hoped it might. A tiny opening? I couldn't be sure.

When the meeting ended, I made some notes and then revised the statement, incorporating some of the students' suggestions without diluting the firm repudiation of Baraka's hate speech. At the end of the memo I called the whole college to account. Especially the faculty, both those who were caught up in this fight and those who sat it out. Behind the measured words I wrote was a heavier-handed message that I dared only imply: you have a choice. You can be at war, or you can be in dialogue.

What I didn't say in writing but did take up in private conversations was that the community as a whole—the majority—had sat on the sidelines and watched these poisoned arrows fly by. As though staying out of the fray—being inactive or passive—was morally neutral. It wasn't. The students were left to make sense of the conflict on their own. They needed to hear from informed grown-ups, from peacemakers who could introduce them to a larger context. The essence of it was that we do not demonize each other. We never—ever—tolerate that.

I was noticing that most often it was the male faculty who indulged the loud ideological rants. And the women faculty who quietly picked up the pieces and knit relationships back together. Of course there were male peacemakers. But few female flame throwers. We needed all the faculty voices, including those of the quiet relationship-menders. But also powerful voices of reconciliation. People willing to stick out their necks. I said at every opportunity to faculty that students needed them in these conversations. Our job at college was in large part to encourage students to tear apart their easy assumptions. But it was unacceptable for faculty, for their own purposes, to recruit students into their private political wars. And equally unacceptable for avowedly impartial faculty to sit back and watch this happen. There was no room for impartiality, no excuse for treating students like objects. I did not want us to look back on this incident as though the students themselves were a crisis.

I also knew that handoffs to others were not enough. I myself needed to develop a clearer understanding of what it would mean for my administration to take up campus divisions in a more genuine way. What was my responsibility, as president, to stand with people in this community who said they had been hurt by others here? If I stood with everyone, pretty soon I would be standing with no one.

The Hillel president made another appointment.

"I used to love Wellesley," she began. "I can't now. The students who invited him here should at least acknowledge that he was hostile and rude. They won't, and you backed them. The message you sent out to the community was not true; their intentions were *not* innocent. There is a double standard here. And it is racial." As she prepared to leave, she turned and asked me a question.

"Is there something written in the job description of an administrator that says you have to be neutral all the time?" This was her parting shot, my last encounter with her. Her points about the double standard were not entirely wrong I had to admit to myself, but I disagreed with her critique of the role I was choosing to play. I was half tempted to send her a writing I'd been incubating about what constitutes trustworthy leadership, five principles that I believed made all the difference. Questioning myself was the first. Honoring my partners, the second. The fourth and fifth spoke to the value of diversity and the cultivation of community. But the third answered her particular question about neutrality: A trustworthy leader makes a conscious choice to avoid the use of force, except as a last resort.

Leadership is by definition the exercise of power. But as tempting as it is to wade in with what looks like decisiveness, over and over I had seen that interventions imposed from on high seldom produced lasting peace. It was hard not to exercise force, painful to look like a weak or clueless leader, easier perhaps to settle for simple solutions to complex problems. But it was even more painful to watch disputes smolder and reignite in debilitating cycles of repetition and escalation.

To avoid the use of force was to commit to being nonpartisan, to be the person whose effectiveness depended on hearing all sides of a dispute. It was my job, as I saw it, to take in the many perspectives that summed to a whole. If I were to become captive of one or more of the many voices, then I'd soon be waging war within myself. My task as the leader was to create conditions within which disputes could be explored and transformed at the most local level possible, the place where those most directly affected could assume responsibility. Here they would be in a position to discover their own resourcefulness and to bring their best selves. That would have been my answer to my student interlocutor. I doubted she was in the mood for a mini-lecture from me on leadership.

Over the Christmas holidays, *Mona Lisa Smile* was released to theaters amid much fanfare. In eager anticipation, the alumnae association had worked with local clubs around the country to organize viewing parties. A major motion picture about *our* college! Within days, we began to hear isolated cries of foul about the film. Alums were *not* liking it. I was not either. The college came across as even more hidebound than it did in the original screenplay, and the students snobbier. The film lacked subtlety, said the early critics. They were right!

And then a great hue and cry rose up from the Wellesley faithful across the country. Graduates from the '50s led the charge. These were gross distortions of the college we know and love. An egregious misrepresentation of the serious students we were then. A review in *Time* magazine began with the fanciful question, "Can a college sue a movie for libel?" It was obvious to them that this was a hatchet job. Our alumnae were asking similar questions. What's the college's relationship to this frivolous and insulting film? Why did you permit the filming? Was it for the money? How much did the studio pony up? How much is it hurting our reputation? What are you doing for damage control?

Mary Ann Hill put together a briefing for reviewers, with demographic comparisons of students in the '50s and the early '00s, and commentary on how and why we were different now. Under a blizzard of alarmed correspondence from riled-up graduates, I sent a letter to the whole alumnae body, already revving in high gear as a volunteer public relations engine determined to clear our good name. I expressed my regret for the distress the film had caused, described the circumstances in which I had consented to the filming, countered the rumor that we did it for the money, which was trivial, cited evidence that applications continued to roll in at the same rate as last year, and that some of the applicants even cited the film as an inspiration. I thanked the many people whose op-ed articles, interviews, and letters to the editor had gone a very long way toward correcting the historical distortions. I appreciated their well-documented and cogent arguments to set the record straight.

Katha Pollitt—a Radcliffe graduate and well-established feminist commentator—took a few swipes at Wellesley in her *New York Times* review of the film but went on to trace the progressive, even radical roots of the college from our inception. It had never been anything like a finishing school—in fact, it was the antithesis. A Wellesley alum and university administrator sent me a copy of her long and irate letter to her local newspaper's editor. She closed it with a flourish: "All of this *mishegas* because of a lousy movie."

I took that as a fitting requiem for this short-lived film until John dropped me a few weeks later at the president's house at Mt. Holyoke College for the annual seven-college conference. I was ready for a few words of sympathy from my sister presidents who knew how enervating the flak catcher role can be. I walked in the room and the first words I heard were: How come Wellesley gets all the breaks? A Julia Roberts movie. *The Oprah Winfrey Show*. A priceless free publicity coup. How did you pull it off?

Dumb luck, I said. Which pretty much summed it up.

15

TO HOLD IN TRUST

I first met Dick Chait in the early months of my presidency. A governance expert well known throughout higher education, he was a Harvard professor who taught at both the business school and the graduate school of education. To launch her term as the incoming board chair, Gail wanted to convene a trustee retreat that would focus on board practices and philosophy. We hired Dick to facilitate it. He would design and lead a process for us to discuss and refresh our committee structures and charters, meeting formats and agendas, and our shared understanding of what it means to be a member of a board whose job is to hold an institution in trust. The president is an *ex officio* member of the board of trustees, as I did know. Beyond that, I was in catch-up learning mode.

As we began to plan the retreat, Dick made a point of meeting initially with me in my office. He recommended that I, as the new president, kick off the retreat with a talk that would set a tone and lay out some of my hopes and aspirations for the college. This was, by then, a familiar topic. He didn't say, but I later recognized, that part of what made him so good at what he did was his sensitivity to the importance of balance in the partnership between a president and a board chair. I did learn much from him during that retreat at the outset of my presidency, much about governance, much about leadership, and more still about that vital partnership with the board.

He must have liked us too, because a few years later he came out with a published case study that portrayed the Wellesley board as an avatar of excellent governance. He taught the case in courses at both Harvard's business school and its education school. When he premiered it at HBS, I sat with Vicki Herget in the back of the classroom, and enjoyed answering students' questions after they'd dissected the case.

Another higher education board came my way in 1999, when Amos Hostetter, Amherst's board chair, came to my Wellesley office to offer me a seat on his. I said yes, and not only because Amos was a persuasive man. Like Wellesley, Amherst College was one of the top liberal arts schools in the country. Amherst had been a single-sex institution until it began admitting women in 1975; Wellesley stayed single-sex. Here was a chance to compare and contrast.

I quickly became a key player on the Amherst board. Earlier that same year I had joined the board of the State Street Corporation and was playing catch-up there on issues of banking and finance. So it was refreshing to participate on a board where I had keen instincts for the nuances of issues. At Amherst I found it exhilarating to test my ideas with a small, cosmopolitan and highly interactive group of trustees, most alums, from many backgrounds, all intellectually engaged. We waded into the thorniest issues facing higher education. I always came away with my thoughts clarified about those issues and, equally, about leadership, about what it took to lead a small and feisty faculty of brilliant, fractious scholars to the satisfaction of a devoted and vigilant board.

The Amherst board was different from Wellesley's in interesting ways— smaller and more male for starters. But it, too, was excellent and an extraordinary opportunity to see first-hand how the voluntary nonprofit sector functioned on its highest plane. These two colleges exemplified the societal benefits of "thinking institutionally," the title of a book by Hugh Heclo that would come out in 2011 and reinforce my belief in the uniquely American model of the liberal arts college, with its indispensable volunteer leadership and support. From my very first interview with the presidential search committee, the Wellesley trustees were essential to whatever success I had in the job.

A case in point: I was starting my tenth year in office, returning to campus from a meeting downtown when the car phone rang. John was driving. I answered and was surprised to hear our outside audit partner on the line, seldom a bearer of cheery news. She called to inform me of a potential problem that seemed to have originated in an innocent question Susan Vogt had raised last year. Susan was the CFO I recruited after I decided to split finance from administration. I'd made that decision in close consultation with Vicki, who, as my second board chair, brought expert knowledge of finance from her years as an investment professional.

Susan had hired the audit firm and they began to raise questions about how we booked endowment gifts. The initial query, it seemed, had ballooned into further doubts. My caller spoke in an argot I needed to check with Susan. She had initiated a preliminary review of our audit controls and it sounded as though something spooky had been unearthed.

"Gee, boss," John said when I hung up, "you sounded worried." I told him I was and asked him to take me home rather than to the office. I wanted to meet Susan at the house, in private.

"Can't do that," he said. "Orders from Jane. She said to be sure to drop you in front of Green Hall. She needs you there. Not sure why." We'd turned into the campus, so I let it go. John rounded the corner at the side of Severance Green and stopped the car. Something was up. It looked like a festival.

No one had mentioned anything to me. John was a picture of studied innocence. He opened the car door and sent me toward the commotion. Ah, it was a stealth party. A fall fest organized by students, Lake Day, a relatively new tradition. They had arranged to surprise me with an early tenth anniversary celebration. Jane promised to deliver me. She had the right impulse, but for the phone call. My head was spinning around the prospect of a donnybrook over our financial management.

There was nothing for it but to join the relay race. A plastic flamingo marked the finish line, a tribute to the quinquennial reunions of my class when the pink birds overran the campus. I pulled on the T-shirt a student handed me and dashed across the green full tilt, to whistles, cheers, and applause.

After several conversations with Susan and then Vicki to sort things out, I called a special meeting of the trustee finance committee, a small and powerful group of senior executives in financial and legal fields. The chair was John Clarkeson, the Boston Consulting Group CEO who had warned me when I first met him that culture is hard to change. He was the ally anyone would want in a pinch, a wise and clear head, judicious and kind. Ed Lawrence, a Ropes and Gray senior partner, had been vice chair of our board and a strong supporter from the day I arrived. He was a key adviser to me, as was Vicki. These were three trustees who ranked very high among my trusted confidantes, partners, and also friends.

Over a period of weeks they led us through a series of tense meetings with one then another audit firm. These were meetings in which I often held my breath. I watched in awe as these skilled trustees provided my new CFO the cover and coaching she needed not only to clean up the problem but also to convert what might have been a rout into a victory. It became a chance for her to learn and to strengthen our finance team and our financial controls for the future. I recognized this as an instance—one of many bestowed on me—of trusteeship practiced as a high art. I'd long known how lucky I was to have this stellar board and, once again, was grateful for their help.

It was not that we were out of the woods financially, I reminded myself. We still had major money worries that would dog us through the year. I'd pushed my Senior Staff, with Susan as the point person, in an all-out effort to eliminate jobs and shrink the operating budget, a potentially poisonous stance for the organizational leader who means to win friends and influence people, especially while also celebrating major new gifts to a capital campaign.

We adopted a new fiscal mantra: growth by substitution, not by accretion. It was slow suicide to watch our costs—and with them our tuition—rise far faster than general inflation as they had been doing for over a decade. If we kept this up, fewer and fewer families would be able to afford us. The trustees were clear about this. So was I. Fiduciary stewardship was the trustees' most essential responsibility in the shared governance of the college. And to complicate matters, the trustees were also our principal source of philanthropic revenue.

Susan hired a new controller, and they resolved the accounting problems. No heads rolled. And we managed the cognitive dissonance of shrinkage in a time of growth as best we could through several years. But whenever I saw the old photo from a crisp October afternoon, it took me back to a schizophrenic moment of joyful abandon with the students. I was in a light blue Lake Day T-shirt that covered the blouse I had worn to town with a wool navy pant suit. White pearls askew, arms akimbo, dashing, laughing. Just minutes before it was shot, I was sure I had big troubles.

How did we manage the dissonance? After a decade on the job my own management approach had evolved. I learned much from and with my partners. From my teams, òne after another, handing off the baton in a relay race through time. I enlarged my understanding of how to work with teams, much of it refined in experiments I ran with Dick Nodell.

I enlisted my colleagues into intentional partnerships, a construct that enabled me to lead from my strengths while I recognized and promoted the strengths of those around me. I found people who were willing to take the ride with me, people who could tolerate uncertainty, who had the self-confidence to open themselves to worldviews that might oppose— even threaten—their own. These colleagues held themselves to high standards of performance and yet forgave mistakes, their own and others'.

I reviewed these commitments with Senior Staff at regular off-site retreats. A week in July; two days in January. We went through our goals for the year, worked through disagreements, and engaged in exercises designed to solidify relationships within the group. I designed the agendas with Dick, who facilitated our conversations. I sought input, always, from Pat and Kate.

Fast forward to April 2004 when the trustees were back on campus for their annual meeting. With Vicki and my senior team, I'd been pushing them hard. We had run two retreats in as many years focused on academic achievement. Were we serving all our students as well as we should? As attuned as I often was to how students were doing outside the classroom—questions that landed them in my office—my larger obligation was how they were doing academically. I wanted to shine a light on the reality that students of color and from low-income families were relatively less successful at Wellesley than were our other students. While we shared this problem with other schools like ours, it deserved our attention. Lee Cuba, as an academic dean who was a social scientist, had a firm hand on data that framed the problem. I had him present the picture to the trustees for discussion at their retreat the prior year. In October, to follow up, we set aside an extra day and a half with the trustees so that they could press academic department chairs on what they could do to ensure the success of all our students. The question continued as an active discussion topic at this April meeting.

We were hearing committee reports when Jane appeared at the door, spotted me at the head of the table next to Vicki, and signaled. How often had I looked up to see Jane in a doorway and known in my gut that something was terribly wrong? These would be some of the most vivid memories of our years together, along with many merry ones. I slipped a note to Vicki, and she called a break. A student had been reported missing—for a few days, unclear how long. Her mother was in the air en route to Boston from the west coast and I was needed at the campus police station to meet her. I told Vicki to make an excuse for me and left.

The rest was an extended nightmare: an interminable wait for any word from the state police, broken by the horrific news that they had found her body on campus. A week later I flew across the country for a funeral at which the many people assembled from every stage of her life could not fathom the coroner's ruling that it had been a suicide. Her high school friends were there, along with high school teachers, siblings, aunts, uncles, friends of the family. They tried to make sense of this calamity, but it was impossible. Several wanted us to know that she seemed happy at Wellesley.

"We knew her much longer than you did," a family friend pulled me aside to say, "and none of us saw this coming. There's nothing you could have done. You didn't let her down."

Three of her Wellesley friends had accompanied me to the service. They provided loving, touching, and quite ordinary accounts of her last few days: a shopping excursion to Tower Records, an ice cream at Newport Creamery, an orchestra practice just before the big concert. She was looking forward to the prestigious summer internship in mathematics she had won. Her Wellesley professor was tremendously proud of her.

"It just doesn't add up," her mother said with each additional detail. Every one of us agreed. We did not know what happened—could not know. We did know that every parent's worst nightmare was to send a child off to college, never to return, and that every educator's worst nightmare was to fail to protect a child whose parents had entrusted her to our care.

Her mother had no doubt about the legacy she wished for her daughter at Wellesley. "Take care of yourselves and each other," she implored our three students as we left. They promised they would. I promised myself that I would remember forever the grace and generosity of this remarkable family in the depths of shock and grief.

Posts appeared on the community conference about stress and sadness, depression, mental illness. Students wrote personal stories of wounds, fears, thoughts of suicide. Many faulted my administration for what students experienced as a cover-up. To guard our reputation, they alleged, we drove suicide underground. We made it worse because we heightened the stigma. Grief gives way to grievance, Victor reminded me again. The weight of holding the sorrow becomes too painful to bear. It explodes in anger.

We had a strong counseling program in the student life division. Our mental health providers in the Stone Center closely followed the science. They worried about suicide contagion, and I did too. I was balancing the expertise of the psychotherapeutic community and our lawyers' liability concerns against the family's privacy rights and students' clamor for open discussions. We were concerned to see increasing mental distress among college students across the country, but I didn't have the foresight then to foresee the worsening crisis this has since become. At the time, I experienced it in part as another uncomfortable tension between conflicting perspectives.

At our summer retreats I brought my Senior Staff together to prepare for the year ahead. Often, this was a time to mark transitions. We had none in July 2003 but several in the offing. Michelle would continue as acting dean of students just until August when Kim Goff-Crews would arrive. Kim had stood out in a national search I conducted the previous year while Michelle brought her sensibilities as a healer to stabilize the division and move it forward. Kim was a great hire, I felt sure. With her partnership, I hoped finally to shape a modern student life division of which we could all be proud.

As I drove the thirty-five miles from my home in North Falmouth to the retreat center in Brewster, I was thinking about the team and the many beds of hot coal we had walked together, barefoot. I felt indebted to each of them, and to each of my teams over the past decade. I was mindful, too, that after five momentous years, this would be Lee Cuba's last summer retreat as dean of the college, the second-ranking officer after the president. Andy Shennan and Andrea Levitt, Lee's two associate deans, would be with us this week, as they had through his deanship. A key priority of mine for the year ahead would be to lead a selection process for the third chief academic officer of my presidency. I was leaning toward Andy as Lee's potential successor but needed to consult with faculty. I knew the trustees had great confidence in Andy, as they had my two previous deans, Nancy and Lee.

The minute I arrived, Dick pulled me aside. Be sure to speak to Susan before we start, he said. He didn't have to warn me that the news was ominous; it was inscribed on his face. Susan told me she had just been diagnosed with lung cancer, small cell. She had never smoked. It was too soon to know the prognosis or what would be involved in the treatment. She was upbeat. She always was. That was part of what we all loved about her. She had joined us only three years ago but had already proven herself a presence. She had been leading the Senior Staff through the minefield of cuts to the operating budget. And with support from the trustee finance committee, she had hit her stride as my CFO. Now this? I could scarcely believe it. I was frightened for her.

I found it hard to be hopeful about lung cancer and was careful not to inflict that bias on her. She was confident in her doctors and wanted to carry on with her work. Susan was a widow and an alumna. When I recruited her, we moved her from New Jersey and set her up in a college-owned house within walking distance of campus. She lived there alone. Her two grown kids lived far away. She felt okay now, she told me, and hoped the treatment wouldn't lay her low. Her job would keep her going, she was sure. She needed it now more than ever.

Will Reed was on a glidepath toward retirement. No longer a member of Senior Staff, he was not at the retreat, but I reached out to him to discuss how to support Susan through her illness without putting the college at risk. He suggested I contact a former CFO he knew from Princeton who had retired to Florida, Ray Clark. I called him and explained our situation. Ray was touched by my desire to enable Susan to continue working as long as she could and agreed to move temporarily to Boston in a consulting capacity—for as long as we needed him.

The trustees were back on campus October 16–17 for their opening meetings of the 2003–2004 academic year. For the resources office, we had scheduled two events around the meetings. This would be a time to honor trustee donors and mark milestones, looking backward and forward. The first event would be a celebration of ten years since the dedication of the Davis Museum and Cultural Center, the building complex I dedicated in my first month on the job. I had become a convert and enjoyed citing the evidence that the Davis had taken root and flourished. Long gone were my worries that too few students saw the museum as a resource to enrich their learning.

The second event we initially conceived as a groundbreaking for the ambitious three-body project in Alumnae Valley: campus center, parking garage, and eleven-acre landscape renewal. On this major project, too, I had begun a skeptic, but became a believer after participating in a decade-long discernment process. We had multiple trustee planning committees, selection committees for architects and landscape architects, multi-constituency campus committees to work with the professionals, and more, much more.

"A great architect and a great client produce a great building," Ed Lawrence said. It takes a partnership. With the trustees and the committees, we had spent hours walking the campus with Michael Van Valkenburgh, our landscape architect, and additional hours circling a massive model created by Mac Scoggin and Merrill Elam, our building architects, and with their many colleagues.

Like the conductor of a symphony orchestra, Pat had led a process that involved alternating solo artists, and multiple small sections, inspired by an attentive audience, in one after another exploration designed to inform a fundamental question: How can a multicultural community that is rapidly changing find its center and common ground? How, specifically, can its physical assets contribute to the realization of this aspiration? Pat was in constant consultation with groups of students about their needs, and with groups of faculty and staff about their ideas.

By now the ground was thoroughly broken, so we improvised an amusing alternative ritual: beam signing. We made speeches—or I mostly did—and we signed our names to a beam that would hold up the garage. The trustees and principal donors, Kathryn Davis, Lulu Wang and her husband, Tony, the architects and landscape architects and developers, other donors and champions of the project all signed the massive steel beam, temporarily dressed up in ribbons and balanced on classy sawhorses for our baptism by Sharpie. It seemed unlikely that anyone would ever see our handiwork once the beam disappeared into the building, but it was the moment that mattered, as was so often the case.

The board dinner was scheduled for the next evening. Jane alerted me that attendance would be heavy, probably because of all the special events, she suggested. Vicki would take care of the program. She would make it low-key. Everyone would be ready to just relax with friends, she said. Fine with me.

But the trustees had my number again and I walked right into the ambush. Vicki had organized a lavish surprise celebration of my tenth year as president. Every trustee had hand-picked a special volume of poetry for me, each wrapped and inscribed with a personal note or card. Each one generously selected, thoughtfully presented. It was a magnificent collection, each book expressing the donor's personality and speaking to mine. They gave speeches—many speeches—of praise, appreciation, thanks. They told stories, many stories. We had many laughs. Nicki Tanner, a dear friend and former vice chair of the board who had a knack for such things, had written an elaborate and hilarious song and made everyone rehearse it. They sang it flawlessly. Pamela Melroy, our astronaut, presented me with a small art glass model of Earth that she had carried in my honor to the International Space Station and back, on a mission of which she was the commander. She told the story of the letter I had written her when I learned of her selection as an astronaut and her response to me. "Holy Cow!" she had written, "I have a letter from the Wellesley president!" Holy cow, I wrote back to her, I've written to an astronaut. I could barely go to sleep that night as I turned the evening's memories over in my mind.

The next morning was the full board meeting, starting as usual with the president's report. "As good as it gets," I opened it, Jack Nicholson's comment to a group of patients in a psychiatrist's waiting room: "Have you ever thought this might be as good as it gets?" I turned Nicholson's sardonic humor on its head. I actually could not imagine it getting better than it was that night. What struck me most was that the words felt so real, so true, because they made no demands or claims on me. They were pure gift. The gift of seeing and being seen, knowing and being known, in these powerful relationships that bound us together in common cause as we held the college in trust.

Susan's cancer was aggressive, formidable. We stayed close to her during her treatment. Too soon she was home with hospice care. Pat and Jane stopped by regularly to sit with her. I joined them at her bedside when I could. In late October we four were there together as the end approached. Susan died that week.

A large crowd showed up for her memorial service in Houghton Chapel. She had many more friends and admirers than we had had the chance to meet, or even hear about. All of us would miss Susan: her spontaneous, upbeat style, her hearty smile. She would pat herself on the back and chuckle when she pulled off a tough assignment. Her outside professional colleagues endowed a "leadership fellowship program" at The Boston Consortium to embody her spirit. Ray was honored to lighten her burdens up to the end. He agreed to stay for the year or until we could find a replacement. A huge gift to us.

At the end of the 2003–2004 academic year, Lee would step down as dean. We celebrated his accomplishments with the trustees at his final board meeting. From the time he joined Nancy as her second associate dean, he and his team achieved amazing results. We updated the curriculum, addressed grade inflation, revitalized the honor code and created two endowed day-long conferences to showcase student work and faculty mentoring. We enhanced the quality of the intellectual community for students, faculty, and staff and invested in interdisciplinary study and experiential learning. We anchored the humanities and the social sciences in two new centers, each endowed by a trustee, that fostered intellectual exchange and interdisciplinary research.

The future of the learning and teaching center was secured with another endowment gift from a trustee. Our faculty were becoming leaders in efforts to engage new learners more successfully, those who came from disadvantaged backgrounds. The center itself had become more effective in helping students sharpen their study skills, to develop the "pedagogic intelligence" essential to success in college. I was especially heartened to see this, I who had arrived at Wellesley with the belief that

I should mask my insecurities, pull up my socks, and sink or swim on my own. A lonely way to learn—and live—as later life taught me repeatedly. The partnership with Lee was pure pleasure.

So was my partnership with Janet Rapelye, my dean of admission from the day I stepped on campus. This was her last board meeting too. Princeton poached her from us, and I named her associate dean, Jenn Desjarlais, acting dean while we conducted a national search. I was sure Jenn would be my choice; Janet had mentored her well as all of us had observed. But the search was in the spirit of due diligence and to ensure that Jenn would have the legitimacy she would need to excel in the role. She did.

As for the new dean of the college, Andy Shennan was the hands-down choice to succeed Lee. There was no doubt in anyone's mind and none whatsoever in mine. He would be exceptional. He already was. For his associate deans, Andy and I selected two scientists, Joanne Berger-Sweeney, a neuroscientist, and Adele Wolfson, a chemist. Both had earned the admiration and respect of faculty across the college. We could tell that from the surprising lack of grousing among humanists and social scientists about the disciplinary imbalance this created in the dean's office, a vote of confidence in the quality of the sciences at Wellesley, and of the work Joanne and Adele were doing to remove barriers to success in the sciences for all students, regardless of background.

In June 2004, I took my new team on a two-day retreat, Joanne's first as a member of Senior Staff. At the break in the morning session she rushed up to me, breathless, incredulous.

"Diana, I had no idea," she exclaimed. "I never imagined that Senior Staff *thinks* so much!" I smiled. I'd long known that faculty everywhere saw administration as mindless make-work. As I once did. As my sister did, and many other faculty, who shunned colleagues if they showed the bad judgment or weakness of character to be lured over to the administration.

Years later I would speak at Joanne's inauguration as president of Trinity College in Hartford, Connecticut. I would tell the story of her epiphany at that first retreat. At Wellesley I watched her bring her fertile mind to the ongoing question of how to improve the experiences of students and faculty, and to advance equity and inclusion. Joanne would now be one of a trio of three impressive and quite different African American women on Senior Staff—Joanne, as the new associate dean of the college; Kim, the new dean of students; and the long-time EEO director, Linda Brothers. With their partnership, we would make headway on the diversity issues that had so often tripped us up.

With that goal in mind, I created a new group in January and gave it a banal name, the January Group. It had no official status and no public face. It would remain under the radar as a place where we could be candid about our efforts to root out racism and discrimination. It would include Joanne, Kim, and Linda and a few others including Victor, and Michelle, who chaired the group at my request. I asked her to poll the members a week before each meeting and select the most meaningful question at that particular moment. The first month's question was: Where is racism most firmly rooted in Wellesley College now? And why there? Everyone had different ideas. Power came up often as the source of the problem, and I did my best not to be defensive. I didn't always succeed at not taking it personally. At a meeting toward the end of the academic year, my colleagues noted a negative tone in my offhand comment about the two extra positions we'd authorized a year earlier in the wake of the WAAM-SLAM protests.

You sound resentful, they told me. As though your hand was forced.

Well, wasn't it?

My colleagues reminded me that at the time I had called it a good solution. They went on to review what had happened since. Student leaders had been especially constructive and collaborative in the past year, they pointed out, and we had results to show it. Almost without controversy, we'd moved issues that had seemed untouchable. Students agreed to eliminate the pre-orientation programs that for years had been segregating incoming first-year students by race and ethnicity upon their arrival on campus. A huge win in a negotiation we had repeatedly lost. The administration and faculty were now back as partners in the management of the honor code, which previous students had carved off as their private preserve, and we had implemented a serious plan to address grade inflation, an especially unpopular topic. Students insisted on referring to it as "grade deflation." They had come a very long way in new and fruitful collaborations with the administration.

A few weeks later, at commencement, I went off script briefly during my charge to the seniors to admit that they had been right. This was an oblique reference to the protests during their freshman year, and the skirmishes that had continued through their next three years. Few of the guests in the tent would have had the slightest idea what the president was talking about. But the seniors knew; some of them surely did.

The trustees knew too; they'd followed the whole drama. They were seated behind me on the dais, as usual. On this day I was channeling their dinner for me in October—how fully seen they had made me feel that night. Recalling that evening brought to mind the developmental process most of us navigate, if seldom consciously, when we discover within ourselves depths that only then we can detect in others: the fullness of who *they* are, their unconditional worth. That gift of appreciative seeing lies at the heart of learning. When someone else sees us in our full potential, bears witness to that capacity, values it in us, relates to it in a way that makes it real, it is then that we come to trust it in ourselves. And this is the beginning of knowing. Before we see, we must be seen. I hoped that some of the seniors who had, during their four years, bumped up against my administration would take in my quick acknowledgement of their efforts, would feel respected for their persistence, appreciated for their determination to make Wellesley more welcoming of all students from all backgrounds.

16

THE TIN CUP

"I could not do your job," strangers would say to me. "I could never ask people for money." Odd, I sometimes thought, that they singled out that one task. As if the rest of the job would be a slam dunk for them? But I held my tongue and kept to myself doubts I had at the start about how *I* would do raising funds.

As a child I was influenced by my mother's Depression-era discomfort with money. Her father's publishing company fell "into the hands of the receivers." A classmate's father threw himself off a roof when his business collapsed. Money and mayhem. Best not to bring either one up, awkward and unseemly. We lived comfortably on Dad's salary and seldom spoke of finances. But I could tell they troubled my mother. She never earned a dime of her own and seemed skittish the few times we ventured into the upscale shops in Chestnut Hill. When the plaid kilt I needed for an ice-skating show was available only at the Dorothy Bullitt Shop, we rushed through the fitting and couldn't escape fast enough. She didn't belong, did not want to be there. And when I lost the wristwatch she gave me, she was furious. "You don't deserve to have nice things!" were the words first out of her mouth. The truth was I didn't want them. They were too dicey. Money was too loaded. I never wanted to be the treasurer of any organization in school or in college. I'd take any other role, but not the money job; it was not my thing.

But then I landed myself in a job that required bringing in big bucks. At BU and at Harvard I'd raised a few million dollars for my research. But this was different. Wellesley was known for its well-oiled resource development operation. It had state-of-the-art practices, a strong staff and volunteer organization and a constituency of loyal alumnae intent on keeping the college "hopping," an image from my first contact with David Stone when he called on behalf of the search committee. My job would be to keep it hopping—higher. The costs of college were rising fast, driven by intense competition among the most selective schools for the best students and faculty. One attracted the other. Success bred success and so did a healthy endowment.

I was coached on how to approach donors at the "leadership gift" level. You'll be meeting with alums and their husbands, the consultants said. Pay attention to dynamics within the marriage. Note who's taking charge but be sure to hear them both. Let them know that they, and only a few other couples, are positioned to make a major difference for the college during your presidency. Build relationships over time. Engage in no transactions, and never a *quid pro quo*.

They had a formula. I'd be successful if I would come to experience interactions with donors as a privilege that was ours to share, an opportunity for us to ensure that our college would continue to thrive. It sounded reasonable, I said to myself, but theoretical. Then I discovered that the donors themselves were going to be my best teachers.

My first development event was week three on the job. I flew to New York City for an intimate dinner party with a dozen or so leadership gift couples at the home of Suzy and Donald Newhouse. Suzy had seated me next to the oil-baron husband of a graduate from her decade, the 1950s. No sooner had I reached for my napkin than he announced gruffly that the college denied admission to both his daughters. I put my napkin down. They went on to other colleges that served them well, he continued. Now, in the prime of life, both were successful business executives and influential community leaders. I looked him in the eye and told him that Wellesley had clearly blown it.

Across the table, I caught his wife's sympathetic gaze. And, for my fourteen years—as for many previous ones—Norma Hess donated millions of dollars to the college. Her husband Leon needed to register his irritation to this new president, and I to acknowledge with regret that it was obviously our loss. Later, when people asked whether big donors bought admission for their children to elite colleges, this story came in handy. Wellesley always kept our admissions decisions separate from fundraising, a principle validated by Norma's loyalty.

The resources office owned a quarter of my calendar. The head of leadership gifts met with Jane every August to block out a series of trips. In year two they cooked up the "Welcome Diana" tour. Working with the alumnae office, the resources team arranged visits to the college's strongholds across the country. I was to meet with the local alumnae club, make a speech, and then dine with one or a few major donors, staffed by the leadership gift officer responsible for that region.

The night before my first trip to Texas I was sitting up in bed going through the briefing book when I was stopped dead by an entry. I read it to Chris. The person I was scheduled to see, the memo said, is "not exactly hostile but certainly disaffected."

"Good luck," Chris chuckled.

Over dinner the following night at an Austin restaurant, I inquired about her college experiences. All good. Where's the hostility, I wondered, and guessed she'd reserved it for the leadership gift officer, the author of my briefing. She asked me about my start-up adventures, and I drew on an expanding trove of stories about learning the ropes. She seemed to relate to those. Early the next morning, the phone on my hotel night table woke me. My dinner companion.

"It's going to be a big job," I heard her say. She wanted to make a big gift to express her early confidence in my ability to succeed. Would I like $100,000?

Indeed.

Chris, meanwhile, had been fundraising for the Dana-Farber Cancer Institute from the time he became president in 1991. When, two years later, we notified Dick Smith, Dana-Farber's board chairman and a business titan, that I'd been offered the presidency of Wellesley, he was appalled. "You can't do that," he insisted, as if I would simply now decline the offer. "Your husband needs you at his side." Dick was used to having his way. Chris and I pretended not to hear him.

But here I *was* at my husband's side in Palm Beach, Florida, both of us on the road raising funds for our two causes. I was channeling the austere

Miss Clapp, my Wellesley president. In my senior year, as a member of the college government cabinet, I met with her often. One day she told us she'd be away the next week. Out on the road with her "tin cup." It wasn't like her to crack a joke. The visual stayed with me.

So I was traveling with Chris, equipped with his-and-hers tin cups. He had the gilded one. Dana-Farber events were rococo. Black tie galas, expensive entertainers, bells and whistles. A photo of Chris holding forth earned a place of honor on the piano in the President's House. Standing on a large stage, he was dressed in a tux and holding a microphone, completely oblivious to the two acrobats dangling upside down above his head. He was *in* his head as usual: the self-contained professor.

Early one morning in Palm Springs, I was seated next to Chris at a lush event for Dana-Farber. Hundreds of attendees attended by legions of uniformed wait staff were feasting on a full breakfast menu of mimosas, eggs, bacon, baskets overflowing with freshly baked goods. As soon as it ended, I was picked up and driven a few miles for a visit with Elisabeth (Lib) Kaiser Davis, an unassuming, gracious and generous senior trustee. A Wellesley graduate in the class of 1932, Lib and her daughter, another alumna, had invited me for a late-morning visit. As we settled in the living room, I glanced at the coffee table and saw three Pepperidge Farm cookies on a small plate. Lib's daughter saw something amiss.

"Ma," she said, "don't you think the Wellesley president deserves a napkin?" Lib stood up, walked with dignity to a sideboard, drew a tissue out of a box and neatly tore it into three equal pieces. One for each of us. I liked her style.

Back in New York City, now in the home of Susan and Sidney Knafel, I was to begin a relationship with one more of the few couples who could make a very big difference. That evening I would deliver my first speech to the mighty New York Wellesley Club. Susan was an officer, also from a class in the '50s. Her husband was a Harvard insider. Both were warm and urbane. Over coffee I told stories about how things were going on campus, what I was learning and seeing and hoping to accomplish. We had a lively and substantive conversation. They knew a lot; I liked them a lot.

As we were wrapping up, Susan told me they had a prior engagement that evening and wouldn't make it to my talk. I assured them that they wouldn't miss a thing—I'd already told them everything I knew so far. We laughed. They said they'd still like to be there, especially now that we'd met; they wanted to cheer me on. They left open the possibility that they'd make a brief appearance on the way to the concert.

The evening club event was in an Upper East Side Manhattan hotel. We had a big turnout. It began with a reception, then my talk. I was at the lectern and into it when I heard a commotion outside. I heard sirens. They have nothing to do with me I thought, and carried on. But as soon as I finished, Peter pulled me aside. He looked dreadful. The Knafels had come to the reception briefly and, as I took the podium, they left. While they were hailing a cab, Susan was struck by a car, badly injured and was now hospitalized. Her health was already precarious. I was heartsick to hear this had happened on the detour they took to support me. I hadn't even seen them.

In Susan's honor and in the hope it might bring her comfort, Sid endowed fellowships for Wellesley seniors to travel and study abroad, as she had loved to do. It was a terrific program, much enriched by the interest Sid took in the student recipients and what they'd learned. And then, too soon afterwards, I was at Susan's memorial service in a Fifth Avenue synagogue. A few years later, at my request, Sid agreed to join our board; he became a wise and beloved leader among the Wellesley trustees. In 2022 I spoke at a beautiful memorial service for him at the New York Harvard Club.

Peter's resignation-letter sat in my desk drawer for nearly five years. When it was time to begin thinking about another campaign, he told me he didn't have the heart to start over again here. He helped me set up a search for his successor. We decided to ask all the candidates if it felt premature to go back to the well so soon after many of our donors had made stretch gifts. I was uneasy about the extent to which big money was moving into higher education. I'd heard about an elite university that closed a big campaign with fanfare over breakfast and launched the next one at a gala that very night. But every job candidate and every expert we consulted warned against "leaving money on the table." To sit out a campaign cycle would put us at a competitive disadvantage with other colleges that were certainly not going to skip any rounds.

I recruited my new vice president. It took a secret search to snatch him out from under the noses of Princeton's fabled development team. He was in the number two slot there and was at first hesitant. We brought him into the President's House through a side entrance and I won him over. Later my heist was repaid by a new Princeton president who poached, serially, our museum director, our chief of police, and then our admission dean.

David Blinder was a catch for us. He began staffing up while I led the Senior Staff in distilling a focused set of priorities. We had five years of intensive self-scrutiny to call upon from dozens of decentralized planning efforts. It was a point of pride to me that this was not a formulaic strategic plan. We'd taken up salient questions one at a time, and delved deeply into each one with the benefit of diverse views from faculty, students and staff. We'd raised up voices that were less often heard, reexamined our values, and emerged with a clear picture of where we wanted to be at the end of our campaign. It would run from 2000 to 2005, preceded by a two-year "silent phase" to nail down a feasible dollar target in conversations with potential high-end donors.

After some wringing of hands, we adopted Women Who Will as the watchword for our campaign. We extracted the three words from the mission statement I inherited from Nan: Wellesley existed "to provide an excellent liberal arts education for women who will make a difference in the world." We debated and then embraced Women Who Will as both provocative and memorable. We emblazoned it on all the campaign materials, on T-shirts, and on colorful banners affixed to lampposts lining the pathways and roads that snaked through the campus. On each banner we imprinted the name and profession of a winner of the annual alumnae achievement award. Before long, students were choosing the alumna in whose footsteps they wanted to follow and standing beneath her banner taking photos of each other.

In June 1998 I took the trustees on a retreat to start a campaign conversation. I was excited when they approved the plan. The package summed to $375 million and change. Should we set the campaign goal there, or round it up to $400 million? As that debate wore on, Vicki groaned.

"We sound like a bunch of women at a restaurant trying to split the lunch check," she said. "Let's be brave and go for $400." We did and Vicki later became my second of two board chairs, succeeding Gail, and my constant companion on the campaign trail.

We identified our dream team of trustee campaign co-chairs, each to represent a decade—the fifties, sixties, and seventies—and a region—greater New York, Colorado and Bel Air, California, and Boston. All much beloved, tremendously generous themselves, well versed in the philanthropic arts, and widely admired. They all said yes.

The resources office arranged small private dinners across the country to be hosted by a leadership-level donor in her home: showcase homes, and elegant meals. But something about these events threw me off. I never mastered the medium. They triggered the shy child in me who suffered in silence at the dinner table for years and froze when called on to speak. In the middle of these dinners, the hostess would chime her glass and invite me to speak. I would stand, make my little pitch and field responses. I spoke without notes of course and had to remember all the names and pretend we'd gathered for a casual conversation. We all knew I had an agenda. Perhaps it was the pseudo familiarity that felt phony to me and made me feel self-conscious. Or the absence of the pulsing energy in the big white tent events. I would be glad when I could put these dinners behind me.

One morning before dawn at the President's House I awoke groggy from a sound sleep and picked up the telephone receiver.

"Is this Diana Chapman Walsh?" asked an unfamiliar voice.

"Yes?"

"I'm calling for your mother. She's here with me. Your father has just died. Peacefully, in his sleep." This was a total shock. Later I would remember a phone call from Dad a couple of years earlier. He was telling me, in his guarded way, that his heart was failing, on top of his lung disease, the result of a lifetime as a smoker and a chemist in an oil refinery. Surgery was out of the question. In retrospect, I could hear the despair in his voice, but at the time I had missed his cue. It was so rare for him to call me, rarer still to reveal any emotion to me, or to anyone. I wished I had caught the next flight to Philadelphia back then.

I made hasty plans to fly there now. Then I called Chris, who was at Princeton to give a lecture. Before lunch, I was at my mother's side. Chris was already there, together with Mom's "kid brother," Uncle Dick, and his wife, Aunt Anne. Mom was stoic, in a state of shock. Dad never wanted any kind of service. He never once attended a funeral. He had donated his body to Penn Medical School. He was quite simply gone without a trace. He and Mom had played duplicate bridge with friends the night before. They went to sleep and he didn't wake up.

I stayed with my mother for three days. My three siblings joined us as they were able to break away from their lives, Sally first, then Bill, and later Muff. We tended to our mother as best we knew how. Bill would handle her financial and legal affairs; Sally, who lived closest, would be her primary support. We sat around, all four of us, and listened to her timeworn stories. I'd been hearing them for years. Yet now I recognized them as surrogates for the grief my mother was repressing. I wished we could all just weep together, but she couldn't tolerate strong emotions. I learned as a child not to cross that line with her. And now I had to leave. I had a flight to LA for a pre-campaign dinner. I didn't want to go. It all felt surreal, incomplete, superficial. We shed not one tear for my father.

I arrived at the Bel Air estate of the campaign co-chair. I didn't tell anyone where I'd been or what I'd been doing. To mention it would cast a pall over the party. I muddled through the night and the next few days in what felt like an out-of-body experience.

In April 2000, our 125th anniversary year, we launched "The Wellesley Campaign" and committed Wellesley—once again—to the most ambitious fundraising campaign any liberal arts college had yet undertaken. We were secure in the knowledge, I often said, that to provide a great education for women was to advance the cause of justice, directly and indirectly, at home and around the world. I spoke often of connections because I saw the capacity to make connections as essential to the ethical lives I trusted our graduates would continue to live. And because the ability to connect new and/or disparate ideas was a fundamental goal of a liberal education.

I presented the campaign as a chance for us to develop new structures— physical, administrative, curricular—that would cut across and connect divisions and silos. We would integrate parts of the curriculum and the community that were isolated or fragmented, and invest in our *collective* intellectual life on campus as a seedbed to prepare whole students for whole lives. If this was a cliché, I believed we had an educational philosophy to stand behind it in the context of a student body that continued to grow far more diverse than it had ever been. We had yet to catch up with the implications of that huge demographic shift. I cast a lot of words into an unknowable future that I saw moving at a faster rate than we seemed able yet to equal.

Early in the campaign I noticed how often we spoke of fundraising in the language of war. We embarked on a campaign, visited strongholds, created strategies and tactics, marshaled the troops, and kept some powder dry. We crafted slogans and banners, logos, and insignia. These we paraded in the service of competition with our rivals. What kind of battle was this anyway?

I wanted to move us away from these bellicose tropes, and yet I wanted us to succeed. Metaphor, I knew from the work of linguists like George Lakoff, was not to be taken lightly. Words created worlds. I'd been thinking about language and leadership, thinking and writing about the kind of leader I wanted to be, and about the cultural environment I wanted to foster at Wellesley. Our faculty were effective, inspiring, passionate about their teaching and scholarship. I wanted to support and enhance those qualities for the future. I believed they would more reliably enact those values when they felt connected to themselves, to one another, to their material, and to their students—as well as to the college, and the larger and deeper meanings of their vocation. That's why we chose to emphasize new connections in our campaign. In addition, though, it seemed to me that *leaders* who wanted to foster those same webs of connection would have to work self-consciously to avoid forces that would tend to drive *them* into isolation. I thought of this purposeful effort to preserve connection as a leadership of peace.

A chance encounter on a busy Friday suggested a fresh metaphor for our campaign. Students' parents and families were on campus for our annual family weekend. I rushed home at around 2:00 to change my shoes. I'd been flat out all day—no, all week—and still had three more public appearances. My feet hurt. Once in the house, I realized I'd skipped lunch, so I passed through the kitchen, found a bagel, and sliced it in half.

The doorbell rang. I opened the door and came face-to-face with six monks in saffron robes. I recognized our new Buddhist advisor, who said brightly, "Oh, we're so glad to find you at home. We've brought you Maha Ghosananda, the Dalai Lama of Cambodia. He wants to meet you." A maroon ski cap pulled down over his ears accentuated twinkling eyes that brightened his face. I was pretty sure there was only one Dalai Lama—and this was not him. Our Buddhist advisor was the expert though, so I didn't challenge her.

I babbled something and brought my hands together in an attempt at a Buddhist greeting, the two bagel halves cupped between them. I laughed and offered the better half of the bagel—the one with cinnamon topping—to the monk. He accepted it with a bow. Our advisor later told me that he ate nothing after noon and passed it to someone else. I dashed off. For the rest of the day, I chided myself for the botched opportunity. I should have canceled the next appointment, invited the group in, and basked in their aura of peace and tranquility.

I felt even worse when I logged onto the internet that night and discovered what an eminence Maha Ghosananda was. No, not the Dalai Lama—there *was* only one—but one of the world's great spiritual leaders, on a global pilgrimage to raise awareness of landmines left in his country after the Vietnam War. Peasants and children were still being maimed and killed by them. I was eager to learn more.

Two days later, I read a prayer in the chapel at the multifaith service for family weekend. Victor was irritated that someone had scheduled another service in the hour just before the program he and his student multicultural council had prepared for their parents and guests. Attendance at our service was spotty. To cheer him up, I invited him to walk with me back to the house for a snack.

"Oh well," Victor said, as we dragged our metal chairs to the edge of the terrace. "Who am I to complain? Maha Ghosananda was here on Friday for a visit with Buddhist students and was perfectly content to spend a couple of hours with the five or six who came to meet him." I took a breath to tell about my Friday surprise, but felt another presence.

I looked up and saw the monk staring at us from the top of the marble steps to the wide terrace. Our advisor told me later that he silently split off from her group again and made his way, alone, up the hill to my house. Victor and I were holding our breath. We had just spoken his name.

We pulled up a third chair. We offered our food to him and talked. His English was limited but we communicated easily. He was playful, warm, and sweet. We shared easy silences that were suffused with spirit, so it felt to me, and his visit inspired gratitude and an impulse to support his journey in whatever way we could.

This was due at least in part to the peace of his presence. His natural, whimsical offerings. He reached into one then another pocket of his down vest and showed us what he'd excavated: a US passport wrapped in an old warranty notice, the German translation of his book, *Step by Step*, folded in a scrap of bubble wrap. He laughed at himself for failing to adhere to the Buddhist instruction to travel light.

When we parted, he walked slowly down the marble steps, turned right at the rose garden, and never once looked back. Victor and I watched him disappear down the hill and into a grove of trees. We knew that this visit had brought us something we had no way of absorbing right away; but that it would stay with us.

Afterwards, I asked myself what it would be like to conduct a fundraising campaign in the spirit of Maha Ghosananda. We would travel to distant places, connect people to an institution I represented by virtue of my role, one with great meaning in my life and in that of the people I would meet. I might empty my pockets, invite stories, sit with memories of the college, reconnect to its values. We would leave space for the unexpected and situate ourselves in a web of continuity, a long stream of connection that extended across many decades, past and future.

"I know this sounds quixotic," I said to the trustee development committee. "New Age. Or maybe Old." I offered the image as an interesting thought experiment. I left them to mull it over.

When I told the story to Pat she saw even more.

"There are many lessons we can take from your encounter, and I'm sure you're right that you will continue to discover new layers of meaning in it. One I see is this: You were given something miraculous when you needed it. I believe we're always given what we need, and that to live this faith is to discern what it is we've been given. It's almost never what we think we want."

We took the campaign on the road. We hosted eighteen events across the country at the Getty Museum in LA, the museums of modern art in San Francisco, Dallas, and Minneapolis. Union Station in Washington, DC, the Shakespeare Theater in Chicago, and, in Cleveland, the Rock and Roll Hall of Fame. In Houston, we gathered in the Johnson Space Center, hosted by our own astronaut whose launch into outer space we had watched in real time on a jumbotron at the campaign launch on campus. And we traveled to Taiwan, Tokyo, Hong Kong, with a stop in mainland China.

Mrs. Ma, as she always called herself, Wellesley's professor and chair of Chinese studies, translated my name for the calling cards I needed for our trip. "What a beautiful name," all of our hosts in China and Taiwan said to me, as they held my card beneath two thumbs. I had no clue what they were seeing, but nodded back. In Taiwan, I gave a speech at the national academy, the Academia Sinica, but, before that, met privately with the Taiwanese president. He asked how many students we had at the celebrated alma mater of Mayling Soong, Mme. Chiang Kai Shek. I told him 2,300 and he looked shocked. I guessed it was the small size of this institution so admired in his country. Then he recovered.

"Ah, you have concentrated on quality," he said, nodding with a knowing look. I quoted him often.

At the Taipei airport, ready to head home, we tore front pages out of local papers for our files. There I was pictured next to the president, the minister of education, and other notables. We couldn't read a word of the accompanying text. On our return, Mrs. Ma deciphered it, and I asked her what my card said. She had translated my name into Chinese characters which read "Holy mountain, Thai, peaceful and serene."

Ah. Lovely. News to me. I smiled. Serenely.

In Philadelphia, my mother joined us. I needn't have worried that she would be ill at ease. I saw alumnae of all ages making a fuss over her, and she basked in the attention. In New York we met at Radio City Music Hall, minus the Rockettes. I neglected to mention to my sister, Sally, that I would be in town that day. She later passed by in a cab with friends. They were amazed to see my name in lights on the marquee. Instead of my usual talk, I was interviewed by Diane Sawyer, Wellesley '64, with my friend Charlie Gibson. In London I dined next to the Rosetta Stone in the Egyptian gallery of the British Museum. We drew capacity crowds across generations in all sorts of venues, high culture and low.

On to Cleveland, Ohio, for another lesson in partnership.

This briefing was upbeat. Dinner with Barbara Ruhlman, another graduate from the '50s who hadn't often been back to campus but was approaching a reunion. She had fond college memories and was ready to consider a serious commitment. Toward the end of dinner, she took charge. She was one of five directors of a family firm. The other four were male and had established endowed chairs at their colleges through the firm's directors' fund. It was her turn. She asked me how much an endowed professorial chair cost and I told her.

"Good," she said, "you can count on $2 million from me for your campaign." But she had a request. If an endowed chair was the most important use for it, fine. But if I had a better idea, she wanted to hear it. "You don't need to tell me now," she said. "You can go away and think about it. My commitment is solid. But I don't want us to look back later and wish we'd done something else."

I took Barbara's challenge back to Lee Cuba, then dean of the college. He and I had been conversing with faculty and students about the quality of intellectual life on campus. We were exploring whether, in our emphasis on academic rigor and hard work, we'd given short shrift to the fruits of that labor, the knowledge, understanding, and rewards of serious intellectual engagement. Was it true, as I heard students grumble, that dutiful Wellesley was "the place where fun comes to die"? I wanted them to know the inherent *joy* of learning.

We returned to Barbara with a creative proposal. It would be an intervention into the culture of the college and would emphasize the results of studies across the disciplines in formats that would foreground the pleasure of intellectual pursuit. As part of our vision, I'd encouraged Lee to flesh out his dream of a daylong conference, an annual all-college celebration of student work. We named it the Ruhlman Conference. Barbara loved the idea, gave us the money for it and henceforth attended every year. Students called it The Ruhlman and treated her like a rock star. She relished the chance later to report to me the reaction of her board colleagues. It sounds mushy, they said to her. You could have had a chair.

Yes, she replied to them. Instead, she had invited her college to think hard about what really mattered. And, with us, had helped create something transformative. She had brought into being an entirely new tradition.

A couple of years later, Nicki Tanner, the board vice chair who had been my campaign wordsmith partner, approached me about her gift. She and Lee designed a companion conference in the fall to showcase the work students did off campus, often over the summer but sometimes extending through the year. These were research projects, internships, service programs, study abroad, other nonclassroom work. Students valued this experiential learning and desired the imprimatur and oversight of faculty, to ground and legitimate it. The Tanner stood the test of time as another opportunity to break down old structures and make way for the new.

As did the gift of Lulu Wang, my classmate and member of the presidential search committee. Now the first female chair of the board's investment committee, a prestigious role, Lulu, herself, was a consummate connector. Through her Wellesley nieces, she was a connoisseur of students' comings and goings, and their dreams. She picked up an urgent need for a gathering space on campus, a space for *all* students. Generations of students had fussed that there was "no there there." I approached Lulu for a transformative gift to fill the need. A big number for a big vision. It was all I could do to get it out of my mouth. She didn't blink and called me two days later to say yes, she would do it. The Wang Campus Center was a resounding success, architecturally, programmatically, and culturally. Shortly after it opened, I was visited by a worried college government president. The students are calling it "the Lulu." Will Mrs. Wang mind? I called Lulu who didn't mind in the least. And she told me how surprised she was by the ask I had made of her. How "bold" I had become.

A return visit to Northeast Harbor convinced me that Lulu was right. I had become bold. My briefing encouraged me to make an "eight-figure ask." Already the largest donor so far in the history of the college, Kathryn Wasserman Davis was now in her late nineties and as sharp as ever. This time I was in Maine to solicit her campaign gift. I would ask her to support international studies—the field in which she earned a PhD after graduating from Wellesley. But not before traveling on horseback through the Caucasus Mountains, the first in a lifetime of adventures in Russia and the USSR and others in Switzerland while her husband was US Ambassador. Our ambitious new initiative in global education would appeal to her, I was sure. I hoped she would want to endow it. That was the easy part of my task.

The other help I wanted from her might prove a harder sell. I was going to seek her support on a major landscape project that included a garage. Not just any garage but one above and below ground, an attractive one. Was that an oxymoron? Maybe. It was certainly pricey. Our architect counseled us to call it a "car storage facility." As if anyone would be fooled by that. Our development consultants were sure we would never raise a dime for a garage. No matter what we called it.

At the end of our lunch at Acadia National Park, where we always went for the popovers, I leaned over to help Kathryn read the check and calculate the tip. We'd had a lovely time. The resources office wanted me to ask Kathryn for $10 million. I'd be a hero if I came back with that. Instead, I decided to present her with a number that would fully cover both projects. I leaned in again and wrote three numbers on a napkin. They summed to $36-million. She didn't flinch but I noticed that my mouth was dry. I explained that we needed the garage to save the landscape from the incursion of cars. She got that right away and liked the global education initiative. Fantastic!

"Let's go back and check with Shelby," she said brightly. Shelby was her son. Back at her home, the two of us trotted down the driveway to Shelby's house, which sat below hers atop Schoolhouse Ledge with a panoramic view of Somes Sound.

"Diana and I have a proposition for you," she sang out happily as we entered his house. I held my breath.

"What is it?" he asked and I spoke the number.

"Sure, Ma," he said. "You can afford that."

Ah, Lulu, yes. I was becoming bold. But, still my mother's daughter, I did not want my presidency to be about the money. It wasn't. It was about the relationships, and the possibilities we dreamed up together.

There were lows. An early morning wake-up in a hotel in some midwestern city. I couldn't remember which. They all melded together; it didn't matter. Another predawn call. This one Chris. I answered in a fog.

My dissertation advisor and mentor, Sol Levine, had died. His family was trying to reach me. I could not believe what I was hearing. I didn't know he was ill. I was not prepared for this. I couldn't take in that he was no longer here. That I would never again hear his voice. And I couldn't make it back in time for the service. I called his wife and we cried together. But then my day began and I stumbled through it. Dissociated again. Later I wrote a tribute to him for the journal *Social Science and Medicine*, and delivered the inaugural annual lecture in his honor at the Harvard School of Public Health. Those opportunities helped me hold him in my heart.

Back in New York, I was headed to dinner alone with Sidney Knafel. By now he was a close friend and a trustee. When I'd first asked him to consider joining the board, he'd said only if he could be helpful. He already was. He was tracking a key characteristic of our faculty culture. Harvard was known for recruiting senior professors from outside. That's how I was tenured there. But Wellesley was committed to "growing our own" through a combination of careful selection and vigilant mentoring of junior colleagues. Sid presented his idea for a campaign gift. What if he were to endow four or five professorships for us to award to assistant professors after their initial evaluation, three to four years in advance of their tenure review? Would this help us retain the very best teacher-scholars we were so carefully cultivating? I told him it was a terrific idea and we discussed it. As he signaled for the check, I said I would carry it back to the academic deans and we would put together a proposal for him. He declined, saying he preferred to write me a letter. I offered again, but he stood firm.

A few days later, his letter arrived. He was eloquent in expressing his intentions for these four new Knafel chairs. I was thrilled. But then I read the last paragraph. It took my breath away. This was why he had insisted on writing the letter himself. He intended to honor my presidency with a *fifth* endowed chair that would carry my name in perpetuity. He wanted to put that in writing to me as a surprise. He had succeeded. I was—again—moved beyond words.

In the early fall of 2004, David came to me looking worried. I paid him to worry and he did it well, but this looked to be beyond the usual. We were on track to meet our overall campaign goal when we closed at the end of the year—the good news. But we had a cavernous hole in Alumnae Valley, literally and figuratively. We'd raised too few gifts specifically designated to support our audacious construction project on the western end of the campus.

Vicki went into high gear and rallied the trustees. Together we filled the hole. And then, through the following year—my last—Vicki secretly went back to her board colleagues again and inspired them to dig even deeper to renovate Alumnae Hall, next to the valley, and rename it in my honor. In case I had any illusions that the campaign had rested solely on my shoulders! It had been the best of partnerships. A far-flung and joyous one. And I had loved it.

To commemorate the leadership gifts to the campaign, the resources office installed a long, curved stone bench at the edge of Alumnae Valley not far from the Lulu and DCW Alumnae Hall. The bench looked across the boardwalk through the new wetlands and out over the lake. In it were chiseled the names of each leadership donor.

When I return to campus, less and less often, I visit the bench. I read every name and recall, as if it were yesterday, the love and generosity behind each of those gifts: the gifts beyond dollars that all those donors—who did become my friends—gave the college and me. In their listening, in their questioning, in their creativity. In their fidelity to an educational vision they embodied in their lives, and continued to nourish and extend for generations to come. In a future we all could sense would be ever more tense and troubled.

17

HOW TO LEAVE A JOB YOU LOVE

I was with Senior Staff in the conference room behind my office when Wanda, who covered the phones, poked her head in the door. Madeleine Albright was on the line.

"Diana! Why are you doing this?!" The voice was familiar. "Why would you leave now? You're on a roll." I inhaled and offered Madeleine the explanation I had given the trustees a few days ago. Part of the art of leading well—and of living well—is to recognize a new cycle making a claim to emerge. As much as I wished I could continue forever, I had concluded that now was the time to begin a transition.

I drew in another breath, ready to say more. But I felt Madeleine with me. She thanked me for my service to our college, offered to help in any way she could, and invited me to DC for lunch to discuss my future. I knew from her memoir how hard it was for her, at the end of the Clinton presidency in 2001, to yield the office of Secretary of State to Colin Powell. There was much more she had wanted to do—and was doing now, in other roles.

Had I offered her more by way of explanation it might have been this: I was heading into my fourteenth year in the presidency. The third longest in the college's history. After we completed the campaign two years ago, I heard from headhunters about openings for university presidents. Those had no appeal. Leading Wellesley had been more a calling than a job.

It had been a protracted decision. I tormented myself with the question of how long I could continue to throw myself into the work. I sensed a sameness creeping in, maybe even a staleness. With that in mind I invented something new at the start of last year. It was a potential capstone project to call the question on whether I was going to move on. I would lead a two-year conversation to engage many Wellesley voices. We would review what we had done over my years in office and project what might lie ahead for the college in the next decade, to 2015. I designed the inquiry with Pat Byrne, who found me a consultant to help track our work. We called it the 2015 Commission. I involved all of Senior Staff in every phase. The team that, after I'd gone, would carry the institutional memory into the next transition.

At the same time, I was careful not to inflict on anyone my waffling about whether to stay or to go. That would have been unfair. I alone was viewing the commission as a decisive data point. If it left me with a sense of completion, then it would be time to go. If not, then I would carry on as president.

I led the commission through the 2005–2006 academic year. We began with a process called "appreciative inquiry." We had conversations across a broad swath of the college community in working groups, plenary meetings, and open sessions with my senior team and trustees, faculty, students, many voices. I was determined to make the most of this 2015 Commission and to keep the focus on it as long as possible. It would be my final gift to the college before I left—if I decided to leave.

The years had been filled with ferment and fruitful change. My leadership teams had been brave and creative. I wanted to codify for the college key lessons we had learned. It would be a framework for the trustees as they designed another search, and, as well, for a new administration as it prepared to set its own priorities. My goal was to surface the important questions but not to tie hands. It would not be a strategic plan that might hide an albatross, like the salary scale handed down to me that the faculty invested with Talmudic authority even after it was no longer affordable. I had something more emergent and porous in mind.

I would bring my synthesis back to campus in the following fall, in September of 2006 and, during that final year of my presidency, we would tease out gaps, disagreements, and uncertainties. We would discuss implications. But now was the time for me to sit with my private question. Is it time for me to go?

I was sure Chris wouldn't mind having our life as a couple back. But he didn't weigh in. I loved him for that zone of discretion he always patrolled for me. I had come to see his distancing as the essence of his love, his respect for my autonomy. He had held the space for each of us to grow within the elasticity of our relationship and that was a key to the success of our marriage. This was my decision to make. I discussed it privately in regular phone calls with Dick. He asked penetrating questions. So did Elaine, who walked with me to the Wings Neck lighthouse and back in the mornings on some early spring Cape weekends. I also savored the more expansive tempo on the Cape. I would plop my zafu on the top boulder of the steps down to our beach on Buzzards Bay. This was my place to sit in stillness and feel the sun rise behind me. And I would meditate. One morning I sensed a presence and, through my left eye, spotted a chipmunk peeking out of a stone crevasse inches away. Was he contemplating me? Hmm, busy little one, what do you see?

In early April 2006, I confided in Vicki that I was leaning toward making an announcement at the end of that academic year, effective a year later. We both knew the trustees would need a year to plan and conduct a new search. But right now, I wanted to keep the lid on my decision. Vicki's goal was to leave me every degree of wiggle room so that I would remain free to change my mind. I knew that as soon as the news went out everything would change. I did not want to ask anyone else—not even my closest colleagues—to share the burden of my inner turmoil.

Vicki left no doubt that she wanted to dissuade me if she could. I knew the board did not want me to leave. The previous August, when we wrapped up the campaign, they said I should take a sabbatical year and do something different, renew myself, and return refreshed. Re-up. That didn't feel right to me. What would that new commitment look and feel like after a year away? My mind kept rearranging itself, as Allison, in her teens, once described herself in the throes of a life decision.

I saw myself as adept at transitions. That irony was not lost on me, I whose job was to preside over life passages, see them coming, feel their impact, name them for others to see, feel, absorb. This had become a personal metabolic process that informed my public role. In summers on the Cape I wrote words to welcome new students as they prepared for the ritual embarking for college. A new cycle began every fall on opening day. It ended four years later in the spring with commencement. I knew the rhythms leading up to a big transition, the clarity and confusion, the ruptures and repairs. I had seen people draw closer together, then pull farther apart, not once but over and over, as if to rehearse an excision they did not know how to endure.

Vicki and I made it through most of April with our secret. I was now ready to take my leave. Why? I was content with the results of the discernment process I'd led, with the candor and depth of the conversations we'd had and the richness of the insights. The commission had set forth a promising future, one that said to me we had done our work well, I and my stellar team. All my teams over the years.

"President Walsh, we think you worry too much," a student said to me one spring day. I was having lunch once a week all semester with small groups of especially remarkable juniors and seniors. I went over the commission report with them and asked why they chose Wellesley when they had many options.

"It was the students who attracted us here," they would tell me. "They showed us that this is where we belong." Now this cohort of students was assuring me that they would do the same for future "prospies," their nickname for prospective students.

"We will take care of Wellesley as generations before us have always done." I took comfort in that. Of course they would. Along with the faculty, and administrators, trustees, and alumnae. I had come to know so many faithful custodians of this college.

The trustees would be back the next week for their quarterly meetings, April 27 and 28. Vicki wanted them to hear first of my decision to leave, before anyone else. But I couldn't leave my senior team in the dark. I pictured them in their seats on the borders of the board room hearing my news for the first time. They would feel disrespected by me, even betrayed, I feared. Their lives, more than anyone's, would be upended by my announcement. So I brought Pat and Jane into my confidence knowing they would keep the secret. They confirmed that to go first to the trustees would violate the trust at the heart of our years together. We four hatched a plan, not a simple one, because Vicki was still hoping I might change my mind.

The board dinner, on the eve of the annual meeting, was to be held as usual in the main dining room of the College Club. At the conclusion of the dinner Jane was to circulate a note to each member of Senior Staff that would ask them to meet me for a brief meeting in the morning a half hour before the board was to convene. We'd never asked anything like this of them. Who knew what they'd infer? Vicki insisted that Jane hold the notes until the last minute. Maybe I would abort the mission. I was to signal her if I was *sure* I wanted to proceed. I did, she signaled Jane, who passed the note to each of our colleagues as they exited the building.

Early the next morning, we convened in a private room in the new campus center, "the Lulu," on the far side of the campus from the College Club, where we wouldn't bump into trustees. I was the last to arrive, my pulse pounding in my temples. They were seated around a table, the chair at the head vacant. I sat and took in their faces. They knew; they'd guessed.

I told my team—my dear friends—that it was going to be a long goodbye. I would continue through the coming academic year. Everything would be different. We would find it hard to lead as a lame-duck administration. We would see breakdowns in connections all over the place, even, inevitably, among ourselves. It would feel as though we were stalled, suspended in a time of disorientation. But that would make it also a time of possibility. If we remained mindful, gentle with ourselves and each other, we would figure it out. I wanted to tell them then how much they had meant to me. But I choked up and couldn't speak. Fortunately, we had to leave to join the trustees.

It was their annual meeting, and we had a full agenda. I managed to fake my way through it. Chris and Allison always laughed at what a terrible poker face I have. Everyone has your number, they would tell me. It's 432–1111. But I kept the lid on this announcement. When the moment arrived, I began by reading a short poem. The trustees were used to poems from me. But this poem, "Silver Star," by William Stafford, was "the tell" in my poker game. "To be a mountain, you have to climb alone," it began, "and accept all that rain and snow." If you last long enough, it ended, you may hear the words, "Well done." I looked up.

Their faces were stricken. I wanted to tell these people who had believed in me that I had to go, to speak the gratitude I wanted them to hear from me. As I scanned the faces, though, I realized that my words were the least of what was happening in the room. It was as though we had stepped into an alternate energy field. We were having a collective experience filled with memory and interconnection and, yes, love. I took this as the ultimate affirmation of the shared meaning we had found in the work we had done together.

Years later I would bring myself back into that moment with the board and recall it as a time when I felt myself immersed in a group that had a wisdom all its own, beyond what any one of us alone brought to it. And I would remember the earlier encounter—with the presidential search committee in 1993—when we realized intuitively that we were going to take this risk together. We knew then that I could believe in them and they in me, that we could trust in the special alchemy we did indeed create together.

If I had known at the outset how steep the learning curve would be, I might have lacked the nerve to start the climb. That would have been a pity because Gail was right—it *was* the plum job. And Chris was right too—my 'yes' *was* a defining moment that did transform my life. I started out believing I could make the work of leading Wellesley my next intellectual project. What I couldn't fully anticipate was the extent to which the demands of the job would call on every resource I had. I could not have imagined the depth of the work I would ultimately do, completely remaking myself. Of course the Wellesley presidency was an irresistible invitation to learn—about higher education, organizations, leadership and world affairs, and more.

I came away with a deeper understanding of the dynamics of a complex system, how to recognize and leverage points of intervention toward positive change. In one challenge after another I had no choice but to expand my ideas about learning and pedagogy, equity and diversity, gender and power, religion and spirituality. I lived the challenges facing higher education at the turn of the millennium and made myself an expert in what the future may hold for institutions that are arguably our nation's last great bulwark against the erosion of democracy around the world.

I and my peerless partners—senior administrators and many more—changed Wellesley for the better during those yeasty years before and after the turn of the millennium. I had no doubt about that. We put our shoulders to the wheel and made the college tougher, wiser, kinder.

And I, as the leader, changed in those directions too. I met amazing people, many of whom would become friends for life. I learned to lighten up, to take myself less seriously, to enjoy the humor—sometimes the absurdities—of situations that would have flattened me in earlier times. I arrived knowing that I wanted to lead with my heart wide open, to understand my work as the essence of love. Over time, I found the language to talk openly about those "soft" aspects of power and generativity.

I led with love as the glue that holds a community together, love as empathy and compassion for others, love as the ability and the commitment to make and sustain connections. It was love as profound respect for others and their autonomy, their humanity. Love, in the definition of Humberto Maturana, as "a manner of relational behavior through which the other arises as a legitimate other (as an other who does not need to justify his or her existence in relation to us) in a relation of coexistence with oneself." I never quoted that esoteric definition, but I saw its meaning implanted in the fertile soil of Wellesley College from its very beginnings. I tried to tend it. Extend it. Live it as best I could. And I did know that we had seen the culture of the college change for the better.

Now I was going to walk away. But why?

Because it was time for me to heed my soul's longing for a change of pace, a more inward rhythm, freedom to relax my attention, time to expand my horizons. I wanted another chance to venture out on unfamiliar terrain, intellectual and spiritual. There was something more I wanted to do still, although I wasn't sure what. But if I waited much longer, a door would close. I knew I craved more time for reflective writing. The shortage of that was my one regret. The only real sacrifice I'd made. The rewards had been beyond reckoning.

The announcement went out from the college. Everything changed.

A Wellesley classmate and friend, Marion Meschter Kane, was soon to retire from her position as head of Boston's leading family foundation. The Barr Foundation was established by Barbara and Amos Hostetter. I knew Amos well as the Amherst trustee who recruited me to that board, when he was chair. As the foundation's first executive director, Marion fixed its trajectory and was both revered and beloved. When she learned I was leaving Wellesley she wondered if I might consider succeeding her at Barr and we had several conversations about departures from jobs we loved.

Marion's assigned freshman roommate, Joan Edmonds, and I had chosen to room together sophomore year. Joan always mothered me in ways that filled a void. Marion, it seemed to me, was put off by Joan's hovering during our freshman year, but I treasured it as I took in the reality that my conventionally middle-class and utterly unremarkable family was lacking in the kinds of intimacy other students seemed to take for granted. Joan became my closest college friend and remained so until she died of metastatic breast cancer at age fifty-one. Her death was the first personal loss that felt unbearable to me. Now Marion was exploring the experience of loss in the context of taking leave.

Leaving a job, she said one day over lunch, a job you have loved, is not so different really from leaving a life you have loved. Marion's husband, Dan, died young of ALS. In the year between his diagnosis and his death in 1995 he made a deliberate effort to be "finished" when he died. Marion's cancer had metastasized now. Her remaining project, she told me, was to think about what she needed to do to finish her life.

"If you care for a smooth transition, then you plan for it in advance so those who are left behind have the ability to carry on. To move beyond the fear of death," she said. I was touched that she wanted to leave the foundation in my hands and I was moved—deeply moved—by the choices she was making. She gave a talk at the forty-fifth reunion of our class in 2011 and enlisted us, her classmates, to "help jumpstart conversations about creatively embracing the end of life with family and friends."

Marion's gift of perspective helped counter the waves of projection that came at me from every direction. It was as though I would let everyone down if I didn't take a much bigger job. A worthy job. One that would redound to the credit of Wellesley.

"You wouldn't leave Wellesley to go do *that*," a trustee said in distress when I mentioned the Barr conversation. Another, a Harvard alumnus, told me how disappointed he was that Neil Rudenstine had retired from Harvard to a low-visibility position at the Mellon Foundation. There was a message for me there. People told me I should be the next president of Harvard. Or—better yet—the United States. *Really?*

At the end of the farewell dinner with Wellesley's New York Leadership Gift Committee, a husband I had just met, a man from India, rushed up to me. He had a message he needed me to hear. He was breathless.

"I don't think you understand how much power you have here," he said in hushed tones. "The influence in this room. The resources. They all love you. They are hanging on your every word. They'd follow you anywhere. You could change the world."

I thanked him and noticed how much these comments grated on me. First of all, the support in the room was not about me; it was about the college. As it should be. I had embodied the institution, and done that well. That was the job. But what really bugged me about the grandiose aspirations for my next gig—well-intentioned though they might be—was that they, too, were about the college, not me. They felt like snares that were baited to hook my ego, to raise my sights up higher toward the next platform of the ziggurat. What I was craving, I realized, was the reverse. I needed time to break loose of others' expectations of me, to decompress and find my own path. I wanted to venture inward, not upward, as Ulysses did at the end of the Odyssey when he ventured inland with his oar.

I took Madeleine up on her lunch invitation. She and I had been talking about an Albright Institute at Wellesley, a possibility I was excited about but would now have to leave to others to develop. That wasn't today's agenda, she was clear. Today was focused on me. As we walked from her office to a nearby restaurant, I watched heads turn as passersby did a double take. I sensed people wondering if I was someone of note. Nope. But it was fun to walk at her side. A Wellesley sister who had reached out in solidarity. An avatar of Wellesley's legendary sisterhood. When we settled at a table, she asked me to tell my story and she listened with a diplomat's ear.

"Well, you've had an interesting career so far," she commented at the end. Crossing disciplines and domains. Blending them. Journalism, reproductive rights, public health, health care delivery, social justice, corporate responsibility, higher education, women's education. That breadth is an asset. She suggested I might want to find a way to preserve and extend those balances.

As we parted, I broached the question of the next year's commencement, my last. She spoke at my second one. After she finished that speech she was rushed to a helicopter idling nearby to transport her to Washington to deal with an international crisis. I explained to her now that the seniors selected their speaker but that I often made suggestions and felt sure they would be delighted if she were able to be there. I couldn't think of anyone with whom I'd rather share the platform one last time and told her so.

Now it was goodbye. May 2007. Faculty and students wrote songs and sang them at a day-long farewell party where we all ate cupcakes iced with my initials and wore big round pins reading "Good Luck Diana" in eight languages. The self-designated poet laureate of the college, a technician on the IT staff, performed an epic poem that chronicled my Wellesley years. That evening, a fireworks display reached its crescendo with my initials emblazoned across the sky over the lake.

A carpenter in the trades shop built a house for Philip, our dog, with a carved wooden replica of the seal of the college. The library book arts program illuminated a favorite poem of mine, "A Summer Day," and the author, Mary Oliver, signed it for me. She and I had the only two copies. It was the poem Parker read to me on the eve of my inauguration, the one that ended: "Tell me, what is it you plan to do with your one wild and precious life."

A first edition of the poems of Rilke came from the faculty. "My life is not this steeply sloping hour in which you see me hurrying," was among my favorite of his lines. From the resources office, I was given a shadow box with three Wedgwood plates: the first building on campus, College Hall, the President's House, and Alumnae Hall, the building the trustees were raising funds to renovate and rededicate in my honor. The feat Vicki had pulled off behind my back with the trustees. I was overwhelmed by their generosity.

I was leaving my name all over the place. A plaque on the wall in the new campus center. Vicki designated her donation to name the cafe for me. A professorship and a scholarship fund in my honor, from two other donors. From another, a stone bench in the valley we created marked with a flagstone that thanked me for reviving the campus. A massive photo montage from the alumnae association. A cover story in the alumnae magazine: "A Very Present President," the title. A farewell video. I couldn't watch it. Cards and notes and letters, hundreds of them. I asked Jane to collect them to send to the college archives with my presidential papers. She was organizing those.

To close the annual sports banquet, the varsity crew team hauled a huge new 8X shell into the dining hall. What was this doing here? They unveiled the bow to reveal my name freshly painted there, and christened it in my honor. Five years later, I'd be back on campus for a dinner, seated next to a first-year student. I asked her what she'd been enjoying.

"I row for the varsity crew," she answered with pride.

"Ah, you must be very good to have made that team. You're rowing in the DCW then."

"Well, no," she said cheerfully. "We have a sleek new shell. That one's being used now by the first-year class." So much for immortality, I chuckled to myself.

Family and friends outside the college prepared to welcome me back. We all knew it wouldn't be easy. After Spring Break the specter loomed larger. I sensed my family wonder what was in store for me. Maybe as much for them. In late May, my sister, Sally, joined me in New York where I'd traveled to receive an award. The Wellesley faithful were out in full force. She emailed me later: "What are you going to do when you're no longer a rock star?"

A few nights later, I overheard Chris laughing on the phone with Allison. A theme was taking wing: What are we going to do about Mom? All this pampering she's received on top of her basic optimist's assumption that wishing things will make them so.

"Okay," Chris said. "Here's the deal." They would play "Hail to the Chief" for me every morning, starting July first. Each day they would drop one note off the end. When the music stops, it's all over, time to stop wishing and start pulling my oar. I threatened to load the song into my iPod for an occasional fix after they cut me off.

At commencement, June 1, 2007, several thousand guests sat in the big white tent on Severance Green. I stood at the podium and watched my last graduating class process in, 560 seniors. When they were all in place, still standing, they took up a chant. It was a minute or two before I recognized the nickname they seldom dared use to my face. Except last month when the improv group advertised their final show.

"You have nothing to fear," their posters said, "unless your name is dcdubs." Of course I went to the show. And loved it. Now the whole senior class was chanting, "dcdubs, dcdubs . . ." on and on. It was all I could do to keep my composure. I finally settled them down. A few days later, an IT guy came to help me set up my civilian email account. I adopted dcdubs for my Gmail address.

In my closing charge to the seniors, I told them that we were about to leap off a cliff together. In the next breath, I assured them that we were "going to fly." But from the recesses of my mind, and I knew from some of theirs, I could hear a murmur.

Sure we are. . . . *Splat.*

That night the trustees hosted a farewell party. An expression of emotion and affection at a pitch I'd never experienced, and doubted I would again. Madeleine Albright, who marched at my side as the graduation speaker, stayed for the dinner. All of us were excited to be with her. Chris was one of the speakers and captivated everyone. Why had I kept him under wraps? The head of leadership gifts declared him "the sexiest man in the room." He told stories about me and Phillip, whose poor dog head hurt when I ran him around the lake in the mornings and pummeled him with my impossible questions.

I was in my element, working the crowd with pleasure. I couldn't help but notice the ease that was natural to me now in this role. *Was it the role?* Who would I be without it? I would still have one practice I learned to fall back on. In times of stress, I retreated to gratitude. When I was depleted or defeated—out of ideas, out of words, exhausted or emotionally drained—one remaining move would bring me back to myself. I would call to mind the people who made my life so rich, who saw me try to find my true self. They were the ones who enabled me to bring my best. They reached out to help me do it. These were people who, in the end, loved me in ways I could never have expected. Or earned.

And now I stood at the podium at my farewell dinner in the historic Main Reading Room of the Boston Public Library. It was the close of an emotional fourteen hours and the climax of fourteen years. I was surrounded for the last time by the people who carried me through. As I surveyed the crowd and took a breath to speak to them, I was nearly upended by a rogue wave of gratitude. I bid farewell to Wellesley on that evening of my last commencement as I departed forty-one years earlier on my own graduation day, with Chris still at my side. Over a lifetime he had become my soulmate. He was my best friend, strongest ally, wisest counselor, number one fan. We two still formed a multitude and were poised to escape—once more—together.

From that high-voltage day of bittersweet celebration I stumbled through my final weeks of sorting and packing, saying goodbyes, and fighting off a darkening sense of impending doom. Before I was done, though, the universe would provide an exclamation mark in my final *minutes* in office. As if I needed an outward sign of the turmoil I was trying to mask, at 6:30 on 6/30, I went out with a bang. This was the coda a wise-cracking campus police officer found the nerve to utter once she sensed that I might be ready to laugh.

For several months previous, in anticipation of having to return the college's car, I'd been asking people what they would buy. Should I get a Prius and be a responsible citizen? Did I want a sporty new car to proclaim my newfound freedom? The decision, as all could tell, was a simplified version of my identity crisis. I kept the conversation going until my closest colleague and confidante, no doubt tiring of the topic, took me aside one day.

"You're thinking about this wrong." Pat's voice was matter of fact. "First of all, you won't be a role model anymore, so if you're thinking the car you drive will influence anyone else, you can forget that. Second, you don't have to keep consulting everyone about your decisions anymore. You just have to decide what you want, Diana, and get on with it."

Perfectly reasonable advice—when you know what you want.

Unable to contain myself, I solicited one more opinion, from a friend with a known affinity for high-performance cars. Dick drove a Saab and a BMW and treasured them both.

"Well, if every American drove a Prius," he answered, "global warming will still be with us. And the jury is still out on how to dispose of their batteries. You're making this a moral decision when it's an aesthetic one."

Bingo.

I went home and told Chris I wanted a BMW. He was so glad I'd finally made a decision that he drove me right to a dealership before I could change my mind. There I ordered a BMW, loaded with bells and whistles—extravagant and flashy in ways that I was not. I picked it up a few weeks later in the afternoon of my penultimate day in office. Chris and I sat in the dealer's lot for nearly an hour that Friday evening with the salesman tutoring me in the car's arcana, most of which struck me as cruelly counterintuitive. By the time the lesson was over, I was not at all sure I'd be able to pilot my ultimate driving machine the three miles to the house in Brookline we'd bought and were just making our own. We'd camped out there on a mattress a few times in secret.

"It's seldom wise to buy a car that's smarter than you are," our friend, Charlie, told me later. I coaxed it home to Brookline, breathed a sigh of relief, and locked it in the garage. There it stayed all the next day. No need to press my luck. That evening, Chris and I were scheduled to return to the town of Wellesley for a retirement party in honor of Jane who was departing with me. We planned to drive the two cars in tandem, my new one, which I would drive, and the college's Acura, which Chris would leave in the garage of the President's House to be picked up the following Monday.

I parked the BMW in front of the main entrance where I took out my house keys for the last time and unlocked the stately front door of the historic mansion I had called home for fourteen years. The house, nearly empty, looked suddenly shabby. The Oriental rugs the trustees bought when I arrived were rolled against one wall waiting to be picked up for cleaning. The drapes were already gone. The walls were bare, and the furnishings displaced.

"Di!" Chris called, and "Di" again more urgently. My childhood nickname was reserved now to get my attention. His next words floated at me in a murky cloud. Like the day Magellan came yelping in from the terrace reeking so strongly of skunk that my senses all shut down.

"Di, your new car just rolled down the driveway into a tree."

What? I left it for just a few moments in front of the house. I stared at him for a second, then dashed past him, through the kitchen and down the back stairs to the side door of the house. There, some distance away, I saw my platinum BMW twinkling in the afternoon sun with the trunk of a small hemlock planted behind its rear bumper. I told myself it wouldn't be too badly damaged; it still looked the same. I sensed that Chris was just behind me, but if he was speaking, I was not hearing.

I ran toward the car and reached the side view mirror first. One of the features the salesman had extolled, the way it adjusted automatically when the car went into reverse. Ha! It had been ripped off the passenger's side and lay on the ground, ragged joint facing upwards. I picked it up as though it was a severed limb that could be reattached. Later, when I told the story, Chris never understood why the mirror mattered. It was nothing compared to the damage to the rear of the car. But finding debris on the ground was a moment of truth for me. When I reached the car, I couldn't open the doors. The automatic locks had completely shut down. I repeatedly pushed the unlock icon on the car key. Nothing. Chris reached for the key.

"Here, let me try." His voice was gentle now. I surrendered it willingly. He remembered that the salesman had shown us the conventional key embedded in the electronic one that had now gone dead. Chris freed the mechanical key and opened the door to the driver's side. I climbed in.

The engine surprised us and started on the first try. Chris slid into the passenger's seat and I shifted the gear to first. When I parked the car by the front door, I now noticed, I didn't leave it in gear. Nor did I set the emergency brake. The college's car I'd been driving had an automatic transmission. My drivers didn't want a manual. Now I had paid the price for that accommodation. I had surrendered hands-on control of my driving and my life in order to be fully absorbed in running the college.

We limped the car along the flagstone path and up on the macadam driveway behind the garage. I hoped the gash in the hemlock would look less raw in a couple of days. Chris and I sat in the car for a long moment, the motor idling, both of us wondering what to say. He was always the cautious one and I chafed at his constant warnings. When disaster really struck it irked me no end to think he might feel vindicated. But today Chris was not going to step in that saw-tooth trap.

"No one was hurt," he ventured. "It's only a thing. The front end seems okay."

I wondered whether I should call the dealer.

"It's Saturday night," he replied. "I doubt we'll find anyone there . . ." I suddenly remembered the "OnStar" button and the trial month of free service the salesman said we'd have. I found the red button below the rearview mirror and pushed it. A man's voice filled the car.

"May I help you?"

Thus did the voice from the ceiling announce my life's remaining project. From here on I would be responsible for deciding how I wanted to participate in my daily life, when I wanted to change gears myself and when I wanted to run on automatic. What help would I want and when? No longer would I have structures, deadlines, projects, production lines or any other duties, just open days to design. Alone, I would have to discern how a worthwhile day might look, and, even harder, how it might feel.

Wendell Berry, a poet with a keen eye for the teachings of nature, offered an answer. "When we no longer know what to do," he wrote, "we have come to our real work. And when we no longer know which way to go, we have begun our real journey. The mind that is not baffled is not employed. The impeded stream is the one that sings."

I decided to allow myself the luxury of having a mind that is baffled. I would settle into the humility and the fecundity of that place of not knowing, a place of great discomfort to scholars who prize knowledge above all else, with scholarly productivity close behind. And yet it was a place I had known all too well through my presidency. I had known bafflement as a doorway to creativity more often than not. A graduating senior I encountered during my last weeks in office inquired about my plans for the future, noticed a certain vagueness, and observed that it sounded like I was headed for a "gap year." I liked the idea and began to wonder what it would mean to be a stream that sings.

18

WHAT MATTERS IN THE END

"They want us to wear our nametags the first week of every month," my mother said in passing shortly after I arrived. We were sitting in her living room. "I approve, so I wear mine. It's only fair to the newcomers. And everyone can use a monthly memory refresher. I certainly can. But Uncle Arthur always complained that this place has more rules than George School."

I'd heard Uncle Arthur's lament dozens of times. But I was listening differently now, listening and watching and wondering how my mother was doing as she approached 90, how she was coping, carrying herself. What did I carry of her, for her? And what did I not? I tried hard to suspend my judgment, too. I labored at that.

"I hate 'critikism,'" my mother often quipped when we were kids. But I knew it wasn't a joke, far from it. Something told me long before I was old enough to apply the word to a person that my mother was "fragile," that she needed me never to hurt her feelings.

I had come down from Boston to visit Mom in her "old folks' home," as she insisted on calling this place. It had a more respectable name: Foulkeways, at Gwynedd. I had made the trip to Philadelphia in my BMW, just back from a month in the body shop after its mishap with a tree. There was no risk of getting lost, as the car was equipped with GPS—an antidote to the issues with time and space that had been my constant companion. Now my wandering mind could be outsourced to a machine. I had planned the visit months ago, when I knew I'd finally have time to do my share for a change. My siblings, Bill, and, even more so, Sally, had been carrying the brunt of caring for our mother since our father's death.

I would spend the week with her, support her, help her run errands, do the things with her that were harder to accomplish now that "they" had taken her license away. The end of her independence, mobility, liberty . . . dignity. I had brought my dog for company and to break the ice. Dad, who needed a prop—or a drink—to lift him out of himself, always had a springer; mine was one of my sole remaining connections to him. I would go with the flow. I had told Mom to make a list of things she wanted to do.

She talked more that afternoon about Uncle Arthur, about the 100th birthday party his women friends planned for him for months. And then he defied them and died two days short of the celebration.

"Arthur was miserable here after Aunt Ann died," she continued and reminded me that he outlived his wife by years, and that this was not the norm.

"We're mostly all widows here if you look around. Arthur and Ann never had children." Mom was plowing familiar ground, pretty much oblivious it seemed to me to the impact of her words. But no judging, Diana.

"After Ann was gone, I came to see that she had spoiled Artie all his life."

A few mornings later, I took my dog Phillip for a walk alone along Shady Ramble, a well-groomed gravel path around the property. The weather was crystalline, one of the first fall days that I so loved, the air sharp, the sky cloudless, all things possible. I was hoping the dawn silence would supply me the respite I needed to corral my own antic thoughts.

Phillip stopped to sniff a tree that was wearing half a nametag. I spotted the other half of the severed scrap of black plastic just off the path in a small pile of leaves. *Ash*, it said, the half wedged in the trunk, and, on the line below, *Americana*. I rejoined the two parts—*White Ash, Fraxinus Americana*—then slipped them into the back pocket of my jeans. I would return them later. For now, I wanted to remember the name of this tree. To learn names in nature might make a worthy pursuit for me now that I had nothing but time. But also I wanted to remember the dumb joke this tagged tree brought to mind: *Hello. My name is White Ash*. I was hyperconscious here of fleeting memory. Ever since I arrived, Mom had been playing a desperate version of twenty questions, searching for elusive words, and, most vainly, phantom names.

"You remember: she was the one who won the golf tournament at the club year after year," Mom would say. "Her daughter was in your class, or Sally's maybe, or Muff's, you know who I mean." I would try to conjure the name, usually without success. We would revert to pantomime when other words failed, and, when we ventured down to the dining room or to pick up the mail, I would simply introduce myself to someone whose name I could tell Mom was unable to retrieve.

When we visited Auntie Phyl she told us her answer to the naming problem was to run through the alphabet and hope the name would appear when she came to its first initial. That worked—sometimes. But it was her gregarious second husband who had the ultimate solution.

"I'm Charlie Biddle," he would say when greeting a friend, "and I hope you can remember who *you* are."

This place where memory fails was laden with memories, and I was awash in them at every turn. As an adult I had watched my father—in the final two decades of his life—reinvent himself privately from the inside out. For a long time, I resisted believing that the change was real. My skepticism, I was loath to admit, was tinctured with resentment. Why was this kind and gentle man not there for me when I needed him? The angry disciplinarian had ossified in my child's mind and prevented me from accepting Dad's mysterious transformation into an older person of serenity and grace.

Never in his life did my father, a chemical engineer, have any time for organized religion. He was a confirmed atheist, pure and simple with no apologies. My mother's explanation on his behalf was that he couldn't believe in a god who would have left him an orphan before he was twelve. He hated ceremonies and cant, never went to funerals, and viewed holidays as commercial exploitation. And he was a man of remarkably few words, as taciturn as anyone I have ever known. It was in his presence that I learned the power of silence.

When I was a child, Mom would take us to Chestnut Hill Friends' Meeting. I would sit in silence on "First Day," taking in what people were wearing—clothes and especially shoes—how the sun angled into the room and how the fire in the fireplace smelled and popped, who was nodding off, the chorus of curious breathing patterns, the deepening silence through the hour as people settled into it, and its collective quality once we all became truly still.

At other times in my childhood, when tensions mounted at home, I fled silences that were hostile and isolating. It is said that Eskimos have numerous words for snow, and my early experiences may have attuned me to the multiplicities and intricacies of silence: how a silence could shift from open and inviting, grateful, hopeful, or curious to fearful, fraught, angry, judgmental. Portentous. In the solitude of this early morning walk with my dog, I am reminded once again that silences occupy a continuum from life-giving to death-dealing, with shades of difference in between.

Before my father died, I kept a little sign on a bookshelf in my study that read, "I am a Quaker. In case of emergency please be silent." After his death I felt that he lived on in the silences to which I retreated in emergencies. A benign and loving presence who said to me now, I held you to the uncompromising standards with which I tormented myself, and you survived. You can handle anything. I made you tough. I made you good.

On awakening that crisp morning, I had taken a quick inventory of the photos in my makeshift bedroom that doubled as my mother's study. The ever-so-familiar images of me and my three siblings, individually and in groups, at key stages of our lives. Posing for school portraits. Lined up by age behind a felled fir tree for the annual Christmas card or hanging ornaments on a living one. Sitting around at birthdays and other holidays, a springer spaniel's head resting in someone's lap. We were sailing on Pocono Lake, or skiing in Stowe, Vermont, and, later, in the Rockies or the Alps. We were communing uneasily with cows we found in a meadow during one of our photography phases. And later we were walking down the aisle multiple times, ourselves, with our siblings, and then with our kids at their weddings.

Many of the photos were faded and discolored, well beyond public presentability, if they ever enjoyed that status. Most were in dime-store frames. A rogue's gallery, Dad called this motley collection that became an organic chronicle of our family's evolution. I often wondered to what extent my childhood memories were amplified and distorted by the happenstance that they were, or were not, recorded on film.

My gaze rested on the snapshot in which Bill and I, in our 30s, were standing knee-deep in Pocono Lake, our trousers rolled just above the water line. I was holding Bill's son, Robert, my nephew, on my hip and we were both looking down at my daughter, Allison, who was maybe three or four. Waist-high in water, she pointed toward something farther out in the lake. It was a happy tableau and it stirred a moment of longing. Maybe I should have had more children, but I chose my work instead. Bill was my "older brother," as he liked to say, a qualifier I told him was gratuitous, since he was my only one. Allison, as I looked at this image, was thirty-four—incredibly—a young oncologist, married and busy, three time zones away.

And there on a desk the elegant portrait of my parents surrounded by their large wedding party in front of a stone wall in a formal garden. They were wed at Charmarie, my great-grandparents' summer home at Buck Hill Falls, a resort in the Pocono Mountains, founded by members of our family with a group of Quaker friends. Far Country, their German-town estate, was sold, eventually, to the Philadelphia parks department and then taken private again and carved up, so I was told, because the city couldn't afford the upkeep. As always, I paused on the portrait, in profile, of my father in his twenties that stood in an antique frame on my mother's dresser, his classic and chiseled good looks confirming, I invari-ably thought, that my mother did make the right decision to quit college after her junior year so she could marry him and move to Virginia when he graduated from Penn.

"We were best friends for as long as I can remember," she had reminded me again yesterday. "I was at his twelfth birthday party. He thought it was horrible that he had to invite a girl, but he was given no choice since our families were friends." Mom was rinsing our breakfast dishes in her small kitchenette, the only remaining vestige of the sprawling domestic sphere that had been her exclusive domain in the five houses she and Dad had occupied over time. "When your father took the job at DuPont in Waynesboro, he was ready to find a wife and settle down. If I hadn't gone to Virginia with him, he might have found someone else."

As certain as I was that Mom had long since told me everything of that story there was to tell, I was proven wrong a few hours later when we went down to dinner. On our way into the dining room, Mom introduced me around, as she had been doing, and made a point of ushering me over to a man she identified as a member of her Swarthmore College class.

"Your mother was the smartest person in the class of '41," he said without prompting, an observation I had never before heard anyone make. He then asked, as nearly everyone else did, whether I was "the one from Wellesley."

"Your mother is so proud of you," they invariably added when I said yes. And I noticed each time that I had finally outgrown the corrosive thought that she had always hid it well from me.

"He probably forgot that I didn't graduate," Mom remarked when we were back in her apartment after dinner. "And I wasn't the smartest, just diligent. I did the work." She must have been reading my mind because I was still wrestling with the experience of hearing one of her stories corroborated independently. All of my life I grappled with unnerving questions about which of my mother's stories had any basis in reality and which were fabrications.

"A few of the girls in my class, my good friends, would have known, and cared, that I left college, and why," she continued. "The boys didn't pay attention."

My mother never spoke directly of any thwarted ambitions, but we knew of her dream to graduate from college and find a job in New York City, checking facts for *Time* magazine where she would mark a dot above each verified word. Every week without fail, for as long as I could remember, my mother read her issue of *Time* from cover to cover, usually on the day it arrived in the mail.

I tallied 52 photos hanging on the four walls in the small study where I was sleeping and dozens more on dressers and desks, tables, the upright piano. They stood on every surface in this room, and in Mom's two adjacent rooms. Fifty-two pictures: the number of cards in a deck. My brother Bill, the first-born, appeared in many of them. Bill went off to Bowdoin and came back on his first Thanksgiving with the news from a sociology class that we were "rich." I can still hear the conspiratorial tone in his voice, conveying this revelation secretly and with pride in a discovery that made no sense to either of us. We grew up in the penumbra of the Great Depression, a generation removed, through my mother's frequent retelling of tragic stories from those traumatic times. Mom was never comfortable spending her husband's money, and she was acutely aware that she had none of her own. Certainly, we were not wealthy by the standards plainly in view everywhere around us in Chestnut Hill, an upscale section of Philadelphia, but, more than that, we were never confident about what we deserved.

Three years after Bill's discoveries as a Bowdoin freshman, he dropped me off at Wellesley for my first year of college. I quickly learned, although not in a course, that families talk to each other. They talk about their feelings, their confusion, their sorrows. They share their secret dreams and exult in their accomplishments. They talk about their bodies, and sex, and longing. They laugh about embarrassing and shameful incidents and speak up when they're hurt or angry and apologize. They talk about their loves, Platonic and carnal. And they express in myriad ways their love for one another. They listen.

I would listen to late-night conversations in my dorm during those first few months of college and marvel at the stories, so casually told, that sounded galaxies removed from anything I'd known or felt, sounded enticing, warm, rich—inconceivably real. I found this amazing and kept it to myself, while I continued to accumulate evidence of how we might be different. I felt my mother stiffen when I hugged her on my arrival home for my first Thanksgiving, both arms straight at her side, her body immobilized.

But this was ancient history, excavated, sifted and sorted *ad nauseam*. It was boring. There was nothing more of interest here, no fresh vein to mine. There was something new I was seeking, though, an old yearning with a new twist. Could this become a season for compassion and gratitude, generosity of spirit, a suspension of critikism? On the cusp of my own reinvention, what potentialities might meet me here?

One night as we were leaving the dining room Mom introduced me to Kitty Porter, her fifth-grade teacher at Germantown Friends School. Kitty taught bridge here and, in her late nineties, was known for her ability to remember cards. I commended her on her prowess, and she shrugged it off.

"Oh, they just think I remember," she smiled, rotating her head sideways and upwards from her dowager's hump to look me in the eye with a glint in hers.

"I'm good at faking it."

I smiled back at her.

My thoughts were about as reliable as my mother's stories, I noted now, I who prided myself on focus and discipline. They were spraying in all directions, like the new garden hose that wasn't screwed in all the way and soaked me in cold water. That happened the other day before I left home, when I turned the spigot to hose the dog after a run in the park. I had been struggling with renegade technology in these three months since I blew up my life. It seemed that there were cold showers at every turn. And for what, I kept wondering.

I thought it was to write, so I had been telling myself, and anyone else—they were legion—who inquired about my plans. But the first three months of transition had been more than disorienting. I'd been trying to shake off the doubt implanted in my mind fourteen years earlier by the outgoing Duke University president. His nonchalant comment, "the words have disappeared," had sent a sickening chill through me at the time. And they weighed now on me like a prophecy, or worse, a curse.

"Now I become myself," May Sarton's poem begins, and then describes her several selves as they converge into one—another of the fragmentary word strings that filled my brain and framed my world. "It's taken / time, many years and places; / I have been dissolved and shaken, / worn other people's faces . . ."

When Phillip and I reached a meadow on our Shady Ramble walk, I dug his ball from my pocket and snapped it into the plastic "chuck-it" toy I had brought from Boston in the trunk of my car. He was frantic with anticipation. I wound up the ersatz lacrosse stick and hurled the ball as far as I could—a good 40 yards—and experienced the familiar pleasure in the athletic prowess that distinguished one of my selves, the coordinated one in the persona my mother had forged for me.

Another of my selves knew that I had been kidding myself about what this visit signified, what was really at stake. May Sarton's challenge had been dogging me ever since I decided to break free of my job and reclaim my life. I had known it would be wrenching to leave the college presidency that had animated and defined me, fueled my energy, my intellect, my passions, opened wide new vistas, re-endowed my sense of self.

I was determined, right up to the end, to remain mindful, taking a cue from the opening lines of Mary Oliver's poem of that name. "Every day I see or I hear something that more or less kills me with delight." So I kept a daily journal tracking that daily delight and worked to ground the final movement of my presidency, as fully as I could, in cadences of appreciation and gratitude. For the most part I succeeded. It was a magnificent ending, celebratory and satisfying. Now that it was over, I felt lonely and utterly lost.

Phillip broke into my reverie. Spent from chasing the tennis ball, he took off toward a large oak at the far end of the meadow to lie down in the shade. The day was warming. I called him back and snapped on his leash for the walk back to Barclay. On the near edge of the meadow was a tiny pet graveyard I had remarked on when Mom and I brought Phillip here to run on the first day of our visit. We skirted it then, but I walked him through it now and smiled at his indifference; how simple life is for a dog.

Phillip's life with me began just weeks before Allison's marriage six years ago. She and I had set aside a rare day together. We had a final meeting scheduled with the wedding planner that afternoon and agreed to start early and do something fun first. I polled friends: What would you do with your daughter on your last day together before she's married? I arrived with many suggestions and pulled up in front of Allison's apartment. She jumped into the car, wearing an oversized green jacket.

"It's going to be warm," I said. "You probably won't need that."

"It belongs to Thomas," she said. "He left it here." Allison tended to run cold and, besides, she looked cute in it. I said I had a list of ideas for our day and started to run through it. She interrupted.

"Dog therapy," she said. I drew a blank.

"You know! That puppy you saw and fell in love with. Let's go see him." Magellan, Allison's cocker spaniel from her latch-key-child days, had died a year earlier after a long life, his final years as a canine celebrity on the Wellesley campus. We didn't plan to replace him. But one Saturday morning when Chris was away, I decided on a whim to go alone to the Cape. I whistled for Magellan, caught myself, shrugged and stayed home. Was it not worth going to the Cape without a dog? A few hours later a springer spaniel puppy appeared on the terrace of the President's House and scratched at the kitchen screen. Behind him raced a little girl, followed by a mortified father.

"We're so sorry to disturb you," the man said, panting. "We were walking around the lake, and he got away." The puppy was jumping all over me, licking my face.

"I grew up with springers! I love them! This is a beauty!" I asked where he found this magnificent creature and wrote the breeder's name and number on the back of the manilla folder in my hand. I had told Allison the story of my unexpected caller, then promptly forgot about it. Apparently, she had not.

We went back to the house where I was relieved to find the folder and called the breeder. She invited us right over when she heard our story. Allison and I played on the floor of Lorraine's house with Phillip, the one puppy still with her from the recent litter, surrounded by three generations of his kin: parents, cousins, uncles, aunts. He was six months old, had been the pick of the litter, trained for show. But his adult teeth were coming in crooked, Lorraine said, and she thought she might sell him if the right owner came along.

I could tell that Allison's dog therapy was just what the doctor ordered, and we stayed a long while with the extended springer family. We lost track of time and had to rush to meet the wedding planner. Chris beat us there. When we finished that meeting, Allison remembered Thomas's jacket.

I called Lorraine and we returned, ostensibly for the jacket, but in truth to introduce Chris to Phillip. He sat on the sofa with four adult springers leaning into each other and his shoulder. They looked like a row of birds on a branch. Phillip was in his lap. We left the second time with Thomas's green jacket and a signed contract with Lorraine. We would be back to pick up Phillip after the wedding. It dawned on me later that Allison, who knew I loved dogs, wanted me to have one when she left home for good, when she moved to California with Thomas. I would miss her, we both knew. And she knew that I would love Phillip.

"You can bring a pet to Foulkeways," Mom had said on the day we passed the pet graveyard. "But you can't get another pet when the one that came with you dies." When I brought Phillip as a puppy home to Wellesley, I recall thinking that he would probably be my last dog, then quickly dismissed the thought as absurdly morose. As I exited the pet graveyard, though, to head back up Shady Ramble, I made a mental note—in the spirit of Uncle Arthur—to remember to adopt another puppy before I agreed to be moved to the place where I would die.

But that was not my story now, I reminded myself. That one was for later. A more immediate story was waiting to be written now, if I could husband the words before they disappeared. *My* name is Diana Chapman Walsh, I smiled to myself. I hope you can remember who *you* are.

Looking back now from California, over a decade since that sojourn in Pennsylvania, much water has flowed through streams under the bridges I have crossed, some breaching their banks and flooding fields and roads. I am finally wrapping up the story I started to tell back then. Some of what I've encountered in the intervening years is summed up in the chapter that follows.

Before we turn to it, though, I want to revisit the question of memory which has been much on my mind through this writing. I myself am 78 years old now and my memory is starting to fail in all the annoying but "normal" ways to which I may be hypersensitive from the agony of witnessing my mother's decline.

At the same time, and possibly in part because of these concerns, I have continued and deepened the mindfulness—mind-watching—practice I started in the years just before my return to Wellesley as president. There wasn't a lot of time for zafu sitting during those frenetic years, but since then I have collaborated with a number of well-known contemplative pioneers, read widely in the contemplative sciences and arts, and less widely but with interest in neuroscience and consciousness. I have meditated, gone on silent retreats, and heard many dharma talks. I'm not a Buddhist, nor am I a Quaker any more. I suppose I am a secular humanist of sorts, spiritual but not religious, as many of our students would say.

As I was completing this chapter, I listened one morning to a talk from May 16, 2019, by a teacher, Matthew Brensilver, recorded by the Insight Meditation Center in Redwood City, California. "Removing the Thorns of Memory and Becoming," he called it and quoted Elie Wiesel, who had such a memorable impact on me during the conflict at Wellesley that colored my early years as president. In his book, *Night*, Wiesel writes: "In the end it is all about memory, its sources and its magnitude and, of course, its consequences." In the "reactivation and recombination of memory traces," from which a thought is thought to arise, Matthew said, "we shape our autobiographies, construct our memoirs, hew our identities. Mindfulness meditation—to dwell in the present—offers an escape from the prison of frozen memories, encased in the amber of our limited wisdom at the time the incidents occurred."

In the decade since I first wrote the words in this chapter—true as they were at the time I set them down, I have escaped from the frozen memory of my mother as I saw her during that visit to Foulkeways. Afterwards, life intervened again and again. As it does. Life and death. And I was immersed over and over in the lessons my friend Marion had so faithfully lived and taught, her lessons of love and loss and what matters in the end. When I took my leave of Wellesley, I had no way to know that I was being called back into my extended family. I found myself in new roles that would stretch me in new directions. They would break my heart open, over and over and again.

On October 6, 2008, my beautiful Indian-American grandson was born, Sean Rohan Kurian. I spent the first three months of his life in California where I discovered the answer to a question that had flashed across my mind when I, as the preoccupied president, would vaguely notice trustees or faculty or staff on the edges of a meeting room ogling over pictures of their grandchildren.

What's the big deal here? I would wonder back then. But now I had caught myself head over heels in love with my grandson in the warm embrace of his parents, Allison and Thomas. I sent Judy Jones, a favorite trustee, a photo of Sean with a comment that he was truly gorgeous.

"Everyone feels that way about their grandchildren," Judy wrote back. Answering the question for me again, in case I'd missed the point. I had been clueless.

When my brother-in-law, Rob Carroll, died at age 56, I was able to make it to St. Louis two days before his death, and to stay afterwards with my sister, Muffy, and my nephew and niece, Greg and Meaghan, aged

13 and 15. The loss of their larger-than-life father, who was their stay-at-home parent, came as a devastating blow. A year later I took Muffy on a photo safari to Africa, a time of healing for her and reconnection for us. She was the baby sister I'd been quite close to before I left for college, and had seen only periodically in the subsequent years when she and I were separated by time and space, and by our demanding lives as successful professional women, wives, and moms.

When my sister, Sally, was diagnosed with aggressive kidney cancer, I was her constant companion up to and through her death just 10 months later, on June 2, 2012. The next June my mother died, a year and ten days after she lost Sally, her very best friend in the world. Sally was my surrogate memory, the only person who always knew all the details of our growing up, all the moments I usually forgot. Losing her may be part of what has driven me to write this story so that I might hold onto some of what I lost when she died.

As Sally lay dying in her apartment in New York, I was there with her, often with Chris and Sally's closest friend, Helene Aguilar. Mom hadn't seen Sally in months and was desperate to see her daughter. She was in tears about it when we spoke every day. The head nurse at Foulkeways advised against a visit. It was too much to ask of my mother, physically and emotionally. I didn't see how we could in conscience deny Mom the chance to see Sally one more time.

So, for my mother's ninety-third birthday on May 24, I cooked up a little party. Bill would drive up from Annapolis, where he lived, to Gwynedd for Mom, and from there to Sally's apartment on the Upper West Side of Manhattan. He would drive Mom back home afterwards. Chris and I improvised a miniature birthday party on Sally's living room table next to the bedroom she hadn't left in weeks, except, with help, to use the wheelchair positioned next to her bed to get to the bathroom and back.

After a desultory lunch where we all picked at our food, I asked Mom if she wanted to sit with Sally in her room for a while before heading back to Foulkeways. She nodded. I helped her perch in the wheelchair and I stood in the doorway. She was looking at Sally's arm, longingly it felt to me, and not daring to touch it, to touch her beloved daughter. Sally was groggy from the morphine that was taking only a tiny sliver off her constant pain. I took my mother's hand in mine and gently laid it on Sally's forearm. She sat there, immobile and in silence, for ten minutes or more. Tears streamed down her cheeks. She never saw Sally again.

At the robing room for Barnard's Commencement a few weeks later, a different wheelchair brought me up short again. This one, in the corner, had CHAPMAN taped to the back in large letters. That was wishful thinking. Barnard College was awarding Sally their outstanding service medal. President Obama was the commencement speaker that year amid much hoopla. The President of Barnard, Debora Spar, hoped very much that Sally would be there in person to receive the award. We all did, up to the last minute. But it was impossible. Chris stayed with Sally next to her bed while I marched in the academic procession with the two presidents, surrounded by hordes of ecstatic students. After President Spar read the citation and handed me the medal in a wrapped package, I held it high and looked into the TV camera.

"This one's for you, Sally," I called out to her. She didn't hear me. She didn't want to watch, Chris told me later, or couldn't.

No more than she would or could talk about her life as it slipped away. I never fully forgave myself for my instant reaction the evening her oncologist stood at the foot of her hospital bed and told her he'd run out of options. He said it was time to consider hospice care. After he left, I started to babble about the huge impact she'd had on so many students. They'd been writing and calling. They were so devoted to her, so grateful. Her faculty colleagues were too. She cut me off. With anger.

"I do not want to talk about that."

I was staying with the Gibsons at the time and when I returned to their home, I was still berating myself.

"I can't believe I said that," I confessed. "How could I have? I triggered the old competitive forces that operated on us when we were kids."

"Stop beating up on yourself," Charlie said. "That's not it at all. That's not why she cut you off. She doesn't want to die."

My sister—smart, strong, and fiercely independent—was tested beyond endurance over those ten months, beyond comprehension even. But she never stopped being Sally, the teacher who expected much of her students but more of herself, the scholar who knew more than anyone knew, the self-reliant feminist who was unfailingly thankful for every kindness extended to her, no matter how small.

She didn't want to make a fuss, or to inflict one on others. She tried to limit as best she could the demands she made on me. "Not now," she would say when I offered to come back down from Boston to New York to help with a new crisis. "I'll need you later." I came anyway. Later I returned. She did need me. And I will be forever thankful for the times I was available—and she allowed me—to offer her the only help that made a difference, my undivided attention and a calm heart that ached for her. The pretty guarded person—as she described herself—let down her guard during her dying. She took in the love—all of it. All who loved her were able to take consolation in the fact that Sally knew that we loved her. And that she loved us back.

After Sally died, we three surviving siblings resolved to speak to our grieving mother by phone every day, in a rotation. I made a practice of signing off my calls with the words "I love you." For a while they provoked an uncomfortable silence until one of us hung up. But after a while she was saying those words back to me.

We three took turns making visits to Foulkeways and stayed in close touch with the staff, who described our mother as subdued and sad, depressed. Just over a year into this, I received a call from Muffy, who was visiting. Mom was in the hospital in intensive care. She had fallen and hit the back of her head. She was unconscious. The doctors were pessimistic. I flew down and found her hospital room. Muffy was there with a couple of nurses. Mom had not regained consciousness since she fell.

"Hi Mom," I called out to her. She opened her eyes, leaned forward, and smiled.

"Love you, love you, love you," she said, with a lilt in her voice. Then leaned back and closed her eyes.

Her last words.

Mom continued in a coma for over a week with no possibility of regaining consciousness, the doctors said. I spent parts of those days on a chair alone by her bedside. Just in case. I recalled two long poems she used to read to us when we were young. Two dramatic poems that especially pleased her: "The Highwayman" and "Barbara Fritchie." I still knew fragments of both and recalled them now as I read the words to her.

I'd never much thought about what they signified to her, what she found in these particular poems. Both were about courageous women, one who died for love, the other who risked her life for love of country. They matched Mom's romantic imagination, I realized now, as I recited them at her bedside. They transported her to the imaginary Walter Mitty world to which she would retreat as a hero when she felt alone or abandoned. To a child growing up, those stories could be confusing. But to an adult with the benefit of hindsight, well, what was the harm? Sitting beside her now I felt a closeness I knew to be real. No barriers stood between us, no projections or regrets. Outside of time and space all that remained was love.

19

A LIFE IN DIALOGUE

When I left Wellesley, I told myself that I would embark on a path of self-renewal. Not only myself; I told my whole world. In the official announcements, I quoted John Gardner as my justification for jumping ship. The self-renewal I now sought would be "an endless and unpredictable dialogue between our potentialities and the claims of life—not only the claims we encounter but the claims we invent." Starting in July 2007, I announced, I would begin "a long-deferred sabbatical to listen for the deeper promptings that I had subordinated to the demands of my job and the constraints of the role."

Chris and I were living in the big house we bought in Brookline. I must have imagined I'd be entertaining a lot. The house was ideal for that: perfect circulation, gracious and stately. We'd worked with a designer and a carpenter, Chris in the lead. But before long, he and I had to admit to ourselves that we'd grown tired of entertaining. Vicki gave me a decorative pillow for the living room sofa stitched with an Irish blessing: "May your home always be too small to hold all your friends." I walked by it in my sprawling, empty home, and I winced.

Byllye Avery invited me to join a small writers' group, ten women of a certain age, close to mine plus or minus a decade. Led by a published memoirist who taught at Tufts, we met weekly around my mahogany dining room table where dinner parties seldom occurred. I began to write my Wellesley story, starting with how hard it was to leave. Then I drafted a chapter about my work with Dick.

"Everyone needs a Dick Nodell," said one of the writers. No one pointed out that I was pretty much missing from the story. That observation would come later, a decade later, from my new coach. Another of the women commented in an offhand way that she didn't know why I was doing this writing. Well, that took the wind out of my sails. She was at work on an account of her life, beginning with her birth a few months after her sister, a toddler, drowned in the Atlantic Ocean off Cape Cod. She'd always lived in that shadow. She knew why she was writing: palliation, possibly exorcism?

Poor Phillip was having as hard a time with the transition as I was. Maybe harder. At the President's House he reigned supreme, with a spacious room of his own in the basement where he slept happily in his dog bed. On the wall was a master chart devised by his student walkers. They tallied his daily exercise, food intake (and outgo), grooming and tooth brushing (twice a day), and the state of his spirits. Some of his walkers were aspiring vets; others just missed their dogs.

In Brookline we would not be keeping a dog log. We fixed him up in the pantry. He howled all night long—every night for weeks. We gave up finally and let him sleep in our bedroom. But in the morning his toenails clicked on the wooden floor and woke Chris. I rushed him out for a walk around a nearby reservoir and imagined him griping: Where is my lake? Do you call this a lake? Where are my student walkers? So I scoped out a nearby dog park, threw balls for him there and struck up conversations with other dog park denizens. I suppose that's what I am now, I said to myself. A DP denizen. I took Phillip to a groomer, a task others had done for me.

"I used to be the President of Wellesley College," I heard myself saying. The groomer gave me a look: half puzzled, half pitying.

I still had my job as a director of the State Street Corporation, in my eighth year. The board met every month in downtown Boston. Jimmy used to drive me there from Wellesley. He hung out with the State Street drivers, mostly retired cops, schmoozed with them through my meeting, then returned me to the college. Now the corporation sent a driver for me in Brookline.

On the morning of the first pick up I took Phillip out early. Chris was away. Back home I realized I'd locked myself out. I had no hidden key. Oh great, just what I need, the State Street driver will arrive in his limo and find me in my sweats breaking into my house. I managed to pry my way through the screen porch in the back with few physical antics. But that left barely time to shower and change for the ride to town.

If it had been Jimmy, we would have laughed all the way to Boston. I didn't say a word about the lockout to this new guy. When I climbed into the back seat of the limo, he asked my preferred route. I didn't have one; it was my first trip from here. I assumed he would know the best way to go. He assumed I would. His beat with the police, he said, was the Boston Harbor, underwater. He was a diver, now a driver. I asked him how his transition was going: up and down, he admitted. We bonded and together found our way. As soon as I was back from the meeting, I searched out a hardware store and bought a spare key with a magnetized box. It was my first hardware store in over a decade. I did not tell the clerk what I used to be: progress.

A few days later I experimented with the remote control for the garage door, left for us in a kitchen drawer. It didn't seem to work. I pushed the button on the gizmo several times. Nothing. I pushed it again. Sirens came from every direction. I looked out and saw two police cruisers pull up to the house and slam on their brakes. An officer jumped out of each and left the car door open. Their hands were on their holsters. I opened my front door.

"What's the emergency?" one officer asked, out of breath. He glanced at the device in my hand.

"Lady, that's the panic button."

I'd never had a panic button. We had our moments at Wellesley, but I never saw a panic button. Maybe Campus PO kept one under lock and key? I apologized to the police, labeled the offending device with a red marker, and stuffed it in the back of the bottom-most kitchen drawer.

There was no mistaking the message that I was feeling lost. I decided I needed to start reassessing my current commitments, beginning with my director's role at State Street, my sole commitment in the for-profit world. I had time now to fill gaps in my knowledge of banking and finance. After six months, I concluded that my gifts—and interests—lay elsewhere. In October, Chris took me to Europe on an itinerary he had meticulously planned so I would be out of the country during the first Wellesley board meeting over which someone else would preside. This was so like Chris. He who arrived home with George the dog lamp to mark my survival in the job one day longer than the shortest presidency. His gift of a trip was to celebrate my newfound freedom. For his own personal reset after he resigned from Dana-Farber, Chris had taken a two-week trip alone around the world, something he'd always wanted to do. This husband of mine, content to read a map for hours at a time, believed in the therapeutic value of world travel.

In Vienna we stayed in the elegant Sacher Hotel where I spent many hours tethered to a phone line into a State Street board meeting: a tedious waste of a day in paradise with my husband. It was time. As soon as we were back in Boston, I called the CEO and resigned my board seat.

After that, a post-presidency picture came into focus over several years, with more or less the approach Madeleine Albright had recommended. I found opportunities to stay abreast of—and to help advance—progress on issues of lifelong interest. I would attend to other peoples' problems I was glad to make my own, work with good people I could learn from, people doing work I cared about, and where I could tell myself I was making a small difference. I would lift up and support the leader's best instincts. I would support women in their leadership. There was satisfaction in that.

I stayed on the Amherst College board and, over time, joined the MIT Corporation and then its executive committee, to continue learning and to be of what help I could in academia. I chaired the board of the Broad Institute of MIT and Harvard as it was forming a new governance structure. I heeded Madeleine's advice to return to earlier roots—in health care and health policy—when I accepted invitations to join the boards of the Institute for Healthcare Improvement (IHI) and the Kaiser Family Foundation (KFF), both in 2008.

But while this governance portfolio was gradually coming together, the first and most dramatic change in my life appeared immediately: family. I suddenly had more time for my husband, daughter, sisters, brother, mother. It was as though I was able to hear claims I was newly available to meet, and to reinvent. Allison invited me to a baby shower her friends were throwing for her in Palo Alto. I was touched to be invited.

I basked in the affection and intimacy that flowed through the group that assembled. Someone mentioned maternity leave. Allison would have three months. An idea popped into my mind. After the party, I floated it, tentatively.

"I could come out here and help with the baby. My October is wide open. My whole calendar is for the most part. Nothing that can't be rearranged."

"Oh, Mom," Allison replied. "You're overqualified."

I might be *underqualified* to be a baby nurse. But to be a hands-on mother for a change? To be part of my adult daughter's life? That would be pretty awesome, for me anyway. It took a few more conversations, with Chris on the sidelines, to work out an arrangement that would minimize disruption. I did see in Allison's instant reaction a concern I would have had in her situation, a concern I recalled having myself as a new mother. Would she want me underfoot while negotiating this new role for herself? To Allison's great credit—and my great joy—she came around.

After Sean was born, I moved into a one-room guesthouse which I rented for three months. It was located in Atherton a few miles from their new home. I left my internal clock on Eastern time and arrived in the dark each morning around 5:00 as Sean finished his early nursing. Allison went back to bed, and I sat in the nursery and rocked her beautiful boy until she and Thomas were up. I loved the smell of his head, as I did Allison's as a newborn. When Sean's infant nurse, Jan, arrived each morning, I departed for the day.

I spent many afternoons at the local Obama campaign headquarters, making calls back east into swing states. It would have been more fun to make them for my friend Hillary whom I had hosted on campus on five occasions during my presidency, one with Chelsea, as the first stop on her college tour. In addition, we had spent New Year's Eve twice at the Clintons' invitation at the Renaissance Weekend in Hilton Head, South Carolina, and sat with them at the head table. A few years later, memorably, Chris and I stayed overnight in the "Queens' Bedroom" following a White House reception Hillary hosted for her class before their fiftieth reunion. But now Obama had edged her out in the presidential primary and I would have to wait another eight years to throw myself into her bid to break the glass ceiling.

This would instead be my opportunity to fall head over heels in love with my first and only grandchild. Sean Rohan Kurian became a centerpiece of my life. I was in awe of his parents, who made him the centerpiece of theirs, even as they advanced their two demanding and amazing careers.

By 2012, I had become quite active on the boards of the five national nonprofit organizations, Amherst, MIT, the Broad, IHI, and KFF. I was ready to get back to my writing and was preparing to scale back my commitments when I was dealt a wild card by a friend, Arthur Zajonc. He had been elected the new president of a small nonprofit organization—miniscule compared to the other five—the Mind and Life Institute. In its first leadership change over a quarter-century history, Arthur had agreed to take the job, he said, on condition that he be authorized to add two new seats to the board. He wanted me as one of his new directors. I demurred.

"How about we fly you out to Rochester, Minnesota, to the Mayo Clinic?" he parried. The board would be there for three days of meetings with the Dalai Lama, in from Dharamsala, India, for his annual medical exam. I could participate as Arthur's guest, get a feel for the organization, decide later if I wanted to join the board. The Dalai Lama was highly committed to MLI, Arthur said, as cofounder and honorary chair of the Institute, and a frequent participant in its programs. MLI was one of his top priorities.

That did sound interesting. I agreed to join them but without anticipating how it would feel to be introduced repeatedly—to the Dalai Lama first, then to the MLI directors and the Mayo brass, and finally to various others who would cycle through the meeting—as a person who had been offered a seat on the board and was sitting on the fence.

MLI was founded in 1991 to host a dialogue between Eastern mind science and Western brain science. A historic conference at MIT in 2003 had taken the dialogue public in a dramatic encounter in Kresge Auditorium. Arthur was there. So was Eric Lander, the Broad president whose board I'd chaired. Arthur knew these as worlds I'd since frequented at MIT and the Broad. Arthur knew, too, that I had a meditation practice that dated back to the 1980s and the Kellogg Fellowship. Parker was a mutual friend, through an oddball foundation, the Fetzer Institute in Kalamazoo, Michigan.

Off and on, we three had supported Fetzer's initiatives in educational reform and had spent time together—beginning always with a period of silence—in small gatherings I hosted at the Wellesley President's House. We explored alternative visions for higher education with colleagues who were also contemplatives: Jon Kabat-Zinn, Peter Senge, Otto Scharmer, and other scholars who chose to position themselves on the edges of the academy and to raise unorthodox questions that cut to its core. We sketched the features of a "New University" that would combine systems thinking, sustainability, and spirituality. We invited others to join us as thinking partners. Our conversations seeded work each of us carried out in new directions. And they cemented permanent friendships.

Now Arthur was back, and he knew what he was doing. Part way through the visit at Mayo I was so self-conscious to be playing hard to get, and so taken by the people I was meeting, that I said yes, I'd be honored to join your board. It was unlike any I'd known. Many of its members were pioneers who, in their youth, had traveled to the East and returned to spread contemplative practices through the West. The board also had six newer members. And me, freshly off the fence.

The first event at the Mayo was a series of interchanges between the Dalai Lama and three postdoctoral fellows, young scholars who had undertaken studies with MLI funding. In that interchange I observed the Dalai Lama immersed in what I would come to know as one of his great pleasures, an enactment of one of his great gifts. He brought those young scholars his innate curiosity and his practiced attention to the dance of an open mind engaging another one, an open mind *and* an open heart.

After the scholarly exchanges, His Holiness, as I noted everyone referred to him, was spirited off to a Mayo media room for a televised interview with the BBC. There I watched him measure his words. Now I was in the presence of the seasoned and canny leader of a nation in exile. The interviewer seemed intent on provoking him to speak ill of China. The Dalai Lama held a firm line on the rights of the Tibetan people to return to their homeland. But he would express only compassion for the invaders.

This Mayo meeting would be the first of dozens of encounters across the United States, and two in India, that would enable me to observe and absorb this personification of wisdom and compassion, to work with him, take him in from up close. Memorable among those was my first trip to India, in January 2013. That my then five-year-old grandson, Sean, was half Indian heightened my excitement to see this country. Thomas had grown up in Bangalore, to the north of where we would be. He had family there still. They had come to Wellesley for his wedding to Allison.

It was magical to watch Allison come into her own as a skilled and confident mother with a deeply intuitive feel for who this sweet boy was and who he might become. She seemed to know what he needed of her at any moment. I watched her nourish his curiosity, always with a light and loving touch. I saw what a devoted father Thomas was, Thomas is.

I loved to listen in on the Bump bedtime stories Thomas wove for Sean in a new installment every night, sometimes via telephone if a business trip had taken him away. They featured Sean, his puppy, Bear, and their companion, Wolfie, cast as three detectives who were awakened from slumber when they heard a bump outside the window. It could be an animal in need of their help to figure out what sort of creature it was. They asked it a series of questions, and accumulated clues. A barn owl, a meerkat, a chinchilla, a red-tailed fox. Once they announced their solution, the lost creature had what it needed, and all could go back to sleep.

Being with Sean and his parents was an immersion into the mysteries of the world, the surprises around every corner, the fascinations under foot, the enticement of each new challenge, the impermanence of heartbreak, and the transcendent sweetness of a spontaneous hug. My grandson at age five was already a master teacher in the lessons of gratitude, of dependence and interdependence, and the slow process of waking up, not once but over and over through the cycles of an evolving day, or month, or year. On top of all of that, he was very funny. He loved a good joke, from an early age.

Gardener Sean, Sunday Sweeper Sean, Mailman Sean. When he was three, he would announce his new identities as he picked up another object. He was not, I gathered, trying on occupations. It was too soon for that. What's an occupation anyway to someone so lighthearted? Rather, he seemed to be expressing his essential nature: Busy Sean. Happy to be purposeful, he was in the zone as he walked out into the garden with his watering can way too full. With intense concentration on his face, he would set out to water his little garden, his left hand unconsciously twisted sideways by his hip, or wrapped around the ping pong ball he carried incessantly: Little White Ballie. This expression of his nature always struck me as the very essence of joy and equanimity, of happiness and of kindness.

We watched Sean continue to grow over the years into a bright and sensitive young boy who imagined he possessed the powers of every known superhero, serially and in combination. He assigned me the role of the bungling sidekick in the intricate productions he cast. A willing Nana was the ideal foil. He was a source of constant delight to me, and Chris, if not always to Allison, who did love him dearly but was responsible for boundaries we had had to hold for her, and were freed now to leave to her, with her son. Among her parental projects had been to persuade him that it was not exactly respectful to call his grandfather Dude. My inability to hide my amusement didn't help. Sean would surely be much on my mind during my first trip to India.

I would travel with the MLI delegation to the remote Tibetan settlement in Mundgod, South India, a protectorate of the Indian government, for a six-day gathering of more than 5,000 monks and nuns, refugees who lived and studied in massive Tibetan monastic universities reproduced in the 1960s on the hot and dusty plains of South India after the Chinese drove the Tibetan people out of their mountain home in the Himalayas.

The Dalai Lama would preside over an historic intellectual exchange that culminated years of effort to expand a 600-year-old curriculum. He wanted Western science included. And I was impatient with the pace of curricular reform at Wellesley! I knew this would be an instructive experience. I didn't know much else.

I did notice that I was approaching the trip with naivete and possibly a touch of hubris. As an educator and a woman leader I had always been more than a little skeptical of the heroic model of leadership. Here was a male leader who was worshiped as a reincarnation of the Buddha, a leader with fealty and fiat power of a radically different origin and nature than I could even imagine. How would that work and where would the women fit?

This visit was the first in decades the Dalai Lama made to this settlement. The enthusiasm of his reception gave new meaning to the word fanfare, beyond anything I'd witnessed. Clerics in the Gelug monastic sect wore huge crested yellow hats that signified wisdom, we were told. Our academic regalia back home paled in comparison. From rooftops we heard the guttural throb of long, curved ceremonial horns. Colorful prayer flags flapped in the breezes. Devoted followers chanted and bowed as the motorcade made its way along the entrance road. The Dalai Lama's translator, Thupten Jinpa Langri, MLI's board chair, told us that as a young monk he tended the saplings that now lined the road as mature shade trees. It struck me that we had been called here to help plant new seeds.

Our small delegation of MLI board members had dispersed into the crowd when a representative of the Dalai Lama rounded us up to join him in his private quarters upstairs. We arranged ourselves in a crowded chamber where he introduced us to the abbots who oversaw this system of monastic education. We were passed cups of butter tea and biscuits.

"I know these people," he was saying to the abbots—of us. "You can trust them," he added. I would come to recognize this first moment in retrospect as the initiation of a process that would continue through the week. The Dalai Lama would communicate by example the path he had forged in his years of dialogue with scientists from the West. He would emphasize that the Buddha instructed his followers not to take his teachings on faith, but to find the truth for themselves through the empirical use of introspection. He would say that Buddhism and Western science have in common this dedication to empirical examination of reality toward the goal of reducing suffering.

And he would tell his personal story. Unexpectedly, I was tapped to moderate several of the sessions, filling in for a colleague stuck in Boston. So I found myself in the special moderator's seat next to the Dalai Lama as he spoke movingly of what it was like, as the young leader of his people, to flee his homeland into a larger world of which he knew next to nothing. He felt the responsibility, he told us, as a teacher and a leader, to learn all he could. I knew this moment of truth; I had lived it on my far smaller stage.

In his exchanges with scholars we brought to the meeting, the Dalai Lama demonstrated for the hundreds of assembled monastics of every age that they could open themselves to the other—to "the new materialists" he called us with a merry laugh. The monks should expect and prepare to be transformed by these encounters, he told them, and yet could remain confident in their distinctive gifts for the West. This was a reciprocal exchange of wisdom, he emphasized: what they brought would be sharpened and deepened, not diluted or diminished, as they entered these new encounters in a spirit of open, "warm-hearted" inquiry. These words he especially liked and often repeated.

My questions about leadership had been laid to rest. I was in the presence of a virtuoso. I was conscious though of one discordant note in the issue of gender. Our time with the nuns reinforced my initial impression of a patriarchal culture just beginning to find narrow spaces for women's voices to be raised up. But I was impressed to watch the Dalai Lama escort the monks across a wide and menacing chasm with compassion, humor, and patience. He asked them to incorporate into Tibetan monastic education selected aspects of modernity, its advances and promise, yes, but equally, its anxieties and distortions. In the next breath, he extended to the West a hand to help us cross our wide divide to pull us back from our overheated materialism, and the grasping that was causing great suffering. We moderns ourselves were suffering, he observed, as were billions less fortunate around the world.

This message was implicit throughout the week. But on the fifth day, as we were to break for lunch, he unexpectedly reached for his microphone. He rocked gently from side to side, commented on how comfortable we were compared to most of the world's seven-billion people, and spoke of his dream of an educational initiative throughout the world that would spread what he called "secular ethics." It would seek to reduce human suffering and promote human flourishing by nourishing students' cooperative, connective, and empathic capacities. It would teach them to be more fully human.

I was moderating and the Dalai Lama was speaking directly to me, and—so it felt—through me. He was addressing his Buddhist followers, the Mind and Life Institute, the larger educational community, the Western world. I felt it as a kind of transmission, a message he wanted me to carry, wanted us to carry. We stand at a crossroads now. Material progress has presented humans with daunting challenges. We may or may not manage to address them in time to avert global tragedy. At the same time, though, we can see that advances in science, when combined with growing respect for historic and indigenous wisdom practices, are opening new possibilities. Can we awaken inner development now as an antidote to decades of preoccupation with outer material growth?

I left India in January 2013 with pressing questions. What will it take to transform human consciousness in time? How can we transform educational systems so that they ignite students' cooperative, connective, altruistic capacities? How can we help the young discover their innate humanity? How can I cultivate my own?

I arrived home clearer than ever that I wanted to be close to our daughter and her family, an unfulfilled desire that drove our joint decision to decamp from Boston. I was savoring much of my post-presidency life—feeling valued and useful—but the geographical and emotional distance from Allison was the one gnawing regret in my life. Chris, ever the scientist, said we needed data.

So he had begun the experiment a full five years before we ran it. With a Stanford friend he arranged a one semester post-career sabbatical to begin in winter 2014. First, he had to shut down his research group, initially accepting only postdocs, who needed two or three years in the lab, compared to the five a PhD generally took. Then he stopped taking new members into the group, which would continue until everyone had a good job. That would be easy. The Walsh group was a powerhouse.

This phase of deliberate deceleration puzzled his professional peers. Why quit so early? His research was as good as ever; he was only 69. Was he sick? No, he had dodged that bullet. I was proud of Chris's clarity that this was the right decision. As institutional leaders, both of us had seen faculty hold on to their jobs too long. He did not want to be one of those. He believed, as I did, that there is a time to step aside and make space for a new generation.

The lab was set to close at the end of June 2013. Current and former members organized a farewell party. Chris resisted, but they insisted. They had a template: in 2004, they had organized a *festschrift*, a day of research talks by group members followed by a dinner. That was to commemorate his sixtieth birthday, the one that might not have been but for the emergency bypass operation. Virtually everyone came back to Boston to pay tribute to Chris on that poignant occasion. They would all come back again for the farewell.

As the date for the party approached, I was increasingly conscious of what the lab had meant to my husband—and to me, the place it had occupied in our shared life. Maybe I was feeling the pain of the rupture on his behalf. He was armored against it. Other than me and Allison, our family and friendships, the Walsh group was the central organizing principle of Chris's life. It was the anchor that enabled him to venture into widening circles in a career that far exceeded his wildest dreams— and ours. It was the expression and nidus of his prodigious creativity, this man I married when we were both kids.

Chris had always been a bundle of contradictions. With a restless and ranging mind and an insatiable appetite for travel, he had lived in one city for all but five years of his life. He was an introvert—except when he was not and then he was full of sparkling bonhomie. A scientist, rationalist, realist, he was stubbornly superstitious. He refused to celebrate any milestone even a day ahead. And yet he was an explorer at heart. At the core of these contradictions, what held them together in a coherent whole, were the structures he assembled, starting with his family, with me and Allison.

After that the next most important structure was the Walsh group, an act not of creation but of *co-creation*. I watched him choose every member for intelligence, curiosity, promise, of course, but also for ineffable qualities of mind and character that he sensed would enrich the lab and, later, the fields in which graduates would make their careers. He trained many women who later went on to influential posts in academic science. Chris was especially proud of them. I watched him give every member the thing he most prized in his own life: freedom. Having broken away from an oppressive father, he wanted everyone he developed and mentored to be free to choose their own paths, free to preserve and also modify the best of what they had created with Chris.

The organizers invited me to speak, and I said some of those things. I expressed my appreciation for these former students, many now well into middle age. I thanked them for what they had been for my husband, for us both, and for carrying forward the legacy of the lab, the mighty Walsh group soon to be a memory. I walked back to my seat at the head table on a wave of emotion in the room. Chris stood to hug me. I saw tears in his eyes.

That summer, 2013, was the awful one in which my mother fell on July 1 and died just twelve days later. Chris and I made multiple trips back and forth between Boston and the Cape, Philadelphia and the Poconos, and, in late July, spent a restorative week in Atherton with Allison, Thomas, and Sean. That visit on the heels of the loss of my mother deepened my yearning to be more present in my grown daughter's life.

Back in Boston in the fall, we began to focus on the sabbatical, scheduled to start in January. Chris went online and found a tiny one-bedroom apartment off Sand Hill Road near Stanford, leased it for three months and rented a few pieces of basic furniture, plus a cheap car. We moved in but didn't bother to hang anything on the walls. This was temporary and I enjoyed the austerity for a change.

In the first month we settled into a weekend routine. Allison would bring Sean over to our spartan apartment. He and I went outside and played his fantasy games on the grounds of the apartment complex. Allison and Chris stretched out on our rented sofa and talked about science and medicine, or traded science gossip. They laughed. They napped. Allison was sleep deprived. Thomas would check in and then catch up on errands. It worked for us all—so well that we decided we had all the data we needed. We would stay.

Between January and April 2014, Chris and I uprooted our Boston lives. We sold the Brookline house in June and bought a small condo in Jamaica Plain, close to our friends Andrea and Jon Clardy. I would walk around the pond with Andrea when back for monthly MIT meetings, spend the week and arrange dinners out with friends I missed. I'd have a *pied-à-terre* and a place to leave our furniture, as much as would fit. We found an all-women moving company that specialized in downsizing and chose the charities that could make the best use of the many large items we sloughed off. I donated my BMW to the local PBS station.

Chris would be back rarely, chiefly for summers on the Cape. It was time to shrink our footprint. Bill and I had taken care of Sally's apartment when she died, and Mom's the next year. I was not going to leave a life's worth of stuff on the east coast for Allison to contend with some day. Channeling my mother, I supposed, I did not want to be a burden on my daughter.

A Kaiser colleague found a house next to hers in Redwood City. It was June 2014. Driving over to take a look, Allison and Sean in the car, I reviewed the bidding. The owner, Mrs. Miller, an elderly widow, was moving north to assisted living near her daughter's home. Her old-style California ranch house on Miller Court sounded ideal for us. Real estate was hot and scarce. We hoped we could lease it. Sean, who was six, picked up on the elderly part.

"*How* old is Mrs. Miller?" he asked several times. Allison was worried he'd embarrass us and suggested I be more guarded. Not my long suit, especially with my grandson.

"The house has a swimming pool," I said, "and a well-tended garden. Mrs. Miller is an accomplished gardener." When we arrived, she greeted us and asked Sean his name.

"Sean," he said. "I am a gardener too." She took him by the hand and walked him all around the yard, pointing out her prize plantings. Sean's gift of gab secured us the house to rent. The Irish side of his family, Allison remarked. We lived there for four years. I took photos of shrubs and trees that bloomed in every season and sent them to Mrs. Miller. The catalpa tree in the driveway amazed me with the volume of greenery it produced every spring.

In her garden on the weekends, I continued to play the foil in Sean's imaginary games. They became more sophisticated. He was into video games and had a taste for war and mayhem. Allison told him that Nana is a Quaker: violence is against her religion. This was a stretch but fine with me. I told him I wanted to play games about preserving nature. He found a video game called Plants v. Zombies and adapted it for our outdoor reenactments. He bounced on the diving board with a bamboo pole in his hand and conjured spirits from the pool to rescue plants and critters under assault. I still lacked magical powers, so he dispatched me to fetch more bamboo wands from the grove along the garden fence.

Chris and I continued to marvel at how strategic and successful Allison had been since her start at Stanford Medical School. Admitted to the 2002 oncology fellowship program in a cohort of five physicians, she was the only one without a PhD. At the end of the three years, she was invited to stay on. She brought her clinical acumen into research collaborations with established faculty in other departments, and found her own mentors who championed her work.

She earned a master's degree in epidemiology and fashioned a bespoke career that combined clinical care of breast cancer patients twice a week with large-scale original research on the genetics of breast and other women's cancers, risk factors, detection, and choices of treatments. She had selected oncology as a specialty that was advancing rapidly and, hence, providing better options to offer her patients. Now she was situated at the crossroads between research and practice. She excelled at both and moved up the ranks from assistant to associate to full professor, publishing an average of fifteen to twenty research papers a year, sometimes more.

As I met new people in and around Palo Alto, the conversation naturally turned to what brought me across the country at this stage in my life. I mentioned my daughter whose name they then asked.

"Allison Kurian is your daughter?!" A common reaction. "She is my doctor," they would say, then assure me that they were okay now, and that all her patients swore by her, loved her.

I loved this reversal. Allison grew up on the Atlantic coast under a shadow cast by two well-known parents. When she struck out on her own to Stanford as an undergraduate, she and some friends invented a whimsical mutual support group. They called it CHIMPS: children of intensely motivated parents. Now, on the Pacific coast, her star power was lighting the way for her parents in the San Francisco Bay area. Hers and her husband's. Thomas was circumspect and modest, and I was careful to respect his privacy. I did mention his name to a close neighbor one day, an MIT graduate from India. Her eyebrows shot up: "Tech Royalty!"

Chris had the ability to move on and never look back. Not I. As much as I loved being enfolded into my daughter's family, for at least five years after we pulled up stakes, I still called Boston home. I missed my friends,

my family, my seasons, my trees, my outwardly radiating circles of connection and affection. I missed the east coast where I was seldom anonymous, where I had left behind so much of what had defined who I was.
When we were abroad together in those years and a stranger asked where
we were from, our replies took some sorting out. We seemed to be a couple, but one of us was a Bostonian, the other a San Franciscan? How did
that work?

The Dalai Lama's questions stayed with me too and, in early 2014, I began
to approach them from a new vantage point with another Boston friend,
Sarah Buie. A Wellesley alum from a class five years behind mine, she was
directing the humanities center at Clark University when I first met her
in 2006. She played the Wellesley card, as she put it, when she visited
me in my office to ask if I would give the opening keynote address at a
conference to kick off a three-year program on Difficult Dialogue that was
funded by the Ford Foundation as part of a national initiative. I did that
and also participated in the closing. I was taken by the quality and range
of the Clark program.

Now Sarah reappeared in my life to talk about the most difficult of the
dialogues, the one that was not happening, the one on climate change.
It was silenced in a cloud of denial except among experts, who were
spooked and didn't want to overwhelm others who might not be ready
to face the reality that we humans are in deep trouble. We could see this
tension through the eyes of a former graduate student of Sarah's, Susi
Moser, a geologist and expert in climate adaptation and communication.
Susi was reluctant to go into detail even with us about all she knew. She
considered it irresponsible to ask others to reckon with the reality of our
situation without a structure to provide intellectual and emotional support, some kind of "container" for a deep dive into dark waters.

The three of us decided to design such a structure. We began with a
circle of twelve women who were active in aspects of climate change,
well-known scientists, artists, writers, scholars from around the country.
We wanted to inquire deeply into the question of what the climate crisis
asked of us. We adapted a dialogic form from indigenous and other practices called The Way of Council. We called our experiment The Council
on the Uncertain Human Future, CUHF.

The women who said yes to our invitation were extraordinary people, accomplished in their fields, and fearless in their determination to wade into the painful truth. Together we pooled our knowledge of what was known and not known about the threat of global warming and about the more general forces of ecocide that were rapidly rendering the Earth uninhabitable. We enumerated implications. We opened to the grief beneath what we, collectively, were seeing and coming to know. And, in the affection and connection of the circle—in the depths we discovered in ourselves and one another—we came out, each of us, with a clearer view of who we could be in this time that we now knew to be a global emergency.

I discovered that once I had seen this reality, I could not look away. It would take time to come to terms with what that discovery meant in concrete terms. To begin, I resolved to read widely, pay attention, and do all I could to support the spread of CUHF circles. We created a website where we curated readings. We made films and posted them. We convened new councils and stayed in close touch, as all of us in the initial circle metabolized the impact it had on us and on the networks to which we returned, changed.

I resolved also to bring my growing concern about climate change into every speech I made. At that time, the subject was still mostly taboo in polite company, and I was giving a lot of speeches. I held myself to that vow even on occasions that required some fancy footwork to justify bringing such a downer. I took this on as a test of whether I could frame the message in words that people could bear to hear. I found that young people were grateful to have the issue out in the open. At Washington University in Saint Louis, as one example, I received a 2014 honorary degree and spoke at the hooding ceremony to recipients of graduate degrees and their families. I could see the audience members furrow their brows as I moved into the topic of climate change. The graduates came up to me later with thanks for giving public voice to a worry that haunted them privately.

In September 2014 I was back in Boston, one year into my monthly meetings of the MIT executive committee, which I had joined at the invitation of the former provost and new president, Rafael Reif. I was interested especially in the role the Institute could play in addressing climate change. MIT, historically, was an engine of the Industrial Revolution, the discipline of chemical engineering, and the rise of the petrochemical industry. Institute scientists had unique access and expertise in energy and had leverage that could make a difference in squeezing fossil fuels out of the world economy while redressing economic and energy inequalities around the globe.

Rafael had a stack of over 3,500 signed petitions, collected by a student organization, Fossil Free MIT. They demanded that the Institute divest its endowment of holdings in fossil fuels as part of 350.org's international campaign. The president was looking for guidance on the petitions. I could tell that he wanted to take them seriously. The committee did not want to see MIT's endowment become a political football. I waded in anyway.

Divestment may not be our answer, I conceded, but we should not take this lightly. The issue is not going away. Nor should we want it to. Global warming is this generation's burden, an existential threat to their future. We have an obligation to prepare them to address it. Of all institutions, the world needs MIT's leadership. We all do. I am certainly counting on it.

I was the only former college president on the committee, the only academic, and one of only three women. I brought a perspective that blended the social sciences and the humanities, and years of intense interaction with faculty, and especially with students. I had spent my adult life listening to young people for their ambitions, hopes and worries, listening deeply. I was now translating some of that to the engineers, financiers, entrepreneurs, and technologists running MIT.

My plea cleared an opening for the president, who picked up where I left off. Several others weighed in with constructive suggestions. We forged a consensus that the muscular call for divestment warranted a response in kind, an articulation of the particular role MIT *should* play as a leader in confronting climate change, as a first step, an Institute-wide conversation.

Rafael enlisted a superstar, his vice president for research, Maria Zuber, to lead a year-long conversation. She and I stayed in conversation, too. When we went over a draft report from her committee, I suggested she think of it not as the "statement" it was but as a plan with deliverables. She released it in June as a five-year plan. Instead of divestment, the committee recommended "engagement" with industrial leaders who would be needed for the transition to clean energy, jawboning with those leaders, helping them see the light. This was where MIT could have its greatest impact, the committee argued. Well, some of the members did.

A student leader in Fossil Free MIT wrote a minority report that held out for divestment. As I read it, I was reminded of Parker Palmer's definition of a "tragic gap," the space between an aspiration we hold as nonnegotiable from the standpoint of our beliefs and values and, at the same time, perceive as impossible from a practical point of view. The report quoted an op-ed I had published in the *Huffington Post* titled "When Students Become the Teachers." In it I wrote: "As they watch the world's leaders stand paralyzed before a window that is closing rapidly on the chance to move fast and far enough, today's students find themselves caught between the impossible—mobilizing action in time—and the unthinkable—a planetary meltdown. What an agonizing place from which to step out into adulthood."

I felt the committee had moved the Institute as far as it was able to go at that point. Maria negotiated an agreement that established a climate change advisory committee on which I sat for the next five years. This enabled me to stay involved from a distance in MIT's climate work, to stand resolutely in Parker's tragic gap and to invite others to join me there.

Meanwhile I was finding new ventures on the "left coast," where, we used to say in Boston, all the loose stuff lands after it rolls across the continent from east to west. I'm not so sure about the geology, but life was surely different out here. I became a senior advisor in a Stanford center on global health founded and led by a Kellogg friend, Michele Barry. I gave a couple of talks at her conferences, ending them, as usual now, with a call to action on climate change. Michele became a convert. Together we wrote a position paper on the health effects of climate change as part of a multidisciplinary Stanford initiative to inform the next US president's agenda on the climate crisis. We worked on it all summer, certain that we were writing for Hillary Clinton. A strong effort wasted, as fate would have it.

On November 8, with Michele and her husband, Mark, Chris, and I watched the election returns before I headed to Kaiser's media center to call back to Wellesley. I had been asked to Zoom in with a few words. A huge party was underway on campus in the Keohane Sports Center. Two jumbotrons were set up and alumnae had gathered from all over the country to celebrate Hillary's historic victory. The returns were coming in slowly in California and we were not overly worried about the outcome. All the pundits had called it for Hillary. But as I headed out the door, Chris called to me.

"Watch out," he said. "It's not looking good. I think you need to measure your words." I did, and later noted that, once again, Chris was right. Unfortunately this time.

In early March 2020, I was back in Boston at the MIT Corporation meeting. It ended with a scientific lecture on the novel coronavirus by a rising star we had recruited to the Broad while I was chair. During the reception we all studiously avoided physical contact, feeling self-conscious as we bumped elbows as a greeting. But it was only two weeks earlier that a Biogen meeting—also in Cambridge and involving some of the same people—left close to 100 of 175 attendees infected with COVID-19. That meeting was believed to have seeded thousands of additional cases.

By the weekend, when I arrived home in California, Chris and I had no doubt that our lives were about to change, radically and perhaps permanently. He had an autoimmune disease, giant cell arteritis. Any risk I took could jeopardize his health, even his life. Zoom would become my portal to the outside world. We would retreat into a "bubble" that included Allison, Thomas, and Sean; our lives were intertwined now, much to my joy. We settled into this new routine and soon found ourselves among the lucky few for whom an extended lockdown was disorienting at first but, in the end, a relatively minor inconvenience, except for the turmoil around us.

I was shaken, from a distance, by COVID-related suffering and inequities, accentuated by the murder of George Floyd and all that followed. The nation was again forced to confront the multigenerational racial wounds of which I had been conscious throughout my life, and had tried to help heal. I participated in the upsurge of Zoom seminars, teach-ins, and book discussions on race and racism and began to feel a glimmer of hope that this time might be different. Finally we might come to terms with our nation's history of racism, patriarchy, colonialism, with the savage inequalities in generational wealth, and personal well-being, with the exposure in "sacrifice zones" to the toxic effluents of extractive capitalism. It was a mere glimmer, but I held tight to it.

With small Zoom groups of close friends and colleagues, I worried about growing threats to democracy, at home and around the world. We saw cracks in so many of the institutional structures we had long had the luxury of serving. Had we taken them for granted? How blind had we been? We explored what we could do to make a small difference in confusing times: mentor the next generation, clear paths for emerging leaders, see them in their brilliance, affirm them in their efforts, resolutely hold the light when the darkness around us was deep.

Chris was on occasional Zoom calls with scientific colleagues seeking a semblance of stability in the pandemic. When I was not on Zoom, I dug back into the personal writing I had been wanting for a long time to make a priority. I had been introduced to a writing coach, who asked, "What would it be like for you to write something beautiful about the hardest thing you have ever had to do? The most painful challenge you have had to face?" I knew instantly what that would be: the time my husband, Chris, the most important person in my life, came close to dying of a heart attack. I was launched.

I was abetted now by an enforced lockdown at home and by the example of my husband, the mad scrivener, who was pecking away at his computer day and night on scientific monographs. He never did learn to touch-type, but had written and published six weighty new tomes in just the few years since we had moved west. He put me to shame. It was time for me to focus. I returned to my memoir.

I thought about the claims of life—of mine, of anyone's. Isn't the first claim to find the courage, whatever the cost, to carry on, to reach out and connect with others, to keep reaching out? Aren't we humans here to cultivate a shared sense of purpose, to listen and be changed, to persist no matter how messy the world seems to be, no matter how intractable the problems might appear at any moment, no matter how indeterminate the future might look?

My life had been one long conversation with a question like this at its center. I'd hosted so many discussions, sat in so many circles, felt myself and others move through so many cycles of self-doubt, disillusionment, despondency, sometimes rage, only to emerge bolstered by the knowledge that we are not alone in our fears and grief. We are not alone in our hopes and visions of a safer, saner world that might work better for everyone. We are interdependent, all of us, woven inextricably together in the chemical and biological logic of life that my beloved Chris Walsh has been delineating for his entire career.

In November I received an email from Jinpa. Mind and Life was arranging the first-ever meeting of the Dalai Lama and Greta Thunberg. Over a million viewers had registered and MLI wanted me to help design, shape, and moderate the online conversation on January 9, 2021. Sean, by then twelve and in sixth grade, was learning about climate change and thought this might help raise awareness. I agreed and set aside my writing again, but temporarily only. I was confident this time that I would return to it immediately, and I was right.

By mid-October 2022, the manuscript nearly complete, the United States was approaching a midterm election that many of us were convinced would be the most important of our lifetimes. I signed up with an organization called Vote Forward to write nonpartisan letters and postcards to eighteen-year-olds encouraging them to vote. We were at Sean's house, celebrating his fourteenth birthday, and I wanted his advice. Which would be more persuasive, I asked, the postcards I'd been writing by hand or the more detailed form letters I could just personalize and mail in envelopes? Sean picked up the postcard and read it: "November 8 is your last chance to make your voice heard in this important election," I wrote in part. "Will you please join me as a voter? I'm a volunteer in my late 70s, and you are a young voter. We need *you* now!"

"Go with that one," Sean replied with certainty, and took a picture of it.

I did, and placed my faith in this new generation, trusting them to learn and to lead.

APPENDIX: TRUSTWORTHY LEADERSHIP

As we watch the unraveling of systems and structures around the world, we hunger for leadership worthy of trust. The times demand pervasive leadership to which all of us contribute our share. So how can we develop trustworthy leadership? Although we should not delude ourselves that this is an easy task, I believe that, as a beginning, we can try to live at least the following five commitments in our various leadership roles.

We Can Question Ourselves. First and foremost, we should question ourselves. Effective leadership comes from an inner core of integrity and yet is not fixed, stubborn, or implacable. Leaders we trust are open to our thoughtful influence. They are aware that they cannot possess all the answers because they can have only one perspective. They are eager to hear responsible critique, and the viewpoints of others.

When leaders inspire us, we experience them as consistently themselves—yes—we sense in them a solid self-confidence, but not one that walls others out. Clear about who they are, they can open themselves to others. They stay attuned to their inner truth through disciplines that keep them honest, knowing, as the ancients did, that the first and most demanding obligation of a leader is the Socratic injunction to "know thyself." Yeats wrote that "we make out of the quarrel with others, rhetoric, but of the quarrel with ourselves, poetry." Trustworthy leaders are poets; they quarrel with themselves.

We Can Establish Partnerships. Second, since even if we know ourselves, we can't know all we need to know from our own limited perspective, we need to establish partnerships as the basic units for accomplishing

work. And they have to be reliable partnerships, which means investing time and energy in preserving their integrity. Reliable partnerships
help prevent the distortions of information that often result from perceived or real imbalances of power—distortions produced by projections onto the leader and/or the tendency to shield her from bad news.
Trustworthy leaders choose their partners wisely, for a range of perspectives and for a sense of shared core values. They negotiate the common
understandings at the heart of these partnerships, which they attend
to regularly, and integrate into a larger understanding of the goals they
are pursuing.

To be trustworthy leaders, then, we need to make a serious commitment to a network of partnerships that are honest and effective, solid and
sophisticated and above all remain capable of receiving candid critique.
Enlisting others—and not just loyal insiders—in these alliances becomes
a major part of the leader's task: inviting a mutual exploration of what
happened when things go awry, coming together to assess behaviors that
may be undermining the alliance, taking explicit steps to reinforce shared
commitments, revisiting the inspiration from which the collaboration
draws its meaning.

We Can Resist the Use of Force. Third, I believe that trustworthy leaders
consciously resist the use of force except as a last resort. Leadership is by
definition the exercise of power, and leaders are constantly called upon
to deploy their power on one side or another of high-stakes disputes.
As tempting as it is to wade in with what looks like decisiveness, in our
hearts we know that interventions imposed from on high seldom yield
enduring peace. Refusing to resort to force is never easy. It's painful to
look like a weak or uncertain leader, a judgment our culture is quick to
apply as we grope for simple solutions to complex problems.

But it's even more painful to watch disputes smolder and reignite in
debilitating cycles of repetition and escalation. Avoiding the use of force
reflects a conception of leadership as nonpartisan, and of the leader as the
person whose effectiveness depends on hearing all sides of a dispute, in
essence taking in the many perspectives that comprise the whole. If we
become captive of one or more of these voices, then soon we are waging

a war within ourselves. As leaders, our task is to create conditions within which disputes can be explored and transformed at the most local level where those most directly affected can assume responsibility and discover their own resourcefulness.

We Can Value Differences. Fourth, knowing that differences of opinion, perspective, and world-view are a crucial part of life and learning, we will be trustworthy leaders if we truly value differences, not only as an ethical imperative and a measure of respect for others (although surely for these reasons), but also as a unique creative resource. In any group, organization, or system, the voices from the margins hold the buried wisdom that can alert us to our self-deceptions.

There are aspects of any culture to which resistance is a healthy response. We need a new language, then, about how we understand differences, and a new kind of leadership that will engage identity struggles in diverse communities by appreciating their complexity and messiness, digging beneath the power dimensions, and opening to profounder meanings and deeper human connections. Only when we have leaders who understand healthy conflict in its inevitability and its productivity will we begin to develop the skills to mine it well. We as leaders need to hone those skills—and that tolerance for complexity—so that others can. And it's never easy.

We Can Cultivate Sustaining Communities. That's why, fifth, and finally, trustworthy leaders need to weave communities that can function as sustaining systems of mutual support. All leaders need places to which they can retreat to grapple with pressures and doubts and the assaults on confidence no one should have to confront alone. I know from years of experience how isolating leadership can be, how sudden, wide, and unnerving, sometimes, the swings can be from elation to despair, how often, even now, I lose and find myself again: my moorings, my equilibrium, my commitment, my heart.

If we can practice our leadership within supportive communities—if we can build and bind those communities—then we can begin to define and experience leadership as a collective project that derives its power

and authority from a cooperative attachment to mutually-defined commitments and values. Having done so, we can perhaps free ourselves and
others of the illusion that we could or should try to accomplish our goals
on our own—to trust that we don't have to carry the whole load, that we
can co-create with each other, that we need do only what we can do, and
bring only what is ours to give. Never forgetting that we must bring our
very best so others can do the same.

EPILOGUE

On January 4, 2023, I spent the day again sitting beside Chris's hospital bed, this time at Stanford University Hospital. He had undergone emergency neurosurgery for a traumatic brain injury sustained from a fall the previous afternoon. The accident was a complete shock, a fluke. He was as fit as he'd been in years, and we were as happy. A week later—it is difficult to write these words—my beloved husband of fifty-seven years died without regaining consciousness.

Chris was grateful to be living what he called a "charmed life." That it ended so abruptly will continue as a mystery and a heartache. But we were consciously living with the awareness that life is fragile and so we left little unsaid or unresolved. And I will always be grateful that he read this memoir in manuscript, that he died in the sure knowledge that I loved him as much as he had loved me from the day we first met in 1964.

When it came to writing this book, Chris was the *sine qua non* in keeping my spirits up; he often said of his own books that he wrote them for himself. In retrospect, it strikes me that I wrote this one in part for him.

Many others have been essential to the making of this memoir. Some, but far from all, appear in the story, Others who don't show up in the book did show up for me, and I thank my many partners, including those whose contributions landed amid the thousands of words (a full half of the submitted manuscript) on the cutting room floor. I trust that many of you know who you are, how much I owe you, how deeply I value your friendship, support, and, especially now, your care.

I thank Byllye Avery for her writing group and her ongoing friendship, Drew Altman, for a courtesy office at the Kaiser Family Foundation during my initial years as a transplant from Boston, and Mollyann

Brodie there, an accomplished younger leader eager to learn from me. I was lucky to learn with close friends in the Kellogg National Fellowship Program, including Michele Barry, Sandra Daley, Rick Jackson, Chris Musselwhite, and Nancy Snyderman who read and commented on drafts. Elaine Ullian did too over the years, as did Dick Nodell and Stephanie Lyness, Pat Byrne and Jane Backman. The book is far better for the generosity of these readers.

Andrew Shennan, as an assistant professor in 1993, served on the Wellesley search committee that selected me as president and has continued at Wellesley in leadership roles, now as provost. A historian with a scholar's eye and a way with words, he commented on several drafts and cheered me on. Thanks, Andy.

At Wellesley College, the alumnae association, resource development office and college archives provided helpful information and materials. Wellesley's President, Paula A. Johnson, MD, is an inspiration and a friend. Madeleine Albright was, too, and I miss her. Joanne Berger-Sweeney brought her own distinctive gifts to a few of the lessons here and became a creative next-generation leader, as did Kim Goff-Crews, Jenn Desjarlais, Mary Ann Hill, and Kate Salop.

Toward the end of the process, three anonymous reviewers for the MIT Press provided vital advice. Their insights improved the book and I thank them. I was encouraged also by new friends out here on the "left" coast: Charlotte Jacobs, Jane Morton, and Michael Jacobs also read drafts, and helped me keep the faith.

Andrea Clardy, another true friend and fellow writer, remained close from across the continent. It was she who supplied the definition of friendship that stands behind this book: a friend is someone who knows the song in your heart and can sing it back to you when you have forgotten the words. On one of our calls, in August 2020, she heard me losing my song and suggested I meet a writing coach/editor who was helping her with her playwriting.

Michele Lowe, who has an uncanny gift for asking just the right question, followed the threads, noted where the reader was lost, and where the writer disappeared. We spoke weekly by phone, not Zoom. I liked that. I liked her. A whole lot. At the outset, she asked me what I wanted to do. I told her I'd written throughout my life, but not yet the beautiful book I wanted to write from the time I was twelve. We set out together to bring that wish to fulfillment and soon found ourselves in a generative partnership that transformed us both. I can't thank you enough, Michele.

Susan Buckley, MIT Press acquisitions editor, helped me bring the project across the finish line. With Amy Brand, director of MITP, she saw the promise in my submission, secured the outside reviews, and made the case for its publication. Then she brought sensitivity and skill to the painful process of pruning an overlong original submission. Susan saw the book I wanted to write but hadn't—yet—and guided me with clarity, efficiency and warmth, to bring it to life. I have Greg Morgan to thank for steering me toward Amy Brand and the MIT Press, and I treasure his continued friendship.

Finally, what matters in the end: family. My older brother, Bill, and younger sister, Muffy, remain as my compact nuclear family of origin, living far away now, but ever present in my mind and heart as I wrote the book. So were Bill's wife, Bonnie; my nieces, Dorothy and Meaghan; Dorothy's husband Justin and their children, William and Julia; Meaghan's husband, Brian; and my nephews, Greg and Robert.

To Allison, Thomas, and Sean, I want to say that Chris and I treasured living out here with you as integral members of your beautiful family. You placed the capstone on a marriage we could not have imagined when we first met and set out together to see what we could make of ourselves. How lucky we were—and I am still—to be here with you in the warm embrace of your family.

Diana Chapman Walsh
Menlo Park, California
February 16, 2023

INDEX